Careers in Manufacturing & Production

Careers in Manufacturing & Production

Editor

Michael Shally-Jensen, Ph.D.

SALEM PRESS

A Division of EBSCO Information Services, Inc.

Ipswich, Massachusetts

GREY HOUSE PUBLISHING

Publisher's Cataloging-In-Publication Data
(Prepared by The Donohue Group, Inc.)

Names: Shally-Jensen, Michael, editor.
Title: Careers in manufacturing & production / editor, Michael Shally-Jensen, Ph.D.
Other Titles: Careers in manufacturing and production | Careers in--
Description: [First edition]. | Ipswich, Massachusetts : Salem Press, a division of EBSCO
        Information Services, Inc. ; Amenia, NY : Grey House Publishing,
        [2016] | Includes bibliographical references and index.
Identifiers: ISBN 978-1-61925-894-5 (hardcover)
Subjects: LCSH: Manufacturing industries--Vocational guidance--United States.
Classification: LCC HD9720.5 .C375 2016 | DDC 338.6--dc23

First Printing

PRINTED IN THE UNITED STATES OF AMERICA

CONTENTS

PUBLISHER'S NOTE

Careers in Manufacturing & Production contains twenty-seven alphabetically arranged chapters describing specific fields of interest in these industries. Merging scholarship with occupational development, this single comprehensive guidebook provides manufacturing and production students with the necessary insight into potential careers, and provides instruction on what job seekers can expect in terms of training, advancement, earnings, job prospects, working conditions, relevant associations, and more. *Careers in Manufacturing & Production* is specifically designed for a high school and undergraduate audience and is edited to align with secondary or high school curriculum standards.

Scope of Coverage

Understanding the wide net of jobs in manufacturing and production is important for anyone preparing for a career within those fields. *Careers in Manufacturing & Production* comprises twenty-seven lengthy chapters on a broad range of occupations including traditional and long-established jobs such as welder and tool and die maker, as well as in-demand jobs including industrial designer, quality control inspector, and power plant operator. This excellent reference also presents possible career paths and occupations within high-growth and emerging fields in these industries.

Careers in Manufacturing & Production is enhanced with numerous charts and tables, including projections from the US Bureau of Labor Statistics, and median annual salaries or wages for those occupations profiled. Each chapter also notes those skills that can be applied across broad occupation categories. Interesting enhancements, like **Fun Facts**, **Famous Firsts**, and dozens of photos, add depth to the discussion. A highlight of most chapters is **Conversation With** – a two-page interview with a professional working in a related job. The respondents share their personal career paths, detail potential for career advancement, offer advice for students, and include a "try this" for those interested in embarking on a career in their profession.

Essay Length and Format

Each chapter ranges in length from 3,500 to 4,500 words and begins with a Snapshot of the occupation that includes career clusters, interests, earnings and employment outlook. This is followed by these major categories:

- **Overview** includes detailed discussions on: Sphere of Work; Work Environment; Occupation Interest; A Day in the Life. Also included here is a Profile that outlines working conditions, educational needs, and physical abilities. You will also find the occupation's Holland Interest Score, which matches up character and personality traits with specific jobs.

- **Occupational Specialties** lists specific jobs that are related in some way, like engraving press operators, graphic designer, and material coordinators. Duties and Responsibilities are also included.

- **Work Environment** details the physical, human, and technological environment of the occupation profiled.

- **Education, Training, and Advancement** outlines how to prepare for this field while in high school, and what college courses to take, including licenses and certifications needed. A section is devoted to the Adult Job Seeker, and there is a list of skills and abilities needed to succeed in the job profiled.

- **Earnings and Advancements** offers specific salary ranges, and includes a chart of metropolitan areas that have the highest concentration of the profession.

- **Employment and Outlook** discusses employment trends, and projects growth to 2020. This section also lists related occupations.

- **Selected Schools** list those prominent learning institutions that offer specific courses in the profiles occupations.

- **More Information** includes associations that the reader can contact for more information.

Special Features

Several features continue to distinguish this reference series from other career-oriented reference works. The back matter includes:
- Appendix A: Guide to Holland Code. This discusses John Holland's theory that people and work environments can be classified into six different groups: Realistic; Investigative; Artistic; Social; Enterprising; and Conventional. See if the job you want is right for you!
- Appendix B: General Bibliography. This is a collection of suggested readings, organized into major categories.
- Subject Index: Includes people, concepts, technologies, terms, principles, and all specific occupations discussed in the occupational profile chapters.

Acknowledgments

Thanks to editor Michael Shally-Jensen, who played a principal role in shaping this work with current, comprehensive, and valuable material. Thanks are also due to Allison Blake, who took the lead in developing "Conversations With," with help from Vanessa Parks, and to the professionals who communicated their work experience through interview questionnaires. Their frank and honest responses provide immeasurable value to *Careers in Manufacturing & Production*. The contributions of all are gratefully acknowledged.

EDITOR'S INTRODUCTION

Introduction

Manufacturing, or the making of finished goods and other products (including parts and materials), employs about 12 million people in the United States. The manufacturing industry as a whole creates all kinds of products, from chemicals and circuit boards to food, machinery, and motor vehicles. Many manufacturing jobs are in large plants or factories, but others are in smaller settings such as custom shops, specialized mills, and small manufacturing facilities.

There were about 265,000 job openings in manufacturing in spring 2014, according to the U.S. Bureau of Labor Statistics (BLS). Although BLS expects that employment will decline somewhat in selected manufacturing industries over the next ten years, industry experts say that there still is a need for workers with the right set of skills in manufacturing. Most job openings are expected to arise from the need to replace workers who are retiring, but others will be created through industry changes and/or growth. Employers have a continuing need for qualified workers such as machinists, welders, food workers, transportation equipment assemblers, and maintenance technicians, among other skilled and semiskilled trades. Moreover, the pay in manufacturing can be good: BLS data show that workers in this industry often earn more overall than workers in other industries.

Industrial Ups and Downs

The tale of manufacturing in the United States is a tale of growth, decline, and recovery. Manufacturing employment peaked in the late 1970s and has been fluctuating, with an overall decline, since then. Although manufacturing growth was especially strong in the 1950s and 1960s, it also held steady in the 1990s, even as goods manufactured outside the United States were starting to compete with those produced domestically. Between 2000 and 2010, manufacturing employment declined significantly, by as much as one-third of its total (or 6 million jobs). The lower cost of producing goods outside the country led many companies to move their manufacturing operations abroad. Additionally, manufacturing, like many other industries, was hit hard during the economic recession of 2008-2009.

Fortunately, in recent years the manufacturing industry has been adding jobs in selected occupations and in selected regions. The nature of the industry has changed, however, with fewer jobs on the assembly line and more jobs operating machines and/or the computer-control devices that run them. Furthermore, some manufacturers have begun moving their operations back to the United States, owing to growing labor costs everywhere, the expense of transporting material and goods, and administrative and other difficulties often associated with sustaining a foreign business. Even so, manufacturing employment has not returned to pre-recession levels, and it is unlikely to do so because technology continues to increase productivity and reduce the need for some types of workers.

All told, then, BLS projects manufacturing to lose about a half million jobs by 2022. Such is the nature of an ever advancing economy such as that of the United States. Yet, even as many of segments of the industry are expected to have slower-than-average employment growth, there will be some that should experience increases at relatively fast rates. For example, employment growth in two segments—engineered wood products and cement and concrete products—is expected to be about triple the average for all workers. Employment in architectural and structural metals manufacturing is expected to nearly double. Among the fastest growing segments are those related to construction, an industry that was hit hard by the recession but has now bounced back. As construction activity expands, so too should manufacturing industries that supply materials for construction projects.

Manufacturing Occupations

Workers in the manufacturing industry work in hundreds of different occupations. A little over half of these are first-line production occupations, such as assemblers, food production, metal and plastic machine workers, woodworkers, and power plant operators. The rest fall into categories such as engineering, maintenance and repair, transportation, and administration. Although all products are made differently, many of them go through similar stages of manufacture and involve a variety of workers performing different tasks.

Production workers help to make a product according to its design specifications, doing such tasks as operating machinery, overseeing product quality, or packaging and preparing finished goods for shipping. Although many production tasks have been automated, some of the largest employment numbers are linked to this group. Occupations such as supervisor and inspector see a steady demand, as do those of machinist, welder, and team assembler. Food production work, too, continues to do well in the industry.

Installation, maintenance, and repair workers keep the production equipment and machinery, as well as the facility itself, functioning properly. As a result of the increased use of automated processes, maintenance and repair work of machinery remains an important component of manufacturing. Industrial machinery mechanics and millwrights, for example, are projected to add about 25,000 jobs over the next ten years. These jobs are expected to be in several manufacturing industries, including motor vehicle parts manufacturing, architectural and structural metals manufacturing, and pharmaceutical and medicine manufacturing. Boilermakers, too, are expected to remain in demand even as the manufacturing industry evolves.

Transportation and material moving workers handle products and raw materials and help to get them from one location—such as a loading dock, shipping and receiving area, or warehouse—to another. The need for workers to do heavy lifting inside factories continues to diminish with the increased use of technology. At the same time, stock laborers and material movers are among the occupations with the largest manufacturing employment. Production and/or shipping coordinator is another slow but steady performer in this area.

Engineering and design professionals are often involved at the earliest stages of manufacturing when they are creating or improving a product's makeup and design. These workers may also help to design the machines, robots, and other technologies used in factories. As manufacturing innovation continues, a few of these occupations are projected to add some jobs over the next ten years. Boilermakers, too, are expected to remain in demand even as the manufacturing industry continues to change.

A Career in Manufacturing

As with any industry, manufacturing has both advantages and disadvantages. The work environment and other factors are worth considering when you are planning a career.

Work environment. Manufacturing worksites often include large rooms with conveyor belts, assembly lines, robotic equipment, and areas for processing or storing materials and products. Most also have areas for office workers that resemble those in other businesses. Production facilities can be hot and noisy, depending on the industry. In addition, some workers have tasks that are repetitive or require long periods of sitting or standing. To protect against injury, workers in manufacturing facilities often must follow strict safety rules and may be required to wear protective gloves, hair nets, or safety goggles. On the other hand, manufacturing offers flexibility for people who want to work a nonstandard schedule. Some facilities run production lines in two or even three shifts, which may involve evening and nighttime work.

Satisfactions. The rewards, in the end, can outweigh the difficulties of the job. Among the former are good pay and benefits along with the satisfaction of having contributed to the creation of a material product. Workers say that it is rewarding to observe the manufacturing process from start to finish. Some workers even seek jobs with a specific manufacturer because they like a product. If you like using your hands and modern technology, and also using your brain, then a career in manufacturing could be a good choice for you.

Education and training. The manufacturing field presents opportunities for job seekers with a range of backgrounds. Depending on the occupation, different qualities and skills are required. Workers usually need a combination of education and training. For example, computer-control machine tool operators typically need a high school diploma or better plus at least a month of on-the-job training. Jobs that require the least amount of preparation and skill have been the most heavily impacted by technological changes, as robots and other equipment have become more sophisticated. Manufacturers tend to need fewer workers today than they once did, but the workers that they do need tend to have higher levels of skills. Preparing for a manufacturing career thus includes education, training, experience, and, often, the learning of licenses or certifications.

Taking technical courses in high school is a good way to start preparing for a career in manufacturing. Additionally, you may want to consider earning a certificate or a degree from a community college or technical school. Keep in mind, however, that employers sometimes focus less on one's credentials and more on what one can do. Manufacturing workers need to be able to cooperate as part of a team. They also need to be detail oriented, dependable, and adept at problem solving. Dexterity and mechanical or technical ability are important, too. Thus, in many cases, a degree or certificate is useful, but employers are often also looking for those who can apply their skills. It is often advantageous to get in the workforce to gain practical experience while also continuing one's education.

Training on the job is one of the most important ways for workers to become competent at many occupations in manufacturing. This training often happens informally, as workers learn from more experienced workers. More structured training sometimes is offered as well. Through on-the-job training, workers get instruction in the tasks specific to their occupations; yet the learning typically comes through doing, through applying the training.

To qualify for an entry-level position in some occupations, you may need either work experience in a related occupation, a professional credential, or both. In other occupations, experience is useful even if it is not required.

—M. Shally-Jensen, Ph.D.

Sources and Further Reading

Killingsworth, William R. *Saving American Manufacturing: The Fight for Jobs, Opportunity, and National Security*. New York: Business Expert Press, 2014.

Torpey, Elka. "Got Skills? Think Manufacturing," *Career Outlook*, June 2014. Washington, DC: Bureau of Labor Statistics.

What Your Boss Wants: Manufacturing. New York: Films Media Group, 2015.

Boilermaker

Snapshot

Career Cluster(s): Manufacturing

Interests: Metalworking, welding, construction, working with your hands

Earnings (Yearly Average): $59,860

Employment & Outlook: Faster than Average Growth Expected

OVERVIEW

Sphere of Work

Boilermakers construct, repair, and install boilers, vats, and other industrial vessels designed to hold liquids and gases. The construction and installation of boilers and vats falls within the larger sphere of industrial manufacturing and maintenance. Boilermakers construct equipment used in home and commercial heating and cooling, industrial food production, scientific development, gas and electrical power generation, and a variety of other industries.

Work Environment

Boilermakers work in specialized manufacturing plants and also perform on-site installation, repair, refitting, and deconstruction services, which can take them into a variety of work environments. They may work independently or in close conjunction with other boilermakers, depending on the requirements of a specific job.

Boilermakers often work outdoors and may face climatic hazards on the job. In other cases, boilermakers may work in cramped, physically limited conditions, such as when repairing the inside of a boiler or working in a boiler room at an industrial facility. Boilermakers encounter significant physical risk during the course of their work and may be required to live away from home, in housing near individual worksites, for extended periods.

Profile

Working Conditions: Work both Indoors and Outdoors
Physical Strength: Medium Work, Heavy Work
Education Needs: On-The-Job Training, High School Diploma or G.E.D., High School Diploma with Technical Education, Apprenticeship
Licensure/Certification: Required
Opportunities For Experience: Apprenticeship, Military Service
Holland Interest Score*: RES, RIE, RSE

* See Appendix A

Occupation Interest

An individual pursuing a career as a boilermaker should have a strong interest in hands-on manufacturing and construction. Those with interest and experience in metalworking and welding will likely have an advantage when seeking employment. Because worksites and conditions vary, prospective boilermakers should be comfortable with a variable workload and should be prepared to encounter unpredictable conditions on the job.

A Day in the Life—Duties and Responsibilities

Most boilermakers work full-time schedules, though overtime work and changing hours are common during certain projects. The typical routine for a boilermaker depends considerably on the nature of the current project. A typical day may be spent in a workshop, fabricating or attaching parts for a boiler or vat, or at a worksite, installing, repairing, or deconstructing a boiler for a customer.

Boilermakers often must follow technical schematics and blueprints to construct the parts needed for a certain vat or boiler. Many of the parts, including tubes, intake and exhaust valves, and the bodies of the vats or boilers, are typically constructed in a workshop. Boilermakers spend a considerable amount of time welding, using either handheld welding tools or computer-aided equipment.

Once the components of a boiler or vat have been completed, the device must be installed in its final location. The installation process can take place in a variety of environments. Many facilities install boilers and vats outdoors or on rooftops. In other cases, boilers and vats may be installed in basements or specialized rooms.

Boilers and vats are constructed to endure years or even decades of continuous use. Boilermakers must therefore spend a considerable amount of time performing regular maintenance and inspections on previously installed vats and boilers. Maintenance often involves using hand-operated welding tools to repair cracks or broken seals in the piping leading to or away from the boiler. In many cases, boilermakers may be required to spend days or weeks working on site.

Duties and Responsibilities

- Locating and marking reference points for columns or plates
- Hammering, flame-cutting, filing, or grinding irregular sections or structures to fit edges together
- Bolting or welding structures and sections together
- Aligning, connecting, and welding water tubes to drums and headers
- Installing manholes, valves, gauges, and feedwater connections
- Assisting in testing assembled vessels for leaks and other defects
- Repairing assembled boilers or tanks

OCCUPATION SPECIALTIES

Boilermakers II

Boilermakers II assemble boilers, tanks, vats, and pressure vessels according to blueprint instructions. They differ from Boilermakers I, who assemble and repair boilers and related pressure vessels.

Boilermaker Fitters

Boilermaker Fitters position, align and temporarily secure structural parts and related assemblies of pressure vessels, such as boilers, tanks and vats, for permanent assembly by Boilermakers.

Boiler House Mechanics

Boiler House Mechanics maintain and repair stationary steam boilers and related equipment, using hand tools and portable power tools.

WORK ENVIRONMENT

Physical Environment

Boilermakers typically spend part of their time in manufacturing facilities and part of their time working on-site in a variety of conditions. Fabrication and construction are conducted indoors, while maintenance, installation, and deconstruction sometimes occur in outdoor environments.

Plant Environment

Manufacturing plants are common venues for the construction of boilers and vats. In addition, many boilers and vats are used in industrial processes and may be installed in plants of various types, including utility and power plants, brewing facilities, and iron and steel construction facilities.

Transferable Skills and Abilities

Organization & Management Skills
- Coordinating tasks
- Making decisions
- Managing people/groups
- Paying attention to and handling details
- Performing duties which change frequently

Research & Planning Skills
- Developing evaluation strategies

Technical Skills
- Applying the technology to a task
- Performing scientific, mathematical and technical work

Unclassified Skills
- Performing work that produces tangible results

Human Environment

Many large-scale projects require boilermakers to work in conjunction with one another. In some cases, boilermakers may work closely with engineers or technical drafters in order to translate design blueprints into a finished product. Boilermakers also work in training groups that include apprentices, or beginning workers; journeymen, workers who have completed apprenticeship requirements; and master workers, experienced boilermakers who supervise lower-level workers during projects.

Technological Environment

Boilermakers often use computer-aided welding machines for construction projects and may also use computer-aided drafting and design (CAD) software to refine and change boiler and vat specifications before construction. In many cases, handheld tools are used for a large number of construction, repair, and installation projects.

EDUCATION, TRAINING, AND ADVANCEMENT

High School/Secondary

Most boilermakers receive on-the-job training through apprenticeship programs and may begin training immediately after finishing high school or an equivalent degree program. High school–level training in mathematics, engineering, and drafting may be helpful to those entering the field. In addition, basic computer literacy skills are often needed for communication with customers and operation of field-specific software and machinery.

Suggested High School Subjects
- Applied Math
- Blueprint Reading
- English
- Metals Technology
- Welding

Famous First

The first boiler inspection law was enacted in Connecticut in 1864. It authorized the governor to appoint an Inspector of Boilers to check every steam boiler used for manufacturing or mechanical (e.g., locomotive) purposes.

Postsecondary

Few apprenticeship programs require postsecondary education for applicants, though some colleges and technical institutes offer programs in mechanical construction that may be helpful to those pursuing employment as boilermakers. In addition, because welding is a frequently used skill among boilermakers, those with certification or training in welding techniques are more likely to be accepted into apprenticeship programs. Many technical institutes offer certification programs that train in the use of hand-operated and computer-aided welding devices.

Adult Job Seekers

Though most boilermakers begin their careers following high school, adults may transition to the field by completing training programs offered at technical institutes or by applying directly to an apprenticeship program. Adults with previous experience in welding, manufacturing, or metalworking may have an advantage in obtaining an apprenticeship in the field.

Professional Certification and Licensure

Boilermakers receive professional certification by completing an apprenticeship program offered by an organization such as the Boilermakers National Apprenticeship Program (BNAP). Most apprenticeship programs require four to five years of training, including at least 144 hours of related technical training and 2,000 hours of paid, on-the-job training per year. Apprenticeship programs cover basic metalworking and welding techniques as well as the technical aspects of construction equipment and computer and manual design. Trainees are also required to learn first aid and safety procedures, as much of the work performed by boilermakers can be physically hazardous.

Following the completion of an approved apprenticeship period, a boilermaker becomes a journeyman worker. A journeyman is considered a professional but still works under the supervision of an experienced boilermaker for several years. Following this period, the boilermaker becomes a master, an independent professional qualified to supervise journeymen or apprentice workers on the job.

Additional Requirements

The construction of boilers and vats is physically demanding, and those seeking a career in the field must be capable of performing the physical tasks the job requires. Boilermakers must typically be capable of lifting heavy objects and have sufficient physical dexterity to complete a variety of tasks safely. Many apprenticeship programs take physical capabilities into account when determining whether to accept an applicant.

Fun Fact

It's a drink that dates back to the 1920s and brings to mind grimy taverns, but the New York Times reports that the "boilermaker"—a shot of whiskey and a beer—is making a comeback in trendy bars.

Source: http://www.nytimes.com/2014/10/15/dining/a-shot-and-a-beer-the-boilermaker-stages-a-comeback.html?_r=0

EARNINGS AND ADVANCEMENT

Earnings depend on the type of industry, union affiliation, and employee's experience and job specialty. Boilermaker installation workers usually earn more than repairers, and those employed in the construction industry generally earn more than those in industrial plants.

Boilermakers had median annual earnings of $59,860 in 2014. The lowest ten percent earned less than $36,000, and the highest ten percent earned more than $87,320. Apprentices started at about half of journey-level wages, with wages increasing gradually to the journey wage as progress is made in the apprenticeship.

Boilermakers may receive paid vacations, holidays and sick days; life and health insurance; and retirement benefits. These are usually paid by the employer.

Metropolitan Areas with the Highest Employment Level in this Occupation

Metropolitan area	Employment	Employment per thousand jobs	Annual mean wage
Houston-Sugar Land-Baytown, TX	1,030	0.36	$54,670
Indianapolis-Carmel, IN	700	0.75	$70,080
Baton Rouge, LA	650	1.71	$48,620
Beaumont-Port Arthur, TX	470	2.98	$60,610
Evansville, IN-KY	440	2.57	$66,120
Pittsburgh, PA	280	0.25	n/a
Cleveland-Elyria-Mentor, OH	260	0.26	$64,370
Savannah, GA	250	1.59	$61,640
Seattle-Bellevue-Everett, WA	240	0.16	$52,640
New Orleans-Metairie-Kenner, LA	170	0.31	$61,700

Source: Bureau of Labor Statistics

EMPLOYMENT AND OUTLOOK

Boilermakers held about 17,500 jobs in 2014. Employment of boilermakers is expected to grow faster than the average for all occupations through the year 2024, which means employment is projected to increase 7 percent to 11 percent. Growth will be driven by the need to maintain and upgrade, rather than replace, existing boilers; the use of smaller boilers, which require less onsite assembly; and automation of production technologies. Demand for more boilermakers may result from environmental upgrades required by federal regulations such as the Clean Air Act. Opportunities are still expected to be best for experienced workers to maintain and repair existing equipment.

Employment Trend, Projected 2014–24

Construction trades workers: 10%

Boilermakers: 9%

Total, all occupations: 7%

Note: "All Occupations" includes all occupations in the U.S. Economy. Source: U.S. Bureau of Labor Statistics, Employment Projections Program

Related Occupations
- Blacksmith
- Elevator Installer/Repairer
- Millwright
- Sheet Metal Worker
- Welder

Related Occupations
- Power Plant Operator
- Powerhouse Mechanic

Conversation With . . .
CRYSTAL LEDFORD

Journeyman Boilermaker, Boilermakers Union Local 83
Kansas City, Missouri
Boilermaker, 10 years

1. What was your individual career path in terms of education/training, entry-level job, or other significant opportunity?

In high school, I learned to weld in a vocational program. After high school I got a job in a shop welding, which I did for seven years. The first shop I worked in focused on handicapped accessible equipment; we made the chairs that go up stairs and elevators for homes. When the shop I was working in went under, I heard the boilermakers were looking for people who could weld, so I went down to the union hall. I started in their apprenticeship program. You do on-the-job training and they start you off at a lower wage and continually bump you up until you're full-fledged. It's supposed to be a four-year program, but I ended up doing it in two by putting in a lot of hours. I did four three-week sessions of school, learning welding processes, math, and blueprint reading, and alternated that with time in the field. At the end, you're a journeyman.

Boilermakers do a lot of welding. We also do heavy rigging—picking up things with cranes and moving them around. Sometimes I work on a forklift; sometimes it's mechanical work and putting things together. I'm in a union and get sent to different sites all the time. I work in refineries, ethanol plants, and nuclear power plants. As a woman, you almost have to show up ready to prove yourself every day when you're traveling around to different states. But in the last five years, I've seen more women come in, younger women. It's good to see that change.

2. What are the most important skills and/or qualities for someone in your profession?

Welding is one of the predominant skills that you need. But a lot of it is work ethic. You also need mechanical skills.

3. What do you wish you had known going into this profession?

I live in Missouri and just three months into the year, I have worked in Wisconsin, California, Kansas, and Iowa, as well as here in Missouri. If I'd known how much travel is involved, I would have done some things differently. I had just bought a house. I might have bought a smaller house that was a little more maintenance-free.

4. Are there many job opportunities in your profession? In what specific areas?

We've had a lot of work the last few years. It feels a little shaky at the moment, not knowing what the Environmental Protection Agency (EPA) rules are going to be for power, but there's still quite a bit of work. A large part of work in the Midwest is in power plants and refineries and ethanol plants, but boilermakers also work in shipyards. And you're not just limited to the United States. If I wanted to I could get on a list to work all over the place. Australia is building a lot of power plants right now. You can also find work in shops, which mainly make some of the smaller parts and pieces and sometimes pre-assemble large pieces of equipment that we put out in the field.

5. How do you see your profession changing in the next five years? What role will technology play in those changes, and what skills will be required?

Technology will either make or break boilermakers, depending on how the U.S. generates its power in the next ten to fifteen years. Are we going to clean up coal or are we going to do something different? If we go completely solar and it's just solar panels and not solar plants, there will be a reduction in the work force. We have a solar power plant in Arizona right now, but it's still experimental. The building and the boiler is basically the same piece of equipment that's on a coal boiler; it's just how the water inside the boiler is heated that's different.

In the last ten years, though, technology really helped us because the process of cleaning coal added massive amounts of work. Our numbers almost quadrupled because what used to be just a power plant now had a whole line of equipment to clean up the coal.

6. What do you enjoy most about your job? What do you enjoy least about your job?

The answer to both is travel. I enjoy going from job to job and meeting different people and seeing different cities. When you're there for a month or so, it's almost like you live there, so you don't see just the tourist traps. But if you have a family, it's hard to maintain a home life.

7. Can you suggest a valuable "try this" for students considering a career in your profession?

There are boilermaker shops where you could go work in the summer. You could go in and help make some of the equipment that they ship out into the field. It would give you insight into what we do.

MORE INFORMATION

American Boiler Manufacturers Association
8221 Old Courthouse Road, Suite 202
Vienna, VA 22182
703.356.7172
www.abma.com

Boilermakers National Apprenticeship Program
753 State Avenue, Suite 151
Kansas City, KS 66101
913.342.2100
www.bnap.com

International Brotherhood of Boilermakers, Iron Shipbuilders, Blacksmiths, Forgers
753 State Avenue, Suite 570
Kansas City, KS 66101
913.371.2640
www.boilermakers.org

International Union, UAW
Solidarity House
8000 East Jefferson Avenue
Detroit, MI 48214
313.926.5000
uaw@uaw.org
www.uaw.org

United Steelworkers of America
Five Gateway Center
Pittsburgh, PA 15222
412.562.2400
www.usw.org

Micah Issitt/Editor

Chemical Equipment Operator

Snapshot

Career Cluster: Manufacturing; Production

Interests: Chemistry, industrial processes, repetitive work, solving problems, analyzing information

Earnings (Yearly Average): $48,090

Employment & Outlook: Decline Expected

OVERVIEW

Sphere of Work

Chemical equipment operators are responsible for the control and monitoring of machines that change raw materials into commercial and industrial products. They control the flow of chemicals through production equipment and are responsible for maintaining equipment, measuring and adding chemicals, and checking tracking gauges that monitor chemical processes. Operators may monitor multiple machines and may be responsible for taking and testing samples to ensure that chemicals are being processed correctly.

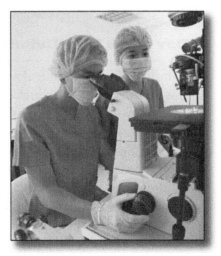

Work Environment

Chemical equipment operators work in a variety of environments, as different chemical processes have highly specialized environmental needs. They often need to climb ladders in order to access tanks and may work in close, tight spaces both indoors and outdoors. Safety equipment varies from industry to industry but often includes respirators, safety glasses, chemical-protection suits, and breathing devices. Chemical equipment operators work in noisy environments and may be subject to extreme lighting and temperature variations depending on the industry in which they are employed.

Profile

Working Conditions: Work Indoors
Physical Strength: Light Work
Education Needs: On-the-Job Training, High School Diploma or G.E.D., High School Diploma with Technical Education, Junior/Technical/Community College
Licensure/Certification: Usually Not Required
Opportunities For Experience: Internship
Holland Interest Score*: RCE

* See Appendix A

Occupation Interest

Individuals drawn to the profession of chemical equipment operator are detail oriented and focused. They are interested in science and chemistry but also in industrial processes, and they do not tire of repetitive, multipart tasks. They are comfortable working with minimal social interaction but are conscious of the safety of themselves and their colleagues. They are independent thinkers and are able to solve problems quickly and analyze complex information.

A Day in the Life—Duties and Responsibilities

The daily duties of chemical equipment operators vary according to the product under production, but operators typically begin by reading ingredient and processing instructions for the machines for which they are responsible and measuring ingredients to add to the machines. Some processes use premeasured ingredients. Operators set and monitor gauges and timers and implement machine operation. Once the process is underway, operators monitor temperature and pressure and may draw samples to test the product using specialized equipment such as pH meters and hydrometers. Operators keep detailed records of chemical processes, often in log format, in which various aspects of the process are noted over the course of production.

Once production is complete, the operator typically cleans and drains the equipment, inspects it for damage or malfunction, and completes the necessary records. They also often perform minor repairs and maintenance, such as lubricating parts and changing filters and screens, and monitor and maintain safety equipment.

Chemical equipment operators may also be responsible for inventorying and ordering supplies and materials and may supervise other workers who deliver and work with supplies. Some equipment, particularly large-capacity fermenting and mixing equipment, is operated from a control room. In this case, operators communicate with maintenance personnel to ensure that cleaning and repairs are completed on the equipment.

Duties and Responsibilities

- Reading plant specifications to determine product type, ingredients needed, and any special procedures required
- Starting equipment to feed raw materials automatically or dumping pre-weighed ingredients into mixing tanks, heating vessels, or onto conveyors
- Drawing samples of the product at specified stages

OCCUPATION SPECIALTIES

Chief Operators

Chief Operators control chemical process equipment from an instrumented control board or other control station. They monitor the recording instruments, panel lights and other indicators, and listen for warning signals to verify conformity of the process conditions to the standards of safety and efficiency of the plant.

Continuous-Still Operators

Continuous-Still Operators control continuous stills from a control station to separate and condense liquids and maintain process control by instrument readings and test results.

Batch-Still Operators

Batch-Still Operators tend batch stills to separate, by distillation, liquids having divergent volatilization temperatures.

Catalytic Converter Operators

Catalytic Converter Operators control catalytic converters to alter chemical composition of liquid or gaseous substances according to knowledge of the process and the sequence of operations.

Saturator Operators

Saturator Operators control saturator tank and auxiliary equipment to precipitate ammonium sulfate.

Kettle Operators

Kettle Operators control heat reaction kettles to process liquid and solid materials into specified chemical products.

Dissolver Operators

Dissolver Operators control equipment that dissolves and precipitates chemicals used in manufacturing chemical products such as butadiene and styrene.

Fermentation Operators

Fermentation Operators control fermentation chambers and tanks to produce enzymes from fungal or bacterial growth for use as industrial catalysts.

Specialties Operators

Specialties Operators control equipment to prepare chemical solutions to meet customer orders or specifications

WORK ENVIRONMENT

Physical Environment

Most chemical equipment operators work in large chemical or manufacturing facilities. Some facilities have both indoor and outdoor components. Outdoor plants are usually covered and protected from the elements. Some facilities are housed within plants that perform multiple tasks in a production chain. Facilities are often brightly lit, and temperatures vary widely. Chemical equipment operators spend many hours standing and moving around, adjusting gauges and pumps and handling water-flow systems used to clean equipment.

Transferable Skills and Abilities

Organization & Management Skills
- Making decisions
- Paying attention to and handling details
- Performing routine work

Research & Planning Skills
- Developing evaluation strategies

Technical Skills
- Working with machines, tools or other objects
- Working with your hands

Human Environment

Chemical equipment operators work alone much of the time, with limited opportunity for social contact while work is being performed. Interaction while on the job is often limited by the noise of the equipment and the attention required to monitor the chemical processes. However, they must be aware of the activities of others on their team, as one chemical process often depends on or affects another. The safety of others in the facility is crucial. Operators often work as part of a team and interact with colleagues and supervisors at set points in the production process.

Technological Environment

Chemical equipment operators must be familiar with computers and various computer systems, as these systems regulate and monitor multiple aspects of chemical processes. They are sometimes responsible for programming software and may use computer systems to log and track information and analyze data.

EDUCATION, TRAINING, AND ADVANCEMENT

High School/Secondary

Students interested in chemical equipment operation should develop a strong background in mechanics, mathematics, and science. Classes focused on industrial mathematics are helpful, as are classes in applied chemistry and statistics. Strong writing skills are important for communicating system information and reporting data.

Suggested High School Subjects
- Applied Biology/Chemistry
- Applied Math
- Chemistry
- English
- Machining Technology
- Mathematics
- Science
- Shop Math
- Shop Mechanics

Famous First

The first dynamite was manufactured in San Francisco, Calif., in 1866. Operating from a site that is now part of Golden Gate Park, Julius Bandmann used patents granted to Alfred Nobel, the inventor of dynamite, to produce the substance under the name Bandmann Nielson Co.

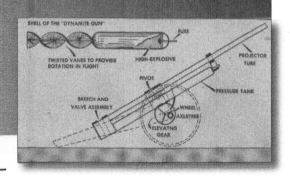

Postsecondary

An associate's degree in applied science or chemical technology is useful when applying for positions in the field of chemical production. These degrees are often paired with on-the-job training in the form of an internship.

Related College Majors

- Physical Science Technologies

Adult Job Seekers

Chemical equipment operators are often promoted from entry-level positions within a plant or factory. Most employers look for two or more years of job experience in a related field. Some companies offer internships or specialized training in lower-level positions that prepare candidates for work as operators. Many community colleges offer night and weekend classes in chemical technology and help to arrange internships with established organizations.

Professional Certification and Licensure

Though formal licensure is not required, many companies require a skill test based on equipment specific to their product lines. Some companies have specialized training and internal certification programs. In addition, a physical examination is often required before employment in this field.

Additional Requirements

Chemical equipment operators are often hired to work forty hours per week and then paid overtime if they exceed that time. Because of this, long hours are possible, though lucrative. Operators are expected to be alert and active and able to remain so for many hours. Good vision and coordination are necessary to ensure that system safety is maintained. In addition, physical strength is often needed to add chemicals to a process, climb ladders to specialized tanks, and react quickly to potentially dangerous situations.

Fun Fact

The best-paid chemical equipment operators in the United States work in Baton Rouge, Louisiana, where the average mean wage was $71,250 in 2014. The lowest-paid operators lived in the East Arkansas area, and earn a mean $41,740.

Source: http://www.bls.gov/oes/current/oes519011.htm

EARNINGS AND ADVANCEMENT

Earnings of chemical equipment operators vary depending on the type and geographic location of the employer, seniority and job classification of the operator, type of product produced and equipment operated. Chemical equipment operators involved in formulating, processing and testing (class A operators) earn more than those primarily involved in tending machinery (class B operators). Those employed in plants producing inorganic chemicals earned slightly more than their counterparts employed in organic chemical plants. Nationally, in 2014, chemical equipment operators had median annual earnings of $48,090.

Chemical equipment operators may receive paid vacations, holidays, and sick days; life and health insurance; and retirement benefits. These are usually paid by the employer.

Metropolitan Areas with the Highest
Employment Level in this Occupation

Metropolitan area	Employment	Employment per thousand jobs	Annual mean wage
Houston-Sugar Land-Baytown, TX	6,130	2.15	$58,230
Philadelphia, PA	2,110	1.13	$47,690
Chicago-Joliet-Naperville, IL	1,540	0.41	$52,380
Dallas-Plano-Irving, TX	1,460	0.65	n/a
Baton Rouge, LA	1,230	3.22	$71,250
Wilmington, DE-MD-NJ	1,020	3.04	$51,690
Cleveland-Elyria-Mentor, OH	960	0.94	$46,870
Newark-Union, NJ-PA	910	0.94	$58,470
Edison-New Brunswick, NJ	890	0.89	$45,140
Pittsburgh, PA	830	0.73	$49,690

Source: Bureau of Labor Statistics

EMPLOYMENT AND OUTLOOK

There were approximately 45,000 chemical equipment operators employed nationally in 2014. Employment is expected to decline through the year 2024. Job openings will occur to replace workers who retire or transfer to other occupations.

Related Occupations
- Power Plant Operator
- Stationary Engineer
- Water Treatment Plant Operator

MORE INFORMATION

American Chemical Society
Education Division
Career Education Program
1155 16th Street, NW
Washington, DC 20036
800.227.5558
www.chemistry.org

American Chemistry Council
700 Second Street NE
Washington, DC 20002
202.249.7000
www.americanchemistry.com

Bethany Groff/Editor

Computer-Control Machine Tool Operator

OVERVIEW

Sphere of Work

Computer-control machine tool operators are responsible for the setup and operation of computer numerical controlled (CNC) machines, including lathes, mills, and turning machines. They operate machines that form, shape, and cut metal and plastic materials used in factories. Operators are responsible for monitoring machines and adjusting them as needed. Computer-control machine tool operators work in a wide range of industries, from automotive manufacturing to machinery and plastics production.

Work Environment

Computer-control machine tool operators work in machine shops. As these shops present a number of safety hazards, operators must wear earplugs for protection from work noise, safety goggles to protect eyes from flying particles, and reinforced boots to protect feet from heavy equipment. Operators are expected to adhere to strict quality control and safety standards. Most computer-control machine tool operators stand throughout the day, but movement is limited and repetitive.

Profile

Working Conditions: Work Indoors
Physical Strength: Medium Work
Education Needs: On-The-Job Training, High School Diploma or G.E.D., High School Diploma with Technical Education, Junior/Technical/Community College, Apprenticeship
Licensure/Certification: Recommended
Opportunities For Experience: Apprenticeship, Part-Time Work
Holland Interest Score*: REI

* See Appendix A

Occupation Interest

Individuals drawn to the profession tend to be independent workers who are interested in complex machinery. They should be able to perform routine tasks without losing attention to detail. Operators are invested in accuracy and precision and interested in mechanical problem solving. Although they work independently, operators must cooperate regularly with colleagues. Individuals interested in the computer-control machine field must be knowledgeable about computer programming, design templates, and computer software. They must work well under pressure and be able to remain focused for long periods.

A Day in the Life—Duties and Responsibilities

The daily duties of a computer-control machine tool operator include inspecting machines for wear and damage before beginning machine operation. Once a machine is in operation, the operator calculates how best to lift and feed materials through the machine and monitors the size and shape of cuts. Some operators may use cranes or lifts to maneuver large pieces. Operators listen for sounds that may indicate worn or faulty components and check for changes in machine vibration and temperature that might indicate a problem. Lubricants and cooling systems are employed to ensure proper machine operation. On occasion, an operator may stop a machine to make minor repairs or to modify or adjust processing according to preset machining sequences

Computer-control machine tool operators use precision tools to install, align, or replace bits and cutting heads. They prepare materials for processing while the machine is in operation, ensuring smooth workflow. They also inspect and measure finished pieces with gauges and calipers to ensure correct machine operation and may work with production lines that include hoists and conveyor belts. Operators are also responsible for cleaning their machines and performing closing inspections at the end of the workday.

Operators are not often required to write, but they must be able to follow complex written instructions. They are often responsible for the input of production data and sometimes the creation of reports. Computer-control machine tool operators may confer with programmers and supervisors to identify problems with machining programs.

Duties and Responsibilities

- Reviewing set-up sheet and specifications to determine operational sequences
- Bolting fixtures to machine bed
- Positioning metal stock in fixture and securing work piece in place
- Assembling cutting tools in tool holders and positioning tools in spindles

OCCUPATION SPECIALTIES

Numerical Control Router Set-Up Operators

Numerical Control Router Set-Up Operators set up and operate
multi-axis, numerically controlled routing machines to cut and shape
metallic and non-metallic workpieces.

Numerical Control Milling-Machine Operators

Numerical Control Milling-Machine Operators set up and operate
multi-axis, numerically controlled milling machines to mill surfaces on
metallic and non-metallic workpieces.

Numerical Control Drill-Press Operators

Numerical Control Drill-Press Operators set up and operate
numerically controlled drill presses that automatically perform
machining operations such as drilling, reaming, counter-sinking, spot-
facing and tapping of holes in metal workpieces.

Numerical Control Jig-Boring Machine Operators

Numerical Control Jig-Boring Machine Operators set up and operate
numerically controlled jig-boring machines to perform such jigging
operations as boring, drilling and counter-sinking holes in metal
workpieces.

WORK ENVIRONMENT

Physical Environment

Most computer-control machine tool operators work in machine shops contained within larger factories. Some operators work with very large pieces of material, such as aerospace components, and must use hoists, cranes, and other lifting devices. Machine shops may contain contaminants such as particulates and hazardous fumes, and operators must wear protective clothing and masks to reduce exposure.

Transferable Skills and Abilities

Organization & Management Skills
- Making decisions
- Paying attention to and handling details

Research & Planning Skills
- Developing evaluation strategies

Technical Skills
- Performing scientific, mathematical and technical work
- Working with machines, tools or other objects
- Working with your hands

Human Environment

Although computer-control machine tool operators carry out their daily tasks independently, they usually work in a team setting, so physical proximity to other workers is common. Noise and vibration make routine communication difficult. Periodic contact may be made with others to ask advice or receive instructions.

Technological Environment

Computer-control machine tool operators must have some knowledge of computer-aided design (CAD) programs, as they may be required to perform basic programming functions. They sometimes use industrial control software that monitors workflow and inventory and enter data into spreadsheets for reporting purposes.

EDUCATION, TRAINING, AND ADVANCEMENT

High School/Secondary

Students interested in the field of computer-control machine tool operation should study mathematics and mechanics and take any available classes in basic engineering, design, and drafting. Courses in shop math and geometry are also beneficial to those interested in the field.

Suggested High School Subjects
- Algebra
- Applied Math
- Applied Physics
- Blueprint Reading
- Computer Science
- Drafting
- English
- Geometry
- Machining Technology
- Shop Math
- Trigonometry

Famous First

The first computer-aided design (CAD) software was developed jointly in 1964 by General Motors and IBM. The system was first used to design the trunk lids of Cadillac automobiles (a GM brand).

Postsecondary

Although postsecondary education is typically not required, aspiring computer-control machine tool operators may benefit from certified training programs available at many community colleges and technical and vocational schools. Training for the field is also available in the military. Professional organizations such as the National Institute for Metalworking Skills (NIMS) provide resources for those interested in pursuing certified training, including lists of accredited programs. Courses in CAD programs and industrial design may also be helpful.

Related College Majors
* Machine Technologist

Adult Job Seekers

Most adult job seekers in this field will increase their chances of finding work by earning certification prior to applying for positions. Training and certification is available through the NIMS Competency Based Apprenticeship System. Adult job seekers may benefit from the on-the-job experience and flexible training schedules that these apprenticeships provide.

Professional Certification and Licensure

Though certification and licensure are not required, some employers may prefer candidates who have earned credentials in various key metalworking skills. NIMS offers fifty-two credentials based on performance and theory tests and also accredits training programs at technical high schools and colleges throughout the United States.

Additional Requirements

Computer-control machine tool operators usually work forty hours per week. They are typically paid overtime if additional work is required. Physical strength is required to work with the materials involved in industrial production. Good stamina is necessary in order to be able to stand for long periods, and attention to detail is crucial.

Fun Fact

These precise and programmable machines are used for dying, jewelry making, drilling, metal molding, and cutting and shaping.

Source: http://www.slideshare.net/elvistaylormark/interesting-facts-about-cnc-machining

EARNINGS AND ADVANCEMENT

Earnings of computer-control machine tool operators depend on the type of machine operated, and the size, geographic location, and extent of unionization of the employer. Median annual earnings of computer-control machine tool operators were $36,440 in 2014.

Computer-control machine tool operators may receive paid vacations, holidays, and sick days; life and health insurance; and retirement benefits. These are usually paid by the employer. In some cases, employers and employees may contribute jointly to union trust funds used to pay for certain additional fringe benefits.

Metropolitan Areas with the Highest
Employment Level in this Occupation

Metropolitan area	Employment	Employment per thousand jobs	Annual mean wage
Houston-Sugar Land-Baytown, TX	5,400	1.90	$39,750
Milwaukee-Waukesha-West Allis, WI	4,010	4.88	$40,790
Chicago-Joliet-Naperville, IL	3,980	1.06	$38,390
Los Angeles-Long Beach-Glendale, CA	3,630	0.89	$37,750
Minneapolis-St. Paul-Bloomington, MN-WI	3,080	1.69	$40,230
Cleveland-Elyria-Mentor, OH	3,080	3.04	$36,950
Warren-Troy-Farmington Hills, MI	2,950	2.58	$40,530
Cincinnati-Middletown, OH-KY-IN	2,250	2.22	$36,640
Philadelphia, PA	2,200	1.18	$41,560
Santa Ana-Anaheim-Irvine, CA	1,770	1.19	$38,110

Source: Bureau of Labor Statistics

EMPLOYMENT AND OUTLOOK

Computer-control machine tool operators held about 120,000 jobs nationally in 2014. Most worked in machine shops, plastics products manufacturing, machinery manufacturing or transportation equipment manufacturing, making mostly aerospace and automobile parts. Employment of computer-control machine tool operators is expected to grow slower than the average for all occupations through the year 2024, which means employment is projected to increase 2 percent to 7 percent. Most jobs will be to replace workers who retire or transfer to other occupations.

Employment Trend, Projected 2014–24

Industrial trades workers: 9%

Total, all occupations: 7%

Computer-Controlled Machine Tool Operators: 4%

Note: "All Occupations" includes all occupations in the U.S. Economy. Source: U.S. Bureau of Labor Statistics, Employment Projections Program

Related Occupations
- Machinist
- Metal/Plastic Working Machine Operator
- Millwright
- Robotics Technician
- Sheet Metal Worker
- Textile Machinery Operator
- Tool & Die Maker

Conversation With . . .
KIDIA TYLER

Instructor, CNC Technology
Gateway Technical College, Racine, Wisconsin
CNC field, 19 years

1. What was your individual career path in terms of education/training, entry-level job, or other significant opportunity?

My mother was a punch-press operator and used to bring her tools, like a dial caliper, home. I was fascinated, but she wouldn't let me play with them. She would tell me: "When you get a little older, you can learn how to use them." So when I got older, I took a blueprint reading class and a gauging class, and learned to read calipers. I told her I was ready and she gave me that caliper. From that point on, I took computer numerical control (CNC) and manual machine classes and graduated in 1997 with a technical diploma in numerical control from Gateway Technical College in Racine, Wisconsin.

I started out setting up manual lathes and mills for a couple of years and then I transferred to my company's CNC department. Over the years, I worked for companies that made parts for the automotive, agricultural, and appliance industries. I worked on horizontal and vertical CNC machines.

I switched to teaching CNC technology because of my family. I have four daughters and a son; as they got older, one of my daughters said: "You're never there. You work twelve-hour days, seven days." She was right. I'm a single mother and I worked a lot of overtime and holidays. Also, I was getting tired carrying heavy tools and getting in and out of machines. I started taking night classes in criminal justice, then saw an opening for this job. I applied and got it, and am now teaching my second semester.

2. What are the most important skills and/or qualities for someone in your profession?

To be a CNC operator, you need to have some math skills. You need to read routings—job instructions on how to complete the process of machining parts—fill out paperwork, follow your work order. You need to pay attention to details.

To work with the machines, you need to know how to operate them, their programs, and how to stop that machine if it's doing something you know it's not supposed to be doing. You'll learn tool offsets, and how to load and unload the offset programs. And you need to know safety on the job. You've got to make sure you are paying attention to your machine and are focused on the job. You have got to be able to look at a part you've made and tell if something's wrong with it.

3. What do you wish you had known going into this profession?

It's not easy to be an African American woman working in a field with predominantly Caucasian men. It was hard to fit in and let them know I could pull my weight. It seems like it's more challenging with skilled work—when you know more than they do. That's when problems came in.

4. Are there many job opportunities in your profession? In what specific areas?

There are lots of CNC jobs within fifty miles of Racine. A lot of employers say they can't get qualified, knowledgeable operators and machinists. They have people coming in who haven't paid their dues and want to make more than $30 an hour in their first machinist job.

5. How do you see your profession changing in the next five years, what role will technology play in those changes, and what skills will be required?

Times are changing and the machines are changing. When I started, you had to make your own programs and blueprints. Now, you go to software for that. I think operators will need to know more programming and how to make blueprints.

6. What do you enjoy most about your job? What do you enjoy least about your job?

I enjoyed working with my hands and figuring out complex blueprints and I loved being a CNC machinist for the 18 years I did it. However, it got to the point I couldn't do it physically mentally or spiritually. When you're a CNC machinist you work a lot of overtime and I needed to make a change to spend more time with my family.

What I love about teaching is training students, and teaching them what I know and what to expect in industry. I love when a student stays in contact, goes out, gets a job, and comes back to say, "Oh, you were right." I like hearing about their successes.

But, I'd never taught before so I've had to learn how to teach from a book when I'm used to doing things hands-on. It's taken some time to learn how to hit competencies, or give tests and homework.

7. Can you suggest a valuable "try this" for students considering a career in your profession?

Take courses in manual and CNC machines. And take tours of manufacturers, talk with supervisors, and watch how a CNC machine works.

MORE INFORMATION

**National Institute for
Metalworking Skills**
10565 Fairfax Boulevard, Suite 203
Fairfax, VA 22030
703.352.4971
www.nims-skills.org

**National Tooling and Machining
Association**
1357 Rockside Road
Cleveland, OH 44134
800.248.6862
www.ntma.org

**Precision Machined Products
Association**
6700 West Snowville Road
Brecksville, OH 44141
440.526.0300
www.pmpa.org

**Precision Metalforming
Association Educational
Foundation**
6363 Oak Tree Boulevard
Independence, Ohio 44131-2500
216.901.8800
www.pmaef.org

Bethany Groff/Editor

Electromechanical Equipment Assembler

Snapshot

Career Cluster: Manufacturing; Production
Interests: Engineering, mathematics, electronics, working with your hands
Earnings (Yearly Average): $32,760
Employment & Outlook: Slower than Average Growth Expected

OVERVIEW

Sphere of Work

Electromechanical equipment assemblers fabricate and construct components that are used in a variety of industries, including construction, retail, computer science, and defense. These components include dynamometers, thermostats, control panels, switches, magnetic drums, tape drives, and appliances. Equipment assemblers also inspect, modify, and test equipment to ensure that it meets standards and specifications. Assemblers use an assortment of tools to position, align, and adjust small parts in electrical and mechanical systems. Detailed schematics, manuals, and blueprints are used during assembly.

Work Environment

Assemblers typically work in manufacturing plants, which vary in size. Although working conditions can differ between industries, an assembler's work normally involves long hours of physical labor while standing or sitting. The presence of machines, tools, and chemicals may pose safety hazards. Proper safety procedures must be followed in order to avoid injury. Electromechanical assemblers routinely wear safety equipment such as goggles and gloves.

Profile

Working Conditions: Work Indoors
Physical Strength: Light Work, Medium Work
Education Needs: On-The-Job Training, High School Diploma or G.E.D., High School Diploma with Technical Education
Licensure/Certification: Required
Opportunities For Experience: Internship, Part-Time Work
Holland Interest Score*: RIE

* See Appendix A

Occupation Interest

Electromechanical equipment assemblers are good with their hands and enjoy working with a team in a dynamic environment. Assemblers have a passion for engineering, mathematics, and electronics and are good at reading schematics and blueprints.

A Day in the Life—Duties and Responsibilities

The daily routine and responsibilities of an electromechanical equipment assembler vary depending on the industry they work in. Day-to-day duties typically involve the modification and assembly of electromechanical equipment. Robotic machinery, power tools, and programmable motion-control devices are utilized in many industries. Tasks performed by assemblers are usually repetitive and can vary in difficulty.

When assembling intricately designed electromechanical equipment, an assembler will refer to schematics and blueprints that detail how the item should be properly constructed. Power tools are used to align, size, and fit equipment components together. In order to connect components, assemblers use bolts and screws or a welding or soldering gun. Throughout the assembly process, assemblers work as part of a team to produce finished products.

Quality control is crucial to the assembly process. After a piece of equipment is complete, assemblers inspect, test, and adjust components to make sure that everything meets the specifications and requirements of the client. If a component needs to be repaired, an assembler takes apart the equipment and performs the necessary maintenance. During maintenance, an assembler cleans and lubricates components and subassemblies.

Duties and Responsibilities

- Examining parts for surface defects
- Positioning parts needed to assemble equipment
- Fastening the parts together using hand tools
- Soldering electrical components in place
- Testing the electrical and mechanical reliability of assemblies using a multimeter, oscilloscope, oscillator, gages, test lights, or other tools
- Drilling, reaming, or tapping holes when needed to complete the assembly of equipment
- Reading blueprints or written instructions

OCCUPATION SPECIALTIES

Final Assemblers

Final Assemblers assemble, install and adjust such electromechanical units as feed drivers, control key assemblies, and printing units on new and rebuilt punched card office machines.

Electromechanical Technicians

Electromechanical Technicians fabricate, test, analyze, and adjust precision electromechanical instruments, such as temperature probes, gyroscope units, telemetering systems, altimeters, and aerodynamic probes.

WORK ENVIRONMENT

Physical Environment

Electromechanical equipment assemblers normally work in manufacturing plants, where working conditions vary depending on the location and industry. Their work is physically demanding and involves long work hours.

Transferable Skills and Abilities

Organization & Management Skills
- Paying attention to and handling details
- Performing duties which change frequently

Research & Planning Skills
- Analyzing information
- Developing evaluation strategies

Technical Skills
- Performing scientific, mathematical and technical work
- Working with machines, tools or other objects
- Working with your hands

Unclassified Skills
- Performing work that produces tangible results

Plant Environment

Manufacturing plants are typically loud and pose numerous safety hazards. The machinery and tools used by assemblers can cause serious injuries, and adherence to safety procedures is essential.

Human Environment

Assemblers work closely with their colleagues, including supervisors, plant managers, and other assemblers. They also communicate with clients in order to ensure that proper product specifications and design elements are being addressed.

Technological Environment

Assemblers use a variety of automated machinery and hand tools, as well as computers, programmable motion-control devices, robotic devices, power drills, and soldering irons. They also use safety gear such as goggles, gloves, and rubber boots.

EDUCATION, TRAINING, AND ADVANCEMENT

High School/Secondary

Some employers require applicants to possess a high school diploma or equivalent certification. Various high school courses are beneficial to individuals interested in electromechanical equipment assembly, including basic and advanced mathematics, computer science, mechanical drawing, drafting, and engineering. Many high schools offer shop classes that can provide students with instruction in the fundamentals of electronics, engineering, and machinery.

Suggested High School Subjects
- Applied Math
- Blueprint Reading
- Electricity & Electronics
- English
- Metals Technology
- Shop Math
- Shop Mechanics
- Trade/Industrial Education
- Welding

Famous First

The first industrial dynamo, or electric generator capable of delivering power for manufacturing, was built in 1881 by the Edison Machine Works in New York City. Called Jumbo No. 1, it weighed 27 tons and had an armature (rotating, electromechanical component) weighing 6 tons. It could generate enough energy to operate 700 lamps, each rated at 16-candlepower. Such a capacity was impressive at the time but now seems rather meager.

Postsecondary

Some employers may require applicants to have a postsecondary degree in technology, engineering, or mathematics. Many community colleges and technical schools offer programs in electromechanical technology and electromechanical engineering technology. These programs, which are designed to give students a strong understanding of electromechanical systems, typically provide a combination of hands-on training and formal classroom instruction. Areas of study include circuit operation, basic troubleshooting, and mechanical principles. Community colleges and technical schools are good places for aspiring assemblers to network with more experienced professionals in the industry, and many also offer job-placement programs.

Related College Majors
- Electromechanical Technology

Adult Job Seekers

Individuals interested in pursuing a career as an electromechanical equipment assembler should enroll in a relevant program at a community college or technical school. Local unions and trade organizations are good places to inquire about job opportunities.

Professional Certification and Licensure

Some employers require certification and licensure. Obtaining certification is a good way for an assembler to prove his or her professional knowledge and skills. Employers are more likely to hire certified or licensed applicants. IPC–Association Connecting Electronics Industries offers several training and certification programs in soldering for electromechanical equipment assemblers. Certification programs offered by the IPC also include electronics assembly and management training.

Additional Requirements

Electromechanical equipment assemblers must be able to distinguish between different colors, as wires are normally color coded. In order to handle the components and tools used on the job, assemblers need to have steady hands and good concentration. The job normally calls for standing or sitting for long periods of time, which can be physically demanding, so assemblers should be in good physical shape and have good stamina.

Due to the complex technologies that are frequently used in the profession, assemblers should have a strong background in basic mathematics and computers. They should also be proficient at reading and understanding the schematics, blueprints, and technical manuals used in the assembly of equipment and components.

Fun Fact

If you want a job as an electromechanical equipment assembler, head for New Hampshire, Colorado, Oklahoma, Iowa or Massachusetts – the states with the highest concentration of such jobs.
Source: http://www.bls.gov/oes/current/oes512023.htm

EARNINGS AND ADVANCEMENT

Earnings of electromechanical equipment assemblers depend on the skill level needed in the assembly process, the type of product assembled, the size and location of the plant and the education of the employee. Electromechanical equipment assemblers had median annual earnings of $32,760 in 2014. The lowest ten percent earned less than $21,710, and the highest ten percent earned more than $48,940.

Electromechanical equipment assemblers may receive paid vacations, holidays, and sick days; life and health insurance; retirement benefits; and tuition reimbursement. These are usually paid by the employer.

Metropolitan Areas with the Highest Employment Level in this Occupation

Metropolitan area	Employment	Employment per thousand jobs	Annual mean wage
Houston-Sugar Land-Baytown, TX	2,260	0.80	$33,850
Los Angeles-Long Beach-Glendale, CA	1,620	0.40	$28,860
San Jose-Sunnyvale-Santa Clara, CA	1,350	1.38	$37,750
Boston-Cambridge-Quincy, MA	1,230	0.69	$39,430
Minneapolis-St. Paul-Bloomington, MN-WI	1,040	0.57	$33,450
Denver-Aurora-Broomfield, CO	1,020	0.77	$34,560
Santa Ana-Anaheim-Irvine, CA	930	0.63	$31,070
Dallas-Plano-Irving, TX	820	0.37	$34,230
New York-White Plains-Wayne, NY-NJ	760	0.14	$35,030
Chicago-Joliet-Naperville, IL	750	0.20	$36,990

Source: Bureau of Labor Statistics

EMPLOYMENT AND OUTLOOK

There were approximately 45,000 electromechanical equipment assemblers employed in 2014. Employment is expected to grow slower than the average for all occupations through the year 2024, which means employment is projected to increase 0 percent to 3 percent. This is due to increased automation and the transfer of companies to countries with cheaper labor. Most job openings will result as workers transfer to other jobs or leave the labor force

Employment Trend, Projected 2014–24

Total, all occupations: 7%

Assemblers and fabricators: -1%

Production occupations: -3%

Note: "All Occupations" includes all occupations in the U.S. Economy. Source: U.S. Bureau of Labor Statistics, Employment Projections Program

Related Occupations
- Biomedical Equipment Technician
- Energy Conservation & Use Technician
- Office Machine Repairer
- Precision Assembler
- Robotics Technician

Conversation With . . . DORI NOUGARET

Manufacturing Technician, Sypris Electronics
Tampa, Florida
Electronics manufacturing field, 29 years

1. What was your individual career path in terms of education/training, entry-level job, or other significant opportunity?

I am originally from western New York and started working in electronics right out of high school. I worked for Motorola for twelve years, starting as an entry level operator. I took every opportunity to learn new processes and some machine setup. Then family members started buying vacation houses in Zephyr Hills, about thirty miles north of Tampa. I came on vacation, liked the weather—as well as the fact that there was so much to do, like golf—so I decided to move to Florida. I delivered mail for about three and a half years, then decided I needed a full-time job and went back to manufacturing.

Seventeen years ago, I started as an entry-level solderer for Sypris Electronics, where we build electronic boards and box-built units for communications satellites and defense communications devices. I advanced to become a work director, then a manufacturing technician. My job is basically the same thing as an engineering aide. I develop processes when we have new products come in; I put change notices in for those, and help train operators.

As an example, a process I created helps us backfill components that are soldered onto a circuit board. I placed a piece of glass on top of the sample board, lifted by spacers to the same height as the component. Using measurements while injecting epoxy from a syringe, I figured out how much epoxy coverage we have when we don't have the glass that allows us to see what we're doing. This way, I know the process is repeatable during production.

I like to create things. At home, my husband is building an airplane and I made the baggage compartments and seats by making my own patterns.

2. What are the most important skills and/or qualities for someone in your profession?

The most important quality to have in any profession is to care about what you are doing. If you take pride in your work and are willing to learn, the skills that are needed will improve with experience. I feel it is helpful to learn from the ground up to be able to develop processes and help others gain the same skills later.

Attention to detail is very important, and you do need to have patience. When training people, I notice that what seems simple to one person—like mechanical assembly, or soldering—isn't always so simple for another.

3. What do you wish you had known going into this profession?

I wish I had known that I was going to make a career out of manufacturing. I would have gone to college for an engineering degree when I was younger, which would have allowed me to advance further in the field.

4. Are there many job opportunities in your profession? In what specific areas?

There are job opportunities in the electronics manufacturing field but it would be a good idea to focus on medical or automotive electronics. Those are the growth areas right now.

5. How do you see your profession changing in the next five years? What role will technology play in those changes, and what skills will be required?

I think the focus will be more on medical and automotive electronics. The skills that are needed will be the same: you're still going to have your basic soldering, mechanical assembly, and machine operators. As for technological changes such as a shift to robotics: I think a lot of that has already taken place. I'm sure better machines will come along, but operators will still be needed.

6. What do you enjoy most about your job? What do you enjoy least about your job?

I enjoy being able to help develop processes and teach operators how to perform each process successfully.

I least like that production schedules fluctuate and can cause a lot of overtime at times. This is not necessarily a Monday through Friday job.

7. Can you suggest a valuable "try this" for students considering a career in your profession?

Spend some time in a manufacturing facility and really see how all of the processes are done. I also think anyone going to school for this type of job should get a part-time job in manufacturing during the summer to learn some hands-on skills. The best engineers are the ones who have a good understanding of the processes from an operator's point of view.

MORE INFORMATION

Fabricators & Manufacturers Association, International
833 Featherstone Road
Rockford, IL 61107
815.399.8700
www.fmanet.org

International Brotherhood of Electrical Workers
900 Seventh Street, NW
Washington, DC 20001
202.833.7000
www.ibew.org

International Union, UAW
Solidarity House
8000 East Jefferson Avenue
Detroit, MI 48214
313.926.5000
www.uaw.org

IPC–Association Connecting Electronics Industries
3000 Lakeside Drive
Bannockburn, IL 60015
847.615.7100
www.ipc.org

Patrick Cooper/Editor

Forklift Operator

Snapshot

Career Cluster: Manufacturing; Production; Shipping
Interests: Heavy equipment, working with your hands, working outdoors
Earnings (Yearly Average): $31,340
Employment & Outlook: Slower than Average Growth Expected

OVERVIEW

Sphere of Work

Forklift operators drive and maintain small industrial trucks and material handlers. Industrial machine operators also use several other types of small-engine and electronic vehicles, including pallet jacks, e-cars, and scissor lifts, in industrial and warehouse settings. Forklift operators are key contributors to the efficiency of warehouses and factories, possessing the ability to move large loads of cargo and inventory without assistance. Misuse of forklifts and other small industrial vehicles can cause great danger to both operators and their coworkers, making adherence to safety procedures an integral part of the job.

Work Environment

Forklift operators work in a variety of commercial and industrial settings, in industries such as manufacturing, transportation, warehousing, construction, and contracting. Forklift drivers and industrial vehicle operators also work in mining, farming, and food manufacturing. Shipping and materials transport is one of the largest industries that employ forklift drivers. While some forklift operators use a forklift as a primary facet of their job, others use the forklift and other vehicles as a supplement to other duties.

Profile

Working Conditions: Work Indoors, Work both Indoors and Outdoors
Physical Strength: Heavy Work
Education Needs: On-The-Job Training, High School Diploma or GED, High School Diploma with Technical Education
Licensure/Certification: Required
Opportunities For Experience: Part-Time Work
Holland Interest Score*: RCE

* See Appendix A

Occupation Interest

Forklift operators come from a variety of professional backgrounds. In the staff hierarchy of warehousing and manufacturing facilities, forklift operators traditionally have seniority over entry-level employees and laborers. Many have worked their way up from entry-level positions in warehousing, storage, or materials handling. Other workers utilize the position as a way to gain experience to become better candidates for future warehouse-supervisor or facilities-management vacancies.

A Day in the Life—Duties and Responsibilities

The day-to-day responsibilities of forklift operators are primarily focused on the receipt and movement of materials. Operators employed in the manufacturing industry are responsible for the intake of supplies used to manufacture goods and objects. Once materials have been delivered to their proper location in the production process, another group of operators stages finished goods for shipment.

Forklift and small vehicle operators in the construction industry deliver building materials throughout jobsites. In addition to transporting loads, forklift operators are often responsible for inspecting loads for accuracy and ensuring they are stored in the proper location. Forklift drivers are also responsible for reporting damaged items and other quality discrepancies to relevant staff members.

Forklift operators may also be required to conduct routine maintenance on the vehicles they operate. Such maintenance tasks include engine maintenance, monitoring tire pressure, evaluating hydraulic and lifting systems, and testing brakes, lights, and mirrors to ensure proper function.

Duties and Responsibilities

- **Operating trucks and controls**
- **Positioning forks or other lifting devices under materials**
- **Unloading and stacking material by raising and lowering lift**
- **Loading and unloading materials manually**
- **Hooking tow trucks to trailer hitches and transporting materials**
- **Taking inventory of materials on work floor**
- **Maintaining records of materials**
- **Performing general maintenance on trucks and filling fuel tanks**

OCCUPATION SPECIALTIES

Straddle-Truck Operators

Straddle-Truck Operators drive four-wheeled vehicles that carry loads of material beneath an elevated frame. Straddle trucks are used for short hauls within or near a plant.

Tractor Operators

Tractor Operators drive a gasoline or diesel-powered tractor to move materials, pull out objects imbedded in the ground or pull the cable of a winch to raise, lower or load heavy material.

Logging Tractor Operators

Logging Tractor Operators drive tractors equipped with hoisting rack, crane boom, bulldozer blade or other device to load or unload logs, pull stumps or clear brush.

WORK ENVIRONMENT

Physical Environment

Forklift operators work in a variety of environments, including warehouses, shipping facilities, factories, trade centers, ports, and manufacturing facilities. Commercial and industrial settings predominate. They also work in and around construction sites and select retail facilities.

Transferable Skills and Abilities

Communication Skills
- Reading well
- Writing concisely

Organization & Management Skills
- Paying attention to and handling details
- Performing routine work

Technical Skills
- Working with machines, tools or other objects

Human Environment

Forklift operation requires strong collaboration, organization, and communication skills. Professionals in this field interact with fellow workers on a near-constant basis, communicating the location, amount, and type of materials that need to be transported.

Technological Environment

In addition to being able to use forklifts and other small motorized vehicles, forklift operators must possess the ability to use shipment-tracking software, inventory-processing systems, and various hand tools such as utility knives, skid steers, and mobile stairs.

EDUCATION, TRAINING, AND ADVANCEMENT

High School/Secondary

High school students can best prepare for a career in materials transport with courses in geometry, chemistry, physics, and introductory computer science. English and writing courses help students prepare for the communication and problem-solving aspects of the occupation.

Suggested High School Subjects
- Applied Math
- Auto Service Technology
- Diesel Maintenance Technology
- Driver Training
- English

Famous First

The first effective forklifts, or fork trucks, were developed around 1919 by Clark Equipment Co. of Lexington, Ky., and Yale Materials Handling Co. of Bridgeport, Connecticut. It was not until about 1926, however, that forklifts began to be used extensively in industry and shipping. By that time, the first skids, or pallets, had also been developed.

Postsecondary

Postsecondary course work is not a prerequisite for a career as a forklift operator.

Adult Job Seekers

Forklift operators can work first, second, or third shifts depending on their industry of employment. Materials handlers in the construction industry traditionally work normal business hours, while those employed in the shipping, manufacturing, or warehousing industry may work at all hours of the day and weekends when necessary. The potentially sporadic nature of shifts may make the job less than ideal for enrolled students or workers with families or young children.

Professional Certification and Licensure

Certification by the Occupational Safety and Health Administration (OSHA) is required for the operation of all powered industrial trucks, including forklifts, tractors, lift trucks, motorized hand tools, and other industrial vehicles powered by combustion engines or electronic motors. Certification can be earned on the job after instruction by a certified trainer or through external courses at training schools or vocational training programs. Most states require certification to be updated every two years.

Additional Requirements

Forklift operators must possess the patience and organization necessary to move potentially hazardous heavy loads with extreme caution. Misuse and abuse of forklifts and other small motorized industrial machinery is a common cause of on-the-job accidents and fatalities each year.

Fun Fact

Precursors to the modern forklift date to the mid-1800s, but it was World War I that saw the usage of powered lift trucks grow due to labor shortages. Today's forklifts were developed in the 1960s.

Source: http://www.themhedajournal.org/2013/03/06/facts-about-forklifts/

EARNINGS AND ADVANCEMENT

Earnings depend on the type, geographic location and union affiliation of the employer and the employee's experience. Pay scales are usually higher in metropolitan areas. In 2014, forklift operators had median annual earnings of $31,340. Annual earnings can be reduced due to the amount of time work can be limited by bad weather.

Forklift operators may receive paid vacations, holidays, and sick days; life and health insurance; and retirement plans benefits. These are usually paid by the employer.

Metropolitan Areas with the Highest Employment Level in this Occupation

Metropolitan area	Employment	Employment per thousand jobs	Annual mean wage
Chicago-Joliet-Naperville, IL	22,320	5.95	$31,770
Los Angeles-Long Beach-Glendale, CA	16,030	3.95	$44,740
Atlanta-Sandy Springs-Marietta, GA	14,340	6.01	$31,220
Riverside-San Bernardino-Ontario, CA	9,360	7.49	$33,060
Dallas-Plano-Irving, TX	9,140	4.08	$28,140
Indianapolis-Carmel, IN	7,610	8.12	$32,640
New York-White Plains-Wayne, NY-NJ	7,360	1.37	$35,970
Memphis, TN-MS-AR	6,960	11.70	$28,460
Minneapolis-St. Paul-Bloomington, MN-WI	6,240	3.42	$35,830
Louisville-Jefferson County, KY-IN	6,090	9.78	$30,300

Source: Bureau of Labor Statistics

EMPLOYMENT AND OUTLOOK

Forklift operators held about 520,000 jobs nationally in 2014. Employment is expected to grow more slowly than the average for all occupations through the year 2024, which means employment is projected to increase 1 percent to 5 percent. Material handling systems in large factories and warehouses will continue to become more automated, reducing the overall demand for these workers.

Employment Trend, Projected 2014–24

Total, all occupations: 7%

Material moving workers: 4%

Forklift operators: 3%

Note: "All Occupations" includes all occupations in the U.S. Economy. Source: U.S. Bureau of Labor Statistics, Employment Projections Program

Related Occupations

- Bulldozer Operator
- Freight, Stock & Material Mover
- Lumber Production Worker
- Ship Loader

Conversation With . . .
NORBERTO PEÑA

Senior Warehouse Manager

Sypris Electronics, Tampa, Florida

Supply Chain profession, 20 years

1. What was your individual career path in terms of education/training, entry-level job, or other significant opportunity?

I got a BBA in accounting from the University of Puerto Rico in Ponce, then went to work for Kmart as operations manager in San Juan. I moved into manufacturing with Hanes as cost accountant, and then became Payroll Administrator for about 4,000 employees a week on the island. I got several promotions until I was a supply chain manager at Hanes, then moved over to Coca Cola. I was a customer service manager; we shipped concentrate to thirty-seven countries around the world which meant that one-third of the world's concentrate came from my team at my plant. After that, I went into electronics with General Electric and was a materials manager. I moved on to become Supply Chain Manager for Cutler-Hammer (now Eaton Electrical), then returned to GE and stayed three more years. At that point I started a food truck business and my brother, a quality consultant, used my business as a model in his training sessions. But the economy was not looking good in Puerto Rico; there is a lot of burglary, and I decided I did not want to raise my kids there.

So I moved to Florida. At Sypris, I'm the Senior Warehouse Manager. Twelve people, including the traffic supervisor, report to me. We start by receiving all the materials for use at the plant and stocking them in the warehouse by program. When we need to send something to production, we pull those items—called "a kit"—and production does the assembly. When they are done, they send the products to my other team, which is packing and shipping. We tie the item to the sales order and ship it to the customer.

2. What are the most important skills and/or qualities for someone in your profession?

To be successful in this profession, an individual must be good at multi-tasking, a quick thinker and decision-maker, and be able to work under pressure because in the manufacturing environment, the supply chain group deals with most of the daily pressure. You need to be a strong person; team-; and goal- and results-oriented all the time. In addition, a person must be open-minded. If you are not willing to listen to different opinions on how to get to a goal, you won't succeed.

Another very important skill is to be good with numbers.

3. What do you wish you had known going into this profession?

I totally love my profession, and am willing to accept any kind of challenge such as working a huge amount of hours a week and/or being blamed for misses, even when they were not really caused by my team. Unfortunately, if you're in supply chain, you will be the one to be blamed for what happens; for instance, if somebody doesn't have a part they tend to say, "They didn't give me the right part." That's one thing I have been battling for twenty years.

4. Are there many job opportunities in your profession? In what specific areas?

Supply chain is a very broad profession. From warehouse operators up to supply chain managers/directors, you will be able to occupy many blue collar as well as white collar positions. Whether at hospitals, supermarkets, or retail, supply chain applies everywhere.

5. How do you see your profession changing in the next five years, what role will technology play in those changes, and what skills will be required?

We can do everything from a phone or iPad or similar device. Even though technology helps a lot, there will always be supply chain personnel needed all around the manufacturing world.

6. What do you enjoy most about your job? What do you enjoy least about your job?

I enjoy everything about my job, although what I least enjoy is when we can't exceed our customer's expectations due to reasons out of our control. For example, we had parts arrive late and my team went the extra mile to put the kit into production right away. We had a time constraint that we figured out how to meet, but something happened during the process and we ended up receiving it back a day later than the scheduled shipping date. Sometimes, that's frustrating, because after putting a lot of effort into the front end, the end result is sometimes not attained.

7. Can you suggest a valuable "try this" for students considering a career in your profession?

Any student considering a career in supply chain should go to an internship in a manufacturing plant, if possible, in the electronics field, since this is a very challenging one due to the huge amount of Stock Keeping Units (SKUs, which are the part numbers—either raw material, sub-assemblies or finished products for sale) that are handled.

MORE INFORMATION

Associated Builders and Contractors
4250 N. Fairfax Drive, 9th Floor
Arlington, VA 22203
703.812.2000
www.abc.org

Associated General Contractors of America
Director, Construction Education Services
2300 Wilson Boulevard, Suite 400
Arlington, VA 22201
703.548.3118
www.agc.org

Building Trades Association
16th Street, NW
Washington, DC 20006
800.326.7800
www.buildingtrades.com

Industrial Truck Association
1750 K Street NW, Suite 460
Washington, DC 20006
202.296.9880
www.indtrk.org

International Brotherhood of Teamsters
25 Louisiana Avenue, NW
Washington, DC 20001
202.624.6800
www.teamster.org

International Union of Operating Engineers
Director of Research and Education
1125 17th Street, NW
Washington, DC 20036
202.429.9100
www.iuoe.org

National Center for Construction Education and Research
13614 Progress Boulevard
Alachua, FL 32615
888.622.3720
www.nccer.org

John Pritchard/Editor

Industrial Designer

Snapshot

Career Cluster: Art & Design; Manufacturing
Interests: Design, consumer culture, technological trends, solving problems, being creative
Earnings (Yearly Average): $64,620
Employment & Outlook: Slower than Average Growth Expected

OVERVIEW

Sphere of Work

Industrial designers, also known as commercial designers or product designers, plan and create new products that are both functional and stylish. They improve older products by enhancing certain features or by making them safer or more user-friendly. They usually specialize in certain consumer goods, such as cars, toys, housewares, or personal grooming accessories. In addition to designing products, some industrial designers also design packaging for the products or displays for trade shows and may even put their creative skills to work on corporate branding campaigns.

Work Environment

Industrial designers are employed by specialized design firms as well as larger companies and manufacturers. Some are self-employed. They spend much of their time in offices or studios where they design products and in conference rooms with members of product development teams, typically comprised of engineers, strategic planners, financial managers, advertising and marketing specialists, and other creative consultants. They may need to spend some time working in factories and/or testing facilities. Most work a forty-hour week, with additional evening and weekend hours as needed to meet deadlines.

Profile

Working Conditions: Work Indoors
Physical Strength: Light Work
Education Needs: Bachelor's Degree, Master's Degree
Licensure/Certification: Usually Not Required
Opportunities For Experience: Internship
Holland Interest Score*: AES

* See Appendix A

Occupation Interest

Industrial design attracts artistic people who look upon consumer products as potential canvases for their creativity. They take satisfaction in products that look good while also being functional and user-friendly. Industrial designers keep up with the latest trends and stay engaged with contemporary consumer culture, design, and technological trends. They must be technically savvy, with strong spatial, communication, and problem-solving skills. The ability to work under deadlines is important.

A Day in the Life—Duties and Responsibilities

The work performed by an industrial designer depends on the size and type of his or her employer and the particular types of products that employer manufactures or builds. Although many industrial designers work for product manufacturers, others work for specialized businesses like architectural firms and medical companies, and still others are self-employed. The work done by industrial designers is increasingly more commercial as companies focus more closely on consumer trends and market research.

Industrial designers are included early on in the corporate product development phase. They may be asked to sketch products that have already been identified or specific details or components for products that need to be upgraded. In some cases, an industrial designer sees a need for a product and recommends the idea to a research and development team for consideration. During the early stages, the designer may research other products, sometimes attending a trade show to view the competition, or survey potential users for desired features.

Once a product has been conceptualized, the industrial designer sketches out designs, either by hand or with design software. The designs might show a smaller model, a product that is easier to hold or more ergonomic, or some other type of innovation. The designer might also create a model from clay or foam board, often first rendering it in 3-D software. The designer suggests specific colors, materials, and manufacturing processes that are within the limitations of the budget. Those who work for manufacturers might render drawings in computer-aided industrial design (CAID) programs that can direct machines to build the products automatically. Industrial designers also communicate their designs and ideas in writing and give presentations to clients or managers.

Before a product is released for the market, the industrial designer might oversee or participate in its testing, at which time he or she may need to make refinements to the design to correct unforeseen issues or improve the quality of the product.

Duties and Responsibilities

- Studying the potential need for new products
- Studying other similar products on the market
- Consulting with sales and marketing personnel to obtain design ideas and to estimate public reaction to new designs
- Sketching designs
- Making comprehensive drawings of the product

OCCUPATION SPECIALTIES

Package Designers

Package Designers design containers for products, such as foods, beverages, toiletries, cigarettes and medicines.

WORK ENVIRONMENT

Transferable Skills and Abilities

Communication Skills
- Expressing thoughts and ideas
- Speaking effectively

Creative/Artistic Skills
- Being skilled in art, music or dance

Interpersonal/Social Skillss
- Cooperating with others
- Working as a member of a team

Organization & Management Skills
- Making decisions
- Paying attention to and handling details
- Performing routine work

Research & Planning Skills
- Creating ideas
- Setting goals and deadlines
- Using logical reasoning

Technical Skills
- Performing scientific, mathematical and technical work
- Working with data or numbers

Physical Environment

Industrial designers usually work in comfortable offices or studios. Those who regularly oversee product manufacturing might be at some risk for health issues related to their factory environments.

Human Environment

Industrial designers usually report to the creative director of the design firm or manager of a department, and they may oversee an intern or assistant as he or she gains experience. Interaction with clients and other members of a product development team may include lively brainstorming sessions as well as harsh criticism about ideas and designs. Self-employed industrial designers interact with others less often as they usually work from home offices.

Technological Environment

Industrial designers use a variety of art tools and supplies to build models and sketch designs, but much of their work is also performed using computer-aided design (CAD) software, computer-aided industrial design (CAID) software, and modeling, animation, and design software.

EDUCATION, TRAINING, AND ADVANCEMENT

High School/Secondary

Students should take a college-preparatory program that includes courses in English, math, and science, including physics and trigonometry. Electives should include drafting, drawing, and other art courses (sculpture, painting, ceramics, and photography) and/ or industrial arts (woodworking and metalworking). Other useful courses include psychology, engineering, and business. Students need to prepare a portfolio for admission to postsecondary art and design programs. Because this is a hands-on field, students should put together models, visit art museums, and engage in other cultural and educational activities that encourage critical and creative thinking skills.

Suggested High School Subjects
- Algebra
- Applied Communication
- Applied Math
- Applied Physics
- Arts
- Blueprint Reading
- College Preparatory
- Drafting
- English

- Geometry
- Industrial Arts
- Mechanical Drawing
- Photography
- Pottery
- Trigonometry
- Woodshop

Famous First

The first patent for a design was issued in 1844 to George Bruce of New York City for a printing typeface.

College/Postsecondary

A bachelor's degree in industrial design or engineering, ideally with a minor in art or design, is the standard minimum requirement for most entry-level jobs in this field; some employers prefer to hire those with a master's degree. Students must acquire skills in drawing, CAD and design software, and building 3-D models by hand, as well as knowledge about industrial materials and manufacturing processes. Courses that build understanding of humans and society, such as psychology, anthropology, human ecology, and philosophy, are also important. Business skills are required for some jobs. Students should plan to apply for an internship and prepare a portfolio of their best work.

Related College Majors
- Industrial Design
- Industrial/Manufacturing Technology

Adult Job Seekers

Industrial design draws on many different abilities, skills, and knowledge. Adults with a close familiarity with industry-specific products, such as medical equipment or sporting goods, could build upon that experience by taking industrial design classes. Adults with a background in art might simply need to add engineering and/or CAD training to their current skill set. Interested adults should discuss options with college admissions counselors.

Most industrial designers begin their careers as interns. They are given assignments of increasing responsibility and prestige as they become more experienced and prove their abilities. In time, an industrial designer may be able to advance to a supervisory position or establish his or her own design firm. Teaching at the college level, writing books, and consulting are other options for those with adequate experience and education.

Professional Certification and Licensure

No professional license or certification is required. Certificates are sometimes awarded upon completion of associate's degree programs.

Additional Requirements

Designers must have good eyesight, including the ability to see different colors. Problem-solving skills, creativity, self-discipline, awareness of cultural trends, and open-mindedness are all desirable. Industrial designers should develop a strong portfolio of their work, as this is often the deciding factor in the hiring process.

Fun Fact

Red Dot Design Awards are like the Oscars of the industrial design world. A few products that won in 2015 include plastic Birkenstock sandals, the Triumph Magic Wire bra, and the BackBeatFIT sports headset.

Source: http://www.dexigner.com/directory/cat/Industrial-Design/Awards.html and http://red-dot.de/pd/online-exhibition/?lang=en&c=0&a=0&y=2015&i=0&oes=

EARNINGS AND ADVANCEMENT

Earnings of industrial designers depend on the individual's education and experience and the type, size, and geographic location of the employer. Industrial designers who have their own consulting firms may have fluctuating incomes, depending on their business for the year. Some industrial designers may work on retainers, which means they may receive flat fees for given periods of time. During any given period, industrial designers can work on retainers for many different companies.

Median annual earnings of industrial designers were $64,620 in 2014. The lowest ten percent earned less than $37,030, and the highest ten percent earned more than $100,070.

Industrial designers may receive paid vacations, holidays, and sick days; life and health insurance; and retirement benefits. These are usually paid by the employer.

Metropolitan Areas with the Highest Employment Level in this Occupation

Metropolitan area	Employment	Employment per thousand jobs	Annual mean wage
New York-White Plains-Wayne, NY-NJ	1,920	0.36	$75,240
Warren-Troy-Farmington Hills, MI	1,900	1.66	$78,240
Detroit-Livonia-Dearborn, MI	1,590	2.21	$81,150
Los Angeles-Long Beach-Glendale, CA	1,510	0.37	$64,120
Chicago-Joliet-Naperville, IL	710	0.19	$67,220
Santa Ana-Anaheim-Irvine, CA	560	0.38	$73,180
Atlanta-Sandy Springs-Marietta, GA	540	0.23	$68,490
Columbus, OH	420	0.43	$63,920
Cincinnati-Middletown, OH-KY-IN	420	0.41	$70,890
Minneapolis-St. Paul-Bloomington, MN-WI	390	0.21	$61,700

Source: Bureau of Labor Statistics

EMPLOYMENT AND OUTLOOK

Industrial designers held about 40,000 jobs in 2014. Employment is expected to grow somewhat slower than the average for all occupations through the year 2024, which means employment is projected to increase 0 percent to 4 percent. Demand for industrial designers will stem from continued emphasis on product quality and safety, design of new products that are easy and comfortable to use and high technology products in medicine, transportation and other fields.

Employment Trend, Projected 2014–24

Total, all occupations: 7%

Art and design workers: 2%

Commercial and industrial designers: 2%

Note: "All Occupations" includes all occupations in the U.S. Economy. Source: U.S. Bureau of Labor Statistics, Employment Projections Program

Related Occupations
- Designer
- Graphic Designer
- Merchandise Displayer
- Multimedia Artist & Animator

Conversation With . . .
JONATHAN DALTON, IDSA

CEO and Co-Founder, thrive
Atlanta, Georgia
Industrial design, 20 years

1. What was your individual career path in terms of education/training, entry-level job, or other significant opportunity?

Originally, I wanted to be an aerospace engineer, but I quickly found I wasn't good enough at math. Growing up I was always very creative, always building and drawing things. My grandfather built me my first drawing board when I was nine. With my engineering ambitions shelved, I started thinking about architecture school. One of my mum's cousins, who is an architect, said, "It sounds great, but the reality is you're going to be working on homes and additions and it's all code and very dry." He suggested industrial design. I found the book, Presentation Techniques: A Guide to Drawing and Presenting Design Ideas by English designer Dick Powell. It's basically how to do great product renderings. I thought, "Wow—you get paid to do that?" I'm from England, and I was doing my A Levels—the three big subjects you do at the end of high school. I was doing chemistry, physics, and math at first, but I dropped math and took design instead. That's where it all began.

Out of college, I worked for Electrolux for three years. A lot of my friends had interned in the States and there were great agencies doing great work that turned all our heads. So after three years, I joined Ziba Design in Portland, Oregon—one of the world's best industrial design agencies. It was an incredible experience. In five years, I went from junior designer to creative director. I then joined Altitude Inc. in Boston and from there, I joined Philips Design, the world's largest design group, in Atlanta. I headed up their industrial design group and outside consulting for four years. It helped me understand how to launch my business—thrive—which I did in 2010. Most of my design work has been appliances and medical products, but I've done lots of other stuff over the years.

2. What are the most important skills and/or qualities for someone in your profession?

The biggest one is problem-solving. You have to be a good analytical thinker. Obviously, you've got to be creative. You have to be empathetic and able to walk in someone else's shoes. Design sits between two worlds in many ways. Designers can be consumer advocates in terms of designing products that people love, but also have to consider engineering and marketing needs. "Design thinking" is a big buzzword in the corporate world.

3. What do you wish you had known going into this profession?

To be successful, you have to put a business lens on design. It can't be creativity for creativity's sake.

4. Are there many job opportunities in your profession? In what specific areas?

It's exploding right now. Chief Design Officer is a title that has become more prevalent in the last five years as organizations start to realize that they can't differentiate their products just on technology and features alone; they have to differentiate on experience.

5. How do you see your profession changing in the next five years? What role will technology play in those changes, and what skills will be required?

We're seeing big shifts. There will always be physical products but physical products now are more often a portal to a digital experience. Industrial design principles are being transferred to the services around a product, the product ecosystem, and a lot of that will obviously be more virtual than tangible. It's a real golden age of design right now. Design is being seen as a strategic business tool and that was never the case before. It was always the lipstick on the product at the end of the day.

6. What do you enjoy most about your job? What do you enjoy least about your job?

You never do the same thing twice. I get easily bored and I have never been bored in this profession. There's always a challenge or a problem to solve.

I'm not very good at helping steer design through bureaucracy. I got good at explaining the value of design, because I had to, but in an ideal world it's something you wouldn't have to do because everyone understood it already.

7. Can you suggest a valuable "try this" for students considering a career in your profession?

The Industrial Designers Society of America (idsa.org) has chapters across the country and many run outreach programs for schools, taking a problem and working as a team to solve it, typically over two weekends. It's sponsored by design agencies and corporations that value design. It's all about teaching kids how to think like a designer. My company, thrive, is an ISDA Ambassador of Excellence. Also, many cities hold a "Design Week" event with various activities like open houses at agencies. It's a great way to peek inside and speak to people who work there and get a sense of what the profession's about.

SELECTED SCHOOLS

Many colleges and universities offer programs in design and illustration. The student may also gain initial training at a technical/community college. Below are listed some of the more prominent institutions in this field.

Art Center College of Design
1700 Lida Street
Pasadena, CA 91103
626.396.2200
www.artcenter.edu

California College of the Arts
1111 Eighth Street
San Francisco, CA 94107
415.703.9523
www.cca.edu

Carnegie Mellon University
5000 Forbes Avenue
Pittsburgh, PA 15213
412.268.2000
www.cmu.edu

Cranbrook Academy of Art
39221 Woodward Avenue
Bloomfield Hills, MI 48303
248.645.3300
www.cranbrookart.edu

Ohio State University
258 Hopkins Hall
Columbus, OH 43210
614.292.5072
art.osu.edu

Pratt Institute
200 Willoughby Avenue
Brooklyn, NY 11205
718.636.3600
www.pratt.edu

Rhode Island School of Design
2 College Street
Providence, RI 02903
401.454.6100
www.risd.edu

Rochester Institute of Technology
73 Lomb Memorial Drive
Rochester, NY 14623
585.475.2239
www.rit.edu

School of the Art Institute of Chicago
37 South Wabash Avenue
Chicago, IL 60603
800.232.7242
www.saic.edu

School of Visual Arts
209 E. 23rd Street
New York, NY 10010
212.592.2100
www.sva.edu

MORE INFORMATION

Association of Women Industrial Designers
P.O. Box 468, Old Chelsea Station
New York, NY 10011
www.awidweb.com

Core77
561 Broadway, 6th Floor
New York, NY 10012
212.965.1998
www.core77.com

Industrial Designers Society of America
45195 Business Court, Suite 250
Dulles, VA 20166-6717
703.707.6000
www.idsa.org

Organization of Black Designers
300 M Street, SW, Suite N110
Washington, DC 20024-4019
202.659.3918
www.core77.com/OBD/welcome.html

University & College Designers Association
199 W. Enon Springs Road, Suite 300
Smyrna, TN 37167
615.459.4559
www.ucda.com

Sally Driscoll/Editor

Industrial Hygienist

Snapshot

Career Cluster: Health Sciences; Manufacturing

Interests: Science, engineering, environment, protecting others

Earnings (Yearly Average): $69,210

Employment & Outlook: Slower than Average Growth Expected

OVERVIEW

Sphere of Work

Industrial hygienists, also sometimes called occupational health and safety specialists, work to ensure employee health and safety on the job. They inspect workplaces for hazards and enforce federal, state, and local regulations governing workplace safety and cleanliness. Hygienists use their particular areas of expertise, such as chemistry or engineering, to determine the safety of a workplace's ventilation system and wiring and to test for radiation, lead, and other dangers. Based on the data gathered, hygienists make recommendations regarding safety protocols and corrective measures to business owners and employees.

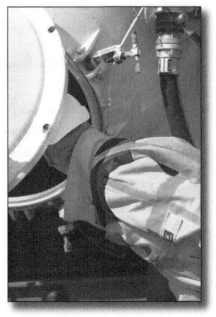

Work Environment

When not working out of an office or laboratory, industrial hygienists may work in a variety of settings, including factories and assembly plants, power plants, hospitals, offices, and mines. They typically work forty-hour weeks and may frequently travel, which can add to their hours. The work is often stressful, as inspections may create adversarial situations when workers and businesses are reluctant to change their practices. Over the course of an inspection, hygienists may be exposed to the same hazards, such as harmful chemicals, as the workers they are trying to protect.

Profile

Working Conditions: Work Indoors
Physical Strength: Medium Work
Education Needs: Bachelor's Degree
Licensure/Certification:
Recommended
Opportunities For Experience:
Internship, Military Service
Holland Interest Score*: IRE

* See Appendix A

Occupation Interest

Individuals interested in the profession of industrial hygienist typically have a strong interest in science. They are committed to protecting workers and the environment, and they must be capable of quickly identifying and solving problems. Prospective industrial hygienists should be attentive to detail, demonstrate mechanical aptitude, and communicate effectively. A calm demeanor is helpful, particularly when conveying negative inspection feedback. Due to the stress and physical risks of the profession, industrial hygienists are usually well compensated.

A Day in the Life—Duties and Responsibilities

Industrial hygienists inspect various workplaces, including factories and offices, and evaluate their safety based on government regulations and relevant occupational safety laws. They test the air quality and make note of any exposed insulation and wiring. Hygienists also test for radiation, chemicals, and lead to determine whether they have reached hazardous levels. In workplaces that require the use of safety equipment, industrial hygienists monitor employee use of equipment such as masks, protective clothing, respirators, earplugs, gloves, and goggles, including how well this equipment fits and blocks exposure to dangerous substances.

Additional responsibilities vary based on the industry in which hygienists work. For example, industrial hygienists working in medical centers may conduct frequent seminars on blood-borne pathogen risks. Those working in factories may spend more time interviewing individual employees about their daily responsibilities in order to understand the risks to which employees are exposed. In addition, some industrial hygienists may spend the majority of their time working in laboratories, testing samples collected during inspections.

If an employee is hurt or sick, industrial hygienists may review reports from physicians in order to assess whether the injury or illness is job-related. They are also responsible for ensuring that all licenses and permits are current. Finally, they review a workplace's existing safety protocols and practices, including any reports on environmental contaminants, waste management storage and disposal policies, and related paperwork. When needed, they offer modifications to those documents and recommend corrective measures beyond existing protocols.

Duties and Responsibilities

- Collecting air, dust, and other samples for study
- Monitoring noise levels
- Measuring radioactivity levels
- Inspecting ventilation, exhaust equipment, lighting, and other conditions that may affect health
- Keeping accurate records of findings
- Testing the reliability of health equipment such as respirators
- Setting up monitoring equipment
- Instructing employees on matters of safety
- Taking air samples and running tests to determine content
- Helping to design factories to avoid exposing employees to dangerous risks
- Advising physicians, toxicologists, engineers, employees, managers, community representatives, and others

WORK ENVIRONMENT

Physical Environment

Industrial hygienists inspect workplaces that may include factories, energy plants, hospitals, offices, construction sites, and mines. When on-site conducting inspections and other routine work, they may be exposed to toxic chemicals, blood and other bodily fluids, radiation, or other hazards.

Transferable Skills and Abilities

Communication Skills
- Expressing thoughts and ideas
- Writing concisely

Interpersonal/Social Skills
- Being flexible
- Cooperating with others
- Working as a member of a team

Organization & Management Skills
- Making decisions
- Paying attention to and handling details

Unclassified Skills
- Using set methods and standards in your work

Human Environment

Industrial hygienists work and interact with a wide range of people, including other hygienists, employees and owners of the workplace being inspected, doctors and other medical personnel, union officials, and equipment technicians. They must therefore be capable of clearly explaining scientific concepts to individuals from different professional backgrounds.

Technological Environment

Industrial hygienists use many types of detection equipment, including air samplers, flowmeters, Geiger counters, carbon monoxide sensors, and particle sensors. They must also use scientific, database, and basic office software.

EDUCATION, TRAINING, AND ADVANCEMENT

High School/Secondary

High school students interested in a career as an industrial hygienist should study natural sciences, including chemistry, geology, earth science, health, and environmental science. Mathematics courses will prepare individuals for the technical aspects of the job. Industrial arts classes, particularly drafting, may also be helpful for aspiring industrial hygienists.

Suggested High School Subjects
- Algebra
- Applied Biology/Chemistry
- Applied Communication
- Applied Math
- Biology
- Blueprint Reading
- Calculus
- Chemistry
- English
- Geometry
- Health Science Technology
- Trigonometry

Famous First

The first federal railroad safety law was the Safety Appliance Act of 1893. It was an act "to promote the safety of employees and travelers upon railroads by compelling common carriers engaged in interstate commerce to equip their [rail] cars with automatic couplers and continuous brakes and their locomotives with driving wheel brakes." The act helped to sharply reduce the number of accidents occurring within the railroad industry.

College/Postsecondary

Industrial hygienists usually obtain a bachelor's degree in chemistry, engineering, physics, or a biological or physical science, although many study environmental health or toxicology as well. Those interested in senior-level hygienist positions should pursue a graduate degree as well. Postsecondary students may find internships in the field especially valuable.

Related College Majors
- Environmental Health
- Environmental Science/Studies
- Environmental/Environmental Health Engineering
- Occupational Safety & Health Technology
- Occupational Health & Industrial Hygiene

Adult Job Seekers

Qualified individuals may apply directly to businesses, consulting firms, and government agencies that list open positions online and in print. Professional trade associations, such as the Association of Professional Industrial Hygienists (APIH), may provide resources and networking opportunities.

Professional Certification and Licensure

Certification and licensure is not legally required for industrial hygienists. However, they may choose to obtain voluntary certification, which is available through many nonprofit organizations. Those interested in becoming certified are advised to consult prospective employers and credible professional associations within the field as to the relevancy and value of any voluntary certification program.

Additional Requirements

Industrial hygienists who travel between sites typically must have a driver's license. All industrial hygienists must keep abreast of changes to relevant government regulations and ensure compliance in the workplace.

Fun Fact

The dangers of working around chemicals or in high places are obvious. But even the guy at the pizza shop is susceptible to the one of the most common hazards—repetitive strain injury—by rolling out dough again and again.

Source: http://smallbusiness.chron.com/top-five-types-workplace-hazards-16112.html

EARNINGS AND ADVANCEMENT

Earnings of industrial hygienists depend on the type and geographic location of the employer and the individual's academic training and experience. Median annual earnings of industrial hygienists were $69,210 in 2014. The lowest ten percent earned less than $40,760, and the highest ten percent earned more than $101,000.

Industrial hygienists may receive paid vacations, holidays, and sick days; life and health insurance; and retirement benefits. These are usually paid by the employer.

Metropolitan Areas with the Highest
Employment Level in this Occupation

Metropolitan area	Employment	Employment per thousand jobs	Annual mean wage
Houston-Sugar Land-Baytown, TX	3,090	1.09	$83,650
Los Angeles-Long Beach-Glendale, CA	1,450	0.36	$74,400
New York-White Plains-Wayne, NY-NJ	1,410	0.26	$76,490
Seattle-Bellevue-Everett, WA	1,110	0.74	$79,730
Dallas-Plano-Irving, TX	940	0.42	$71,370
Minneapolis-St. Paul-Bloomington, MN-WI	910	0.50	$75,130
Phoenix-Mesa-Glendale, AZ	910	0.50	$66,550
Washington-Arlington-Alexandria, DC-VA-MD-WV	880	0.37	$81,220
Denver-Aurora-Broomfield, CO	770	0.58	$78,600
Chicago-Joliet-Naperville, IL	740	0.20	$66,840

Source: Bureau of Labor Statistics

EMPLOYMENT AND OUTLOOK

Nationally, there were approximately 70,000 industrial hygienists employed in 2014. Federal, state and local government agencies employed nearly half of all industrial hygienists. Employment is expected to grow slower than the average for all occupations through 2024, which means employment is projected to increase 2 percent to 6 percent. This reflects a balance of continuing public demand for a safe and healthy work environment and quality products against the desire for smaller government and fewer regulations.

Employment Trend, Projected 2014–24

Other healthcare practitioners and technical occupations: 10%

Total, all occupations: 7%

Industrial Hygienists: 4%

Note: "All Occupations" includes all occupations in the U.S. Economy. Source: U.S. Bureau of Labor Statistics, Employment Projections Program

Related Occupations
- Industrial Engineer

Related Military Occupations
- Environmental Health & Safety Officer
- Environmental Health & Safety Specialist

Conversation With . . .
DANIEL ANNA, PhD

Senior Industrial Hygienist
Johns Hopkins University Applied Physics Laboratory
Laurel, Maryland
Industrial hygiene, 27 years

1. What was your individual career path in terms of education/training, entry-level job, or other significant opportunity?

After completing a Bachelor of Science in safety science, I worked as an entry-level health and safety professional with Quaker Oats. My degree could have led to great opportunities, but I wanted to specialize in the industrial hygiene aspect. So, I completed a master of science in industrial hygiene at Texas A&M University, then worked as an industrial hygienist for Amoco Corporation, which later became BP. After a few years, I pursued a PhD in occupational health at the University of Michigan and obtained a faculty position teaching courses related to industrial hygiene.

After 15 years as a professor, I began working at Johns Hopkins in a cutting-edge research laboratory where I evaluate risks associated with proposed projects. It's the job of industrial hygienists to recognize and evaluate job hazards—chemical, biological, physical and ergonomic—and to recommend controls. Chemical and biological materials can be toxic when inhaled, ingested or absorbed through the skin. Physical hazards include excessive noise, vibration, illumination, temperature or radiation.

I am a Certified Industrial Hygienist (CIH), a Certified Safety Professional (CSP), and I serve as president of the American Industrial Hygiene Association.

2. What are the most important skills and/or qualities for someone in your profession?

Successful industrial hygienists have a natural curiosity, excellent observational and analytical skills, and enjoy solving problems. They need a fundamental knowledge in several basic sciences—chemistry, biology, and physics—and a good mathematics foundation. Basic business skills are also valuable, because industrial hygiene touches every aspect of an organization and benefits a company through increased productivity, improved morale, and reduced costs. Industrial hygienists work with employees at all levels and must genuinely care about people and the environment.

3. **What do you wish you had known going into this profession?**

Many industrial hygienists wish they had known about the profession and job opportunities prior to going to college. Many started in a different major and many began their careers in a different profession before learning about industrial hygiene careers.

4. **Are there many job opportunities in your profession? In what specific areas?**

Yes. Job diversity is a major benefit for anyone considering a career in industrial hygiene. Industrial hygienists are employed in a wide variety of organizations, including internationally. There are jobs working for corporations, consulting firms, and federal or state government agencies. A study by the National Institute for Occupational Safety and Health indicated that there will be a shortage of qualified industrial hygiene and safety professionals in the near future.

5. **How do you see your profession changing in the next five years? What role will technology play in those changes, and what skills will be required?**

Because the role of an industrial hygienist is to protect worker health through the recognition, evaluation and control of job-related hazards, changes to all jobs and workplaces impact the profession.

Industrial hygienists have seen their jobs expand to include risk assessment, environmental protection, product stewardship, safety, and a variety of related areas. Job titles and degree names have started to change to reflect the additional value that we bring to the workplace. Most new industrial hygienists have an undergraduate degree in industrial hygiene or environmental health and safety or in one of the basic sciences, such as chemistry or biology, plus a graduate degree in industrial hygiene.

Future industrial hygienists will be asked to solve more complex problems. New manufacturing technologies—including 3-D printing, robotics, and nanotechnology—will result in different types of hazards. Advances in sensor technology will have an impact on industrial hygienists as they try to evaluate potential exposures and other risks to worker health. The proliferation of "big data" will create a need to be able to evaluate and interpret that new information.

6. **What do you enjoy most about your job? What do you enjoy least about your job?**

My favorite part of industrial hygiene has always been the vast diversity of work. Every day brings different challenges and different potential hazards to control in different environments. In the end, our solutions help to ensure that workers go home to their families and friends healthy and safe each day.

I can honestly say that answering the "worst part of the job" question is difficult for me. But I do wish the value that industrial hygiene brings to workers and business received more recognition. Not everyone appreciates why certain controls are recommended. It's disappointing to see workers make choices that put their health or safety at risk.

7. **Can you suggest a valuable "try this" for students considering a career in your profession?**

Observe people at work. Watch for things that could impact their health and safety. Observe their interactions with equipment, materials, tools, and other people. Talk to them about any concerns they have about their health and safety on the job. Think about their activities, their clothing, and their surroundings. Look for ways to make their job easier and more productive.

SELECTED SCHOOLS

Many colleges and universities offer programs in general health and safety; some provide more specialized programs in industrial hygiene. The interested student may find a list of accredited programs on the website of the American Industrial Hygiene Association (see below).

MORE INFORMATION

American Board of Industrial Hygiene
6015 West Saint Joseph, Suite 102
Lansing, MI 48917-3980
517.321.2638
www.abih.org

American Conference of Governmental Industrial Hygienists
1330 Kemper Meadow Drive
Cincinnati, OH 45240
513.742.2020
www.acgih.org

American Industrial Hygiene Association
2700 Prosperity Avenue, Suite 250
Fairfax, VA 22031
703.849.8888
www.aiha.org

American Society of Safety Engineers
1800 East Oakton Street
Des Plaines, IL 60018
847.699.2929
www.asse.org

Association of Professional Industrial Hygienists
P.O. Box 21565
Chattanooga, TN 37424-0565
888.481.3006
www.apih.us

U.S. Occupational Safety and Health Administration (OSHA)
200 Constitution Avenue NW
Washington, DC 20210
800.321.6742
www.osha.gov

Michael Auerbach/Editor

Industrial Machinery Mechanic

Snapshot

Career Cluster: Engineering; Maintenance & Repair; Manufacturing

Interests: Machinery, mechanics, working with your hands, solving problems, using tools and computers

Earnings (Yearly Average): $49,560

Employment & Outlook: Faster than Average Growth Expected

OVERVIEW

Sphere of Work

Industrial machinery mechanics maintain industrial machines including factory equipment, conveying systems, and production and packing machinery. Most of their job is preventive—an industrial machinery mechanic tries to diagnose problems with a machine before it breaks down—but they are also trained to make repairs when a machine does stop working. When machines break, production is slowed or stopped, so mechanics must make repairs quickly and efficiently.

Industrial machinery mechanics are also known as industrial machine repairers or maintenance machinists. They are responsible

for keeping a number of complex machines in a factory or plant in working order. Industrial machinery mechanics are also responsible for keeping factories or plants stocked with the proper machine parts necessary to make repairs.

Work Environment

Industrial machinery mechanics work in factories, power plants, and on construction sites. They are sometimes required to work overtime, or on nights and weekends, if a machine breaks down outside of regular workday hours. The job of an industrial machinery mechanic can be dangerous. They are required to follow specific safety precautions and wear protective gear while working.

Profile

Working Conditions: Work Indoors
Physical Strength: Medium Work
Education Needs: On-The-Job Training, High School Diploma with Technical Education, Technical/Community College
Licensure/Certification: Recommended
Physical Abilities Not Required: N/A
Opportunities For Experience: Apprenticeship, Part-Time Work
Holland Interest Score*: REI

* See Appendix A

Occupation Interest

Industrial machinery mechanics are interested in how machines work. They analyze and solve complex problems on a daily basis and enjoy working with their hands. Industrial machinery mechanics apply instructions from manuals and diagrams to machines and machine parts, and they are adept at using a number of tools. They will often use computers or other electronic devices to analyze equipment.

A Day in the Life—Duties and Responsibilities

Industrial machinery mechanics work regular work hours, though they are sometimes required to work overtime. Throughout a normal day, they perform a number of tasks related to the maintenance and upkeep of machines in factories and production plants. These machines include conveyor belts, robotic arms, and hydraulic lifts.

When there is a problem with a machine, industrial machinery mechanics must diagnose the issue and figure out the best way to solve it. They talk with machine operators and inspect the machinery. They check initially for loose connectors or worn parts. If a part needs replacing, industrial machinery mechanics will replace it. They are also responsible for having the right parts on hand for such a situation. If there are no loose or worn parts, industrial machinery mechanics must perform tests to determine the problem. Sometimes these tests involve computer programs or electronic testing equipment. Industrial machinery mechanics analyzes the test results to decide his or her next course of action.

Sometimes, industrial machinery mechanics must take entire machines apart and put them back together. This is often done by following a manual or diagram. Industrial machinery mechanics routinely use hand tools. They also use larger tools like lathes, grinders, and drill presses. Some industrial machinery mechanics perform welding tasks. After they have replaced an old part or performed a repair, they will test the machine to make sure it works.

Duties and Responsibilities

- Observing and inspecting equipment regularly to locate causes of trouble
- Oiling, greasing, and cleaning machine parts
- Dismantling machines and equipment
- Repairing or replacing defective parts
- Installing special parts
- Sketching a required part to be manufactured by the plant's machine shop
- Operating basic tool machines to make needed parts
- Adjusting controls on machinery and equipment
- Reassembling machinery and equipment
- Starting and testing equipment
- Keeping maintenance records of the equipment serviced

WORK ENVIRONMENT

Physical Environment

The most common environments of industrial machinery mechanics are factories, plants, and construction sites. These sites can often be noisy and dirty. It is important for industrial machinery mechanics to be able to tune out the distractions of their environment in order to focus on making repairs.

Relevant Skills and Abilities

Organization & Management Skills
- Following instructions
- Making decisions
- Paying attention to and handling details
- Performing duties which change frequently

Technical Skills
- Performing technical work
- Working with machines, tools or other objects

Human Environment

There are a number of people working around industrial machinery mechanics, performing any number of tasks at any given time. They must work well with others, including colleagues and clients. They must also be adept at dealing with machine operators. Often, industrial machinery mechanics will have to ask an operator questions to diagnose a problem with a machine. In a factory environment, every person performs a specialized task in service of a larger production scheme. Industrial machinery mechanics monitor equipment to keep the whole operation running smoothly and are an important part of this equation.

Technological Environment

Industrial machinery mechanics regularly use computers, computerized machines, and testing devices in their work. The majority of industrial machines have computerized components, and many are operated by way of computer software.

EDUCATION, TRAINING, AND ADVANCEMENT

High School/Secondary

An aspiring industrial machinery mechanic should enroll in courses focusing on mathematics, physics, computer science, and English. Shop courses, which instruct students on basic engineering and machinery operation, are also important for aspiring industrial machinery mechanics. Most employers require industrial machinery mechanics to have a high school diploma or pass a General Education Development (GED) test.

Suggested High School Subjects
- Applied Math
- Applied Physics
- Blueprint Reading
- Computer Science
- Drafting
- Electricity & Electronics
- English
- Industrial Arts
- Machining Technology
- Mathematics
- Mechanical Drawing
- Physics
- Shop Mechanics

Famous First

The first heavy-duty cable factory was built in 1841 in Saxonburg, Pennsylvania, by John A. Roebling, who also created the machinery. Roebling's "wire rope" consisted of wire that was wound into strands and then turned onto great reels. Several of these strands were then themselves wound together to form a thick rope or cable. The cable was used in the construction of suspension bridges, example shown here, including the Brooklyn Bridge.

College/Postsecondary

Most industrial machinery mechanics need at least one year of postsecondary education or specialized training in their field. Courses in such a program include blueprint reading, computer programming, mechanical drawing, mathematics, or electronics. Many employers require industrial machinery mechanics to have advanced degrees. Most industrial machinery mechanics are required to be familiar with and trained in repairing all types of industrial machinery.

Some industrial machinery mechanics complete a two-year associate's degree in industrial maintenance at a technical school. Others begin working in a different factory job and take classes provided by their employer in order to become industrial machinery mechanics. In either case, hands-on training is a very important part of any training program. Industrial machinery mechanics must be comfortable with the machines they spend their time monitoring.

Related College Majors
• Heavy Equipment Maintenance & Repair

Adult Job Seekers

A person who has had a job in a factory or has been a mechanic in a different field is a good candidate for becoming an industrial machinery mechanic. The career also draws on a number of other transferable skills, including knowledge of computers or experience working with heavy machinery. Individuals with no background in a related field should enroll in a college or a technical or vocational school that offers a program in industrial machinery mechanics. Technical schools are also a great place for job seekers to network. Communication technologies and standards are always changing, so mechanics should be willing to continue learning throughout their career.

Professional Certification and Licensure

Though it is not required, industrial machinery mechanics can acquire certification through the Society of Maintenance and Reliability Professionals (SMRP). A program called Certified Industrial Maintenance Mechanic, or CIMM, is offered by SMRP. Certification exams test a candidate's knowledge of their field. Those who gain certification must maintain it by participating in fifty hours of skill development and training (offered through SMRP) over the course of a three-year period, or they simply retake the exam.

Additional Requirements

Because troubleshooting is a large part of an industrial machinery mechanic's job, a person in this career must be a creative thinker. He or she must be willing to test different solutions and identify problems based on little information. Industrial machinery mechanics must also keep their cool in stressful situations. A broken machine shuts down production, so mechanics must work quickly, yet efficiently, to keep the factory up and running on schedule.

Fun Fact

The Industrial Revolution, when human- and animal-power was replaced by machines, began in Britain for three major reasons: it had plenty of coal and iron ore to run machines; it was a politically stable coutnry; and it was a major colonial power that could reach across its empire to find necessary raw goods and markets.

Source: http://hubpages.com/education/12-Facts-on-the-Industrial-Revolution#

EARNINGS AND ADVANCEMENT

Earnings of industrial machinery mechanics depend on the type, geographic location and union affiliation of the employer and the employee's skill. Mean annual earnings of industrial machinery mechanics were $49,560 in 2013. The lowest ten percent earned less than $31,090, and the highest ten percent earned more than $71,930.

Industrial machinery mechanics may receive paid vacations, holidays, and sick days; life and health insurance; and retirement benefits. These are usually paid by the employer.

Metropolitan Areas with the Highest Employment Level in this Occupation

Metropolitan area	Employment [1]	Employment per thousand jobs	Hourly mean wage
Houston-Sugar Land-Baytown, TX	11,230	4.07	$24.70
Chicago-Joliet-Naperville, IL	5,490	1.48	$26.83
Los Angeles-Long Beach-Glendale, CA	5,320	1.34	$28.84
Atlanta-Sandy Springs-Marietta, GA	4,020	1.74	$22.25
Cincinnati-Middletown, OH-KY-IN	3,990	4.01	$25.44
Philadelphia, PA	3,740	2.03	$23.51
St. Louis, MO-IL	3,380	2.62	$24.37
Dallas-Plano-Irving, TX	3,330	1.55	$23.02
Gary, IN	3,160	11.82	$26.31
New York-White Plains-Wayne, NY-NJ	3,090	0.59	$25.83

[1]Does not include self-employ ed. Source: Bureau of Labor Statistics

EMPLOYMENT AND OUTLOOK

There were approximately 320,000 industrial machinery mechanics employed nationally in 2012. Employment is expected to grow faster than the average for all occupations through the year 2022, which means employment is projected to increase up to 20 percent. As more companies introduce new automated equipment, these workers will be needed to ensure that these machines are kept in good condition. However, many new machines are capable of self-diagnosis, increasing their reliability and reducing the need for these workers. Many job openings will result from the need to replace workers who transfer to other occupations or retire.

Employment Trend, Projected 2012–22

Industrial Machinery Mechanics: 19%

Total, All Occupations: 11%

Maintenance Workers, Machinery: 11%

Note: "All Occupations" includes all occupations in the U.S. Economy. Source: U.S. Bureau of Labor Statistics, Employment Projections Program

Related Occupations
- Diesel Service Technician
- General Maintenance Mechanic
- Heavy Equipment Service Technician
- Machinist

Conversation With . . .
TRICIA KEEGAN

Facility Manager
Tiverton Power Plant, Tiverton, R.I.
Industrial Machinery Mechanic & Manager, 21 years

1. What was your individual career path in terms of education/training, entry-level job, or other significant opportunity?

I went to high school at Boston Latin School, then went to Boston University to be a math teacher. A friend of mine wanted to visit the Massachusetts Maritime Academy and asked me to drive her down for Women's Day. A woman who spoke there had graduated from Mass Maritime and was a math teacher. I always wanted to travel and always loved books about ships and decided to apply without even telling my parents. I gave up a full academic scholarship to B.U. I had no idea what I was getting into in terms of engineering. I just knew I could still become a math teacher, go to this school and travel all over the world. We did a term at sea each year. I graduated with a bachelor's degree in marine engineering, with a concentration in facilities engineering. A power plant has the same engine as a ship, just on a larger scale. It's the same equipment and the same philosophy. Upon graduation, I was hired by General Electric (GE) Power Systems. I worked as a field service engineer, working on gas turbines, mostly. Then I became a control specialist, working on electronics that run the plant and doing mechanical work. GE manufactures the power-generating equipment that power plants own. I worked on equipment in Oklahoma, Iowa, Newfoundland, the Netherlands, the Dominican Republic, Panama. After I got married and had kids, I went part-time for a while. In 2009, I became the plant manager in Tiverton.

2. What are the most important skills and/or qualities for someone in your profession?

You have to have mechanical aptitude, and that comes with experience. Early on in your career, you're really learning from the people around you. You have to be able to identify preventive and predictive maintenance, rather than unplanned maintenance, by recognizing trends when things go wrong. You have to keep good, detailed logs—how you fixed something, who you worked with. I still refer back to a log I had in 1996.

As a facilities manager, the four things I'm always focused on are: safety of employees and contractors; compliance with environmental and other regulations; productivity; and people. I'm learning more and more how important it is to communicate well and to get input and ideas from many people—the operations department, the maintenance department, the electronics department.

3. What do you wish you had known going into this profession?

One thing I wish I had done more is seek advice, just about day-to-day things. Also, I would be myself more. Being a woman in a male-dominated field, I always tried to tone it down and keep it serious. If people were all going out to dinner after work, the normal me would have gone, but I felt that I had to draw a line. I didn't want to give the wrong impression.

4. Are there many job opportunities in your profession? In what specific areas?

In power generation, the sky's the limit. I could work at a refinery, at a manufacturing facility, a hospital, a natural gas facility, an airport.

5. How do you see your profession changing in the next five years? What role will technology play in those changes, and what skills will be required?

We're looking at renewables, wind power and solar, and we're waiting for that break-through for better storage and transmission, probably through nanotechnology—but it probably won't happen in the next five years. Right now they're studying how your clothes can charge your cell phone, using friction, where the fibers carry electronics to the phone. So what's our future look like? Probably micro-systems where your house will run on a battery pack and doesn't have to be attached to the grid.

6. What do you enjoy most about your job? What do you enjoy least about your job?

There's a new challenge every day. And there's no shortage of work to be done; we're very busy people. What I enjoy least is time away from my three children. Finding that work/life balance is challenging. Also, you worry a lot, you take it home with you, worrying about the safety of your coworkers. You're under a lot of pressure.

7. Can you suggest a valuable "try this" for students considering a career in your profession?

Reach out to someone in the field, maybe through alumni associations at schools. You can visit a power plant, do a tour, or tour ships. I think most people would be willing to give you a couple of hours. If you know a nurse, ask her about arranging for you to visit the hospital's facilities department: they have a back-up generator, they have water sterilization. Or if your father works in the Financial District, all the big buildings have facilities departments. You may think, "Oh, they're just custodians," but they're doing all kinds of important stuff.

SELECTED SCHOOLS

A college degree is not necessary to work as an industrial machinery mechanic. For those interested in the field, however, a technical or community college is a good place to start. Many commercial trade schools are also available. Students are advised to consult with their school guidance counselor or research area post-secondary schools to find the right program.

MORE INFORMATION

International Association of Machinists & Aerospace Workers
Apprenticeship Department
9000 Machinists Place
Upper Marlboro, MD 20772-2687
301.967.4500
www.iamaw.org

National Association of Manufacturers
733 10th Street NW, Suite 700
Washington, DC 20001
202.637.3000
www.nam.org

Society for Maintenance and Reliability Professionals
1100 Johnson Ferry Road, Suite 300
Atlanta, Georgia 30342
800.950.7354
www.smrp.org

Molly Hagan/Editor

Lumber Production Worker

Snapshot

Career Cluster: Forestry/Logging; Manufacturing; Production

Interests: Working with your hands, using heavy machinery, travel, performing dangerous work

Earnings (Yearly Average): $35,160

Employment & Outlook: Decline Expected

OVERVIEW

Sphere of Work

Lumber production workers sort and arrange lumber according to size, grade, and other categories within a timber facility. Some work at logging sites, selecting trees for harvesting. They also work in sawmills, plywood mills, and other lumber production facilities, where they maintain cutting machines, assist in the construction of finished products, and fulfill to the manufacturing needs of the customer. Production workers cut timber according to specifications using a wide range of machines, power tools, and hand tools. Lumber production workers ensure that the facility itself adheres to standard operating procedures, which may involve filling out inventory sheets, properly labeling lumber, and following mandated storage and handling practices. Some

lumber production workers supervise other facility staff, purchase supplies, and procure lumber shipments.

Work Environment

In addition to working at logging sites, lumber production workers are employed at various types of wood production centers. Some work at "primary" sawmills, which are located in or near forest resources, usually in rural areas—these sites are the first stop for harvested lumber. At primary mills, workers may be surrounded by heavy trucks and machinery as well as massive logs that are being delivered, stored, and processed. Other production workers work in "secondary" mills, at which items like furniture, doors, and other wood objects are manufactured. Lumber production workers are also found at mills that produce reconstituted products, such as particleboard and similar, low-quality wood products, that are assembled using the shavings, dust, and chips that are discarded from primary mills. Still other lumber production workers are employed by paper and pulp mills, which use waste products from primary mills to produce paper, cardboard, and other materials. In each of these settings, production workers must follow strict safety protocols, often requiring the use of masks, goggles, and gloves. There remains a physical risk of dust inhalation, machine-related accidents, and other injuries.

Profile

Working Conditions: Work Outdoors
Physical Strength: Heavy Work
Education Needs: High School Diploma or G.E.D., High School Diploma with Technical Education
Licensure/Certification: Usually Not Required
Opportunities For Experience: Part-Time Work
Holland Interest Score*: RCE, RES, RSE

* See Appendix A

Occupation Interest

Lumber production workers rarely experience a routine day. Depending on work location, production workers may be assigned several tasks at once, which can alleviate tedium in a manufacturing environment. Additionally, lumber production workers use saws and cutters, cranes, and other heavy machinery, which adds to a level of excitement at the workplace. Because the work is demanding, requires a significant amount of travel, and can be dangerous, lumber production workers receive an above-average hourly wage, and there are many opportunities to work extra hours. Lumber production workers spend most of each day working with their hands.

A Day in the Life—Duties and Responsibilities

Lumber production workers' daily duties and responsibilities vary largely based on the facilities at which they work, but all involve physically demanding and potentially dangerous work. Workers at primary sawmills, for example, must inventory incoming logs according to tree species, client batches, grade markings, and size. Pulp mill production workers, on the other hand, may focus more on operating heavy machinery that dissolves wood pieces into pulp and re-forms it into paper and other products. Those individuals who visit logging sites select trees for clearing and work with loggers to cut down and transport logs to primary mills.

In general, lumber production workers sort incoming wood according to its grade and species, size, and other categories. They pay strict attention to customer orders to ensure that the client's needs are met in storage and processing. Using forklifts and other machinery, lumber production workers transport wood to cutters, pulp processing machines, and other areas of the facility. They also operate saws and heavy cutters, pulping equipment, and smaller tools. Lumber production workers also have a few administrative tasks, such as issuing special orders for coworkers on customer needs, monitoring machine maintenance schedules, and filling out order and inventory sheets on a periodic basis. Some lumber production workers are supervisors as well, and as such must oversee the activities of lower-level workers in addition to their own tasks.

Duties and Responsibilities

- Determining when trees should be harvested
- Cutting down trees in specified direction
- Removing limbs and tops of trees
- Trimming and dividing trees into set lengths
- Fastening chains or cables to logs
- Driving logs to landings
- Loading logs on trucks or rail cars
- Inspecting and evaluating logs
- Assessing logging conditions and value of timber

OCCUPATION SPECIALTIES

Fallers

Fallers cut down trees with chain saws or other mechanical felling equipment.

Buckers

Buckers trim branches and tops off trees and then cut the logs into the specified lengths.

Rivers

Rivers split logs to form posts, pickets, shakes and other objects.

Tree Cutters

Tree Cutters fell trees of specified size and species, trim limbs from trees and cut trees into lengths for firewood, fence posts or pulpwood, using axes, measuring tools and chainsaws.

Chainsaw Operators

Chainsaw Operators trim limbs, tops and roots from trees and saw logs to predetermined lengths using chain saws.

Log Markers

Log Markers determine the points at which logs will be sawed into sections.

Log Graders

Log Graders inspect logs for defects, determine quality and volume and estimate the market value of logs.

Logging Supervisors

Logging Supervisors manage one or more crews usually consisting of four or fewer workers.

Cruisers

Cruisers hike through forests to assess logging conditions and estimate the volume of marketable timber.

WORK ENVIRONMENT

Physical Environment

Lumber production workers generally work in sawmills and other mills as well as wood processing facilities. Primary mills may be located in rural locations near forests, while secondary production sites are found in a wide range of environments. Although safety guidelines are strictly enforced, there are risks of physical injury at such sites. Workers either live in temporary housing at the job site or commute long distances. Both situations may be stressful at times for those who must spend days or weeks away from their families.

Transferable Skills and Abilities

Interpersonal/Social Skills
- Being persistent
- Working as a member of a team

Organization & Management Skills
- Making decisions

Technical Skills
- Working with machines, tools or other objects

Work Environment Skills
- Working outdoors

Human Environment

Depending on the type of facility at which they work, lumber production workers interact with mill managers, customers, government officials (including the Occupational Safety and Health Administration), union representatives, truck drivers, and loggers.

Technological Environment

Lumber production workers use a wide range of heavy and light equipment. Among these pieces of technology are chippers, digesters (which mix chemicals and wood to cook and form into pulp), fourdriniers (massive automated paper processors), lathes, sanders, hand tools, and many different types of cutters and saws. Many lumber production workers also operate forklifts, cranes, and similar transport equipment.

EDUCATION, TRAINING, AND ADVANCEMENT

High School/Secondary

High school students should study agriculture and forestry. They must also have a strong knowledge of woodworking tools through industrial arts courses. Applied mathematics is useful for taking inventory of and producing properly configured lumber products for customers.

Suggested High School Subjects
- Agricultural Education
- Applied Math
- English
- Forestry
- Mathematics
- Woodshop

Famous First

The first log-rolling national championship tournament took place on a lagoon near Omaha, Nebraska, in 1898. Six competitors entered the tournament, which was won by Tommy Fleming of Eau Claire, Wisc..

Postsecondary

Some lumber production workers pursue additional training in heavy machinery and/or forestry through vocational or technical postsecondary schools. Such training can give a worker a competitive edge in the job market.

Related College Majors
- Forest Harvesting & Production Technology
- Natural Resources Conservation, General

Adult Job Seekers

Prospective lumber production workers may apply directly to a mill or company that announces openings. Some jobs are also posted online, in local newspapers, and/or at the entrance to the mill. Furthermore, some timber industry-oriented professional trade associations and unions post job openings in newsletters or on websites.

Professional Certification and Licensure

Lumber production workers may be required to obtain state commercial licenses and certifications for the use of cranes, forklifts, and other heavy machinery. Much of the experience required for such certification is obtained through on-the-job training.

Additional Requirements

Lumber production workers must be physically fit, as they will be expected to do heavy lifting and other strenuous physical activities. They should also be able to work in a team and follow instructions, especially with regard to safety. Knowledge of tools and mechanical systems is also useful for these individuals. Those who wish to advance to supervisory positions and those working as independent contractors should also have an understanding of business and management.

Fun Fact

The annual World Lumberjack Championships, held each year in Wisconsin, awards more than $50,000 in prizes for events like logrolling and a variety of chopping and sawing contests.

Source: http://www.lumberjackworldchampionships.com/lumberjack-history.php

EARNINGS AND ADVANCEMENT

Earnings depend on the size and geographic location of the employer, the type of job and the experience of the employee. Large companies pay much more than small companies. Lumber production workers in Alaska and the Northwest earn more than those in the South, where the cost of living is generally lower. This occupation is seasonal, with the highest employment in summer and the lowest in winter.

Lumber production workers had median annual earnings of $35,160 in 2014. The lowest ten percent earned less than $25,160, and the highest ten percent earned more than $49,320.

Lumber production workers who work for large, private firms generally enjoy more generous benefits than do those working in smaller firms. Small logging contractor firms generally offer lumber production workers few benefits beyond vacation leave. However, some employers offer full-time workers basic benefits, such as medical coverage, and provide safety apparel and equipment.

Metropolitan Areas with the Highest Employment Level in this Occupation

Metropolitan area	Employment	Employment per thousand jobs	Annual mean wage
Eugene-Springfield, OR	280	1.99	$35,340
Portland-Vancouver-Hillsboro, OR-WA	180	0.17	$36,140
Salem, OR	80	0.56	$36,060
Corvallis, OR	80	2.27	$38,110

Source: Bureau of Labor Statistics

EMPLOYMENT AND OUTLOOK

Lumber production workers held about 54,000 jobs nationally in 2014. Most lumber production workers are employed by companies that operate timber tracts, tree farms or forest nurseries, or for contractors that supply services to agriculture and forestry industries. Employment of lumber production workers is expected to decline relative to all occupations through the year 2024, which means employment is projected to decrease 2 percent to 5 percent. Most of the job openings will result from replacement needs, since many lumber production workers transfer to other jobs that are less physically demanding and dangerous, or they retire.

Employment Trend, Projected 2014–24

Total, all occupations: 7%

Forest, conservation, and logging workers: -2%

Logging and lumber production workers: -4%

Note: "All Occupations" includes all occupations in the U.S. Economy. Source: U.S. Bureau of Labor Statistics, Employment Projections Program

Related Occupations
- Farm Worker
- Forestry Worker
- Forklift Operator
- Freight, Stock and Material Mover

Conversation With . . .
DUSTIN RIGDON

Optimization/Quality Control, Shuqualak Lumber Company
Shuqualak, Mississippi
Lumber production, 17 years

1. What was your individual career path in terms of education/training, entry-level job, or other significant opportunity?

After watching my grandfather and my father work in the timber industry all my life, I knew that I wanted to play some sort of role along those lines. I attended college for forestry and worked part-time at Shuqualak Lumber Company in the summer. Being around the plant during those summer months, I could see that things were slowly creeping more and more toward computers and electronics. I noticed that most of the older workers were having a hard time adjusting to the new and improved machinery and catching on to how the machines work. It also seemed that everyone my age was also going into forestry, so I decided to stop going to school and to work at Shuqualak Lumber full time, focusing on the missing link they needed, which was understanding the computers and the optimizers that determine the "optimal" way to cut lumber. Charlie Thomas III, the mill manager and vice president, decided that each time we upgraded to a new system he would send me to classes to learn all that I could about that equipment. That way, I could teach the operators and others at our plant how it worked, plus I'd be able to troubleshoot any issues that would arise. This has really helped us stay in the game and be more productive as a company.

2. What are the most important skills and/or qualities for someone in your profession?

Someone in this profession has to be computer knowledgeable and able to adapt to new technology; have great verbal communication skills; understand the sawmill process and how lumber is made; and have great troubleshooting skills.

3. What do you wish you had known going into this profession?

I underestimated the electrical knowledge that would sometimes be needed when troubleshooting problems. Over the years, I've gained hands-on experience and have learned things from our electricians that helped me do my job better, but I would have benefited greatly if I had gotten an electrical degree or at least taken a few electrical classes years ago.

4. Are there many job opportunities in your profession? In what specific areas?

As long as lumber is being produced, there will always be job opportunities for computer programmers, electricians, and for people who understand optimization. Optimization uses laser measurement devices and computer algorithms to determine the actual size of the stem, log, or board being measured, and the best possible way to cut it to provide maximum recovery. The sawmill industry can't operate without them anymore.

5. How do you see your profession changing in the next five years? What role will technology play in those changes, and what skills will be required?

The sawmill industry has changed so much just over the years I have been here. Lumber is being scanned better, faster, and more accurately each year. We have devices that will send us text messages and emails if our parameters are off by just thousandths of an inch. We have sensors that will move equipment automatically if the lumber is trending off our set parameters. We have replaced a lot of old hydraulic systems with high-performance electric variable speed drives. Daily lumber reports from each machine are automatically emailed to us at the end of each shift. The list just goes on about how technology has replaced manual labor from the past.

6. What do you enjoy most about your job? What do you enjoy least about your job?

What I love most about my job is figuring out how to improve things on a daily basis. Every machine has the ability to perform smoother and faster while still cutting the high-grade lumber we produce. I'm constantly tweaking speeds, machine movement, and parameters to see just how good I can get it. I also love troubleshooting problems. When a machine is not performing correctly, I love the challenge of figuring out why and figuring out how to fix it.

I guess if I had to list what I love the least it would be that I'm on call all the time. If something happens at the plant, I'm usually involved in one way or another.

7. Can you suggest a valuable "try this" for students considering a career in your profession?

Most companies will give tours to college students to let them see and get a feel for how the plant operates and the type of products they produce. Most of the time I give the tours here and I personally take the time to explain how every machine operates.

MORE INFORMATION

American Forest and Paper Association
1111 19th Street, NW, Suite 800
Washington, DC 20036
202.463.2700
www.afandpa.org

Loggers Council
P.O. Box 966
Hemphill, TX 75948
409.625.0206
www.americanloggers.org

Technical Association of the Pulp and Paper Industry
15 Technology Parkway South
Norcross, GA 30092
770.446.1400
www.tappi.org

Michael Auerbach/Editor

Machinist

Snapshot

Career Cluster: Manufacturing
Interests: Mathematics, engineering, metalworking, computers
Earnings (Yearly Average): $39,980
Employment & Outlook: Average Growth Expected

OVERVIEW

Sphere of Work

Machinists use a variety of computer-guided and hand-operated machines to cut and shape raw metal and other materials into tools and parts used in engineering and mechanical projects. Traditionally, machining is described as the process of removing metal from a metal object, though some machinists also fashion plastic or wooden parts for certain projects.

Machinists also conduct quality-control measurements to ensure that the parts or items created through the machining process conform to the specifications of the designers and engineers. Machining can be considered part of the construction and technical manufacturing industries.

Work Environment

Machinists work in machine shops and specialty manufacturing shops. They may also work in larger factories, completing machining tasks as part of a broader manufacturing process. Machinists may work alone, or they may work in close proximity to or conjunction with other machinists and manufacturing specialists. Many machinists also work closely with engineers and designers to complete certain tasks. A small number of machinists work independently, contracting their services to designers who require specialized parts for a project.

Profile

Working Conditions: Work Indoors
Physical Strength: Medium Work
Education Needs: High School
  Diploma with Technical Education,
  Apprenticeship
Licensure/Certification:
  Recommended
Opportunities For Experience:
  Apprenticeship, Military Service
Holland Interest Score*: RIE

* See Appendix A

Occupation Interest

Those interested in a career in machining should be detail oriented and have some basic familiarity with mathematics. Precise measurement is essential to the machining process, and manual machining requires a high degree of coordination to ensure exact specifications. Machinists need to utilize complex equipment, and a background in metalworking and engineering can be helpful in learning the tasks characteristic of machine work. In addition, modern machinists often use computer-aided machines, so familiarity with computer operations is an advantage to those interested in pursuing a career in machining.

A Day in the Life—Duties and Responsibilities

While some machinists may work on one project at a time, others may work on a number of different projects during a typical day. The daily hours for most machinists vary according to the type of company that employs them, but most machining work can be done during regular business hours. Evening, weekend, and overtime work is common in the machining industry, as it is not unusual for a machining shop to accept contracts with short deadlines for completion.

During a typical day, machinists may spend time studying blueprints or diagrams and creating computer-generated models or schematics for various projects. Machinists also perform a variety of measurements and tests to determine the tolerances and dimensions of the parts or devices that emerge from the machining process. A machinist must dedicate a certain amount of time each day to setting up or calibrating manual or computer-guided machines. Once prepared, a machinist may complete anywhere from one to several hundred projects per day, depending on the complexity of the project. In many cases, machinists may also be required to buff, polish, file, or refine their products after the machining process.

Duties and Responsibilities

- Studying blueprints, sketches, or other specifications to determine necessary materials and procedures
- Developing specifications from general descriptions
- Assembling parts to make lathes, milling machines, shapers, or grinders
- Verifying dimensions, alignment, and conformity of workpieces using measuring instruments
- Testing machines for malfunctions
- Calculating where to cut or bore into the metal
- Using machine and hand tools to set up, repair, and adjust metalworking machines
- Measuring and marking dimensions and reference points to lay out stock for machining

OCCUPATION SPECIALTIES

Automotive Machinists

Automotive Machinists set up and operate a variety of general or specialized metalworking machines to repair automotive engine parts such as transmissions, springs or brakes.

Maintenance Machinists

Maintenance Machinists set up and repair machines, equipment and tools; fit and assemble parts to make machine tools; and maintain industrial machines.

WORK ENVIRONMENT

Physical Environment

Machinists may work in a machine shop or on a factory floor. They typically have a workbench or a desk with a computer. Machinists must also have access to a workroom containing a variety of industrial manual and computer-guided machines, which they use to cut, etch, shape, bend, and otherwise manipulate various materials.

Transferable Skills and Abilities

Organization & Management Skills
- Paying attention to and handling details
- Performing duties which change frequently

Technical Skills
- Performing scientific, mathematical and technical work
- Working with machines, tools or other objects

Plant Environment

Some machinists work in factory environments, where the machining area is housed near where other workers assemble, decorate, and process the factory's products. Machining in the factory environment tends to be different, as factories may have hundreds of employees and typically assign each employee a small number of specific tasks.

Human Environment

Machinists typically work as part of an engineering team that may include project managers, engineers, designers, and a variety of others who help to manage the office area or the marketing portion of the business. While some small shops may hire as few as one machinist, in other cases, a machinist may be part of a larger team that works together to complete projects.

Technological Environment

Computer-aided design (CAD) tools allow machinists and engineers to plan products on a computer and translate digital designs into instructions for machines or schematics for construction projects. Modern machinists also use computer-numeric-controlled (CNC) equipment, which can perform a variety of specific tasks, including metal and wood cutting, planing, and routing, with digital guides and plans.

EDUCATION, TRAINING, AND ADVANCEMENT

High School/Secondary

Machinists typically hold a high school degree or the equivalent. Many machinist positions do not require higher levels of education for starting employees. High school courses such as mathematics, drafting, metalworking, and computer science can be helpful for those looking to pursue machining as a career.

Suggested High School Subjects
- Algebra
- Applied Math
- Blueprint Reading
- Drafting
- English
- Industrial Arts
- Machining Technology
- Mechanical Drawing
- Metals Technology
- Physics
- Shop Math
- Trade/Industrial Education
- Welding

Famous First

The first tool factory to specialize in the making of tools for machinists was the Nashua Manufacturing Company of Nashua, NH, which was established in 1838 by John H. Gage.

Postsecondary

There are a variety of vocational career programs aimed at helping students to pursue a career as a machinist. In addition, some community colleges offer programs for machining, including both computer-aided and manual machining techniques. Generally speaking, an associate's or bachelor's degree is not required for those seeking to become machinists, but colleges and universities offer courses in engineering, mechanics, and mathematics that provide helpful skills for professional machinists. Those with postsecondary degrees may have an advantage in the job market.

Related College Majors
* Machine Technologist

Adult Job Seekers

Adults attempting to transition to machining from other fields are advised to pursue classes at a technical institute or community college. For some adults, classes in basic computer skills may be necessary, depending on the individual's level of familiarity with digital machining programs. Some retired or former architects and engineers may choose to work as machinists on a contract basis.

Professional Certification and Licensure

Technical institutes and vocational schools often offer certificate programs for professional machinists. These programs may last from two to four years and typically introduce students to both manual and computer-oriented machining techniques. In addition to academic training, machinists typically receive on-the-job training for periods ranging from six months to one year. Some machinists enter the profession by apprenticing with a professional machinist for several years before attempting to find work as a professional.

Additional Requirements

In addition to academic and on-the-job training, machinists may be required to engage in further education in an effort to stay abreast of new developments in their field. Many employers offer continuing-education programs or seminars designed to introduce machinists to new technological developments.

Fun Fact

St. Hubert, a French hunter-turned-priest, is the patron saint of many: hunters, archers, mathematicians, machinists … and anyone stricken with rabies.
Source: http://www.thecross-photo.com/Hubert-Patron_Saint_of_Hunters-Written_by_Mitch_Ballard.htm

EARNINGS AND ADVANCEMENT

Earnings depend on the type, geographic location and union affiliation of the employer and the employee's skills. In 2014, median annual earnings of machinists were $39,980. The lowest ten percent earned less than $24,620, and the highest ten percent earned more than $60,740.

Machinists may receive paid vacations, holidays, and sick days; life and health insurance, and retirement benefits. These are usually paid by the employer. Some employers also provide hand tools, safety glasses and extra pay for late shift and overtime work.

Metropolitan Areas with the Highest
Employment Level in this Occupation

Metropolitan area	Employment	Employment per thousand jobs	Annual mean wage
Chicago-Joliet-Naperville, IL	16,680	4.45	$40,130
Houston-Sugar Land-Baytown, TX	13,140	4.62	$42,780
Warren-Troy-Farmington Hills, MI	9,460	8.27	$41,980
Los Angeles-Long Beach-Glendale, CA	9,240	2.28	$37,360
Minneapolis-St. Paul-Bloomington, MN-WI	7,590	4.16	$47,040
Cleveland-Elyria-Mentor, OH	6,480	6.39	$39,640
Santa Ana-Anaheim-Irvine, CA	6,050	4.08	$41,370
Milwaukee-Waukesha-West Allis, WI	5,670	6.90	$41,590
Seattle-Bellevue-Everett, WA	4,920	3.30	$50,020
Dallas-Plano-Irving, TX	4,790	2.14	$36,150

Source: Bureau of Labor Statistics

EMPLOYMENT AND OUTLOOK

There were approximately 400,000 machinists employed nationally in 2014. Employment is expected to grow about the same as the average for all occupations through the year 2024, which means employment is projected to increase 7 percent to 12 percent. The use of computer-controlled machine tools and new technologies allows fewer machinists to accomplish work more quickly. Most job openings will be due to the need to replace experienced workers who transfer to other occupations or retire.

Employment Trend, Projected 2014–24

Machinists: 10%

Total, all occupations: 7%

Metal workers and plastic workers: -5%

Note: "All Occupations" includes all occupations in the U.S. Economy. Source: U.S. Bureau of Labor Statistics, Employment Projections Program

Related Occupations
- Apparel Worker
- Computer-Control Machine Tool Operator
- Industrial Machinery Mechanic
- Millwright
- Precision Assembler
- Tool & Die Maker

Related Military Occupations
- Machinist
- Welder & Metal Worker

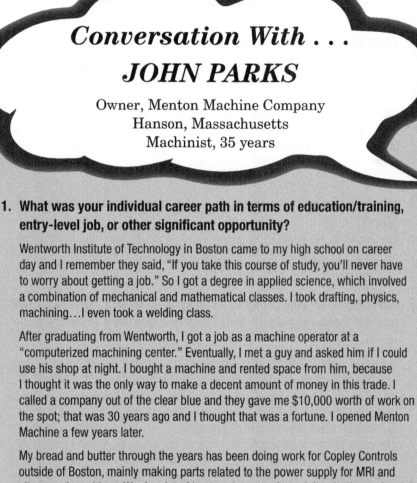

Conversation With . . .
JOHN PARKS

Owner, Menton Machine Company
Hanson, Massachusetts
Machinist, 35 years

1. What was your individual career path in terms of education/training, entry-level job, or other significant opportunity?

Wentworth Institute of Technology in Boston came to my high school on career day and I remember they said, "If you take this course of study, you'll never have to worry about getting a job." So I got a degree in applied science, which involved a combination of mechanical and mathematical classes. I took drafting, physics, machining…I even took a welding class.

After graduating from Wentworth, I got a job as a machine operator at a "computerized machining center." Eventually, I met a guy and asked him if I could use his shop at night. I bought a machine and rented space from him, because I thought it was the only way to make a decent amount of money in this trade. I called a company out of the clear blue and they gave me $10,000 worth of work on the spot; that was 30 years ago and I thought that was a fortune. I opened Menton Machine a few years later.

My bread and butter through the years has been doing work for Copley Controls outside of Boston, mainly making parts related to the power supply for MRI and ultrasound machines. We do a lot of heat-resistant and specialty plastics and metals for clients in robotics, biotechnology, electronics, health care and other industries. We do a lot of prototyping, which people think of as one or two parts, but you can have as many as fifty parts with a prototype. Whenever you're designing something new, you have to build a prototype and make sure it works right. We built the prototype for the first monitors for Virgin Atlantic's in-flight entertainment. We also do production machining, which involves a large quantity of a few hundred or more parts.

2. What are the most important skills and/or qualities for someone in your profession?

It's important for machinists to be meticulous regarding both the accuracy of measurements and the finish of the parts they machine. You must constantly inspect parts both dimensionally and for looks. Looks are important, especially if something's on the front of a machine and especially when you're dealing with medical parts.

People want their finished machines to look really nice, almost like jewelry. Also, there are calculators on most of the machines, but you do need basic math skills.

3. What do you wish you had known going into this profession?

I wish I had known that the pay is relatively low for the amount of knowledge required to be a good machinist. For what machinists have to know, they're really underpaid. You could work at actually building the machines or doing mechanical assembly or mechanical engineering and be better off. I was able to open a shop and make money, but nowadays it costs a minimum of $50,000 to buy a machine and some of them can cost as much as $500,000 or more. A plumber or electrician doesn't have those kinds of start-up costs.

4. Are there many job opportunities in your profession? In what specific areas?

Machining—like a lot of manufacturing industries in America—has lost a lot of jobs to overseas competition.

5. How do you see your profession changing in the next five years? What role will technology play in those changes, and what skills will be required?

The major change in machining is 3D printing. It's mainly used for prototype work now, but will probably be used for production work down the road. A 3D printer can make very complex parts, but right now they're just not fast enough to handle production. Computerized machining centers have seen advancements in speed and in machines that perform multi-operations on a part. You can put a plate in a machine and it will cut it to a certain shape, drill holes, tap threads, and so on, rather than moving the part from machine to machine. The machines can move in multi-axes at one time. Think of an airplane propeller and all the curves; there are machines that can make that all at once.

6. What do you enjoy most about your job? What do you enjoy least about your job?

I enjoy this work only because I'm self-employed. I always try to make parts in the quickest possible time to make as much profit as possible. The least enjoyable part is when we have large quantity production orders. It's often monotonous.

7. Can you suggest a valuable "try this" for students considering a career in your profession?

Call a local machine shop and ask if you could visit and get information. We do hire part-timers and summer help who do things like check parts.

MORE INFORMATION

American Machinist
1300 East 9th Street
Cleveland, OH 44114
216.696.7000
www.americanmachinist.com

International Association of Machinists and Aerospace Workers
9000 Machinists Place
Upper Marlboro, MD 20772-2687
301.967.4500
www.goiam.org

National Tooling and Machining Association
1537 Rockside Road
Cleveland, OH 44134
800.248.6862
www.ntma.org

Precision Metalforming Association
6363 Oak Tree Boulevard
Independence, OH 44131
216.901.8800
www.pma.org

Micah Issitt/Editor

Meat Cutter

Snapshot

Career Cluster: Food Production
Interests: Food processing, culinary arts, working with your hands
Earnings (Yearly Average): $28,660
Employment & Outlook: Average Growth Expected

OVERVIEW

Sphere of Work

Meat cutters prepare meat, fish, and poultry for consumption. Some meat cutters perform initial butchering on recently slaughtered animals, while others trim commercially prepared meat sections into smaller pieces for retail display and consumer purchase. Retail meat cutters are traditionally known as butchers. In addition to the receipt and storage of meat, fish, and poultry products, meat cutters are responsible for inspecting food items to ensure quality and freshness. While industrial meat-cutting jobs are often conducted in processing plants away from consumer environments, butchers often interact with customers directly and must be knowledgeable about meat quality, residential storage requirements, and recipes.

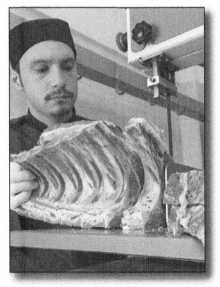

Work Environment

Meat cutters work primarily in temperature-controlled food-processing plants. A large amount of initial meat-cutting work is conducted in refrigerated environments to ensure food freshness. Industrial-grade meat processing requires an extensive array of machinery and equipment that can be potentially dangerous. Butchers and retail food preparers also use a variety of potentially dangerous tools and equipment, such as bone saws, cutlery, and professional-grade meat slicers.

Profile

Working Conditions: Work Indoors
Physical Strength: Light Work, Medium Work, Heavy Work
Education Needs: On-The-Job Training, Apprenticeship
Licensure/Certification: Required
Opportunities For Experience: Apprenticeship, Part-Time Work
Holland Interest Score*: RSE

* See Appendix A

Occupation Interest

Meat cutting and industrial-grade food preparation attract workers from a wide variety of backgrounds and career interests. While entry-level positions are primarily filled by unskilled laborers, specialty meat-cutting positions and management roles are often done by those with a professional background in food processing, culinary arts, small-business management, or commercial food distribution.

A Day in the Life—Duties and Responsibilities

The responsibilities of meat cutters can be divided into three major functions: initial processing, preparation for shipment, and retail preparation. Meat cutters and industrial food preparers are also responsible for a variety of safety and anti-contamination measures throughout this process.

Initial meat processing involves preparing animal carcasses for further processing. This work is traditionally completed in slaughterhouses or food-processing centers. These workers must inspect food products for defects and prepare them for shipping to locations where they will be further processed.

Once the meat has been prepared for shipment, it is received by secondary processors, such as wholesalers and food companies, who further break down the specimens into salable items and food products. This involves cutting the meat into still-smaller salable portions; canning fish, meats, and poultry; and adding ingredients to prepared food items containing the meat.

Retail and display preparation of meat items falls under the responsibility of butchers. These meat cutters receive large portions of meat, fish, and poultry and trim them for retail sale. Meat cutters and butchers at this end of the processing spectrum grind meats for use in cooking; marinate meats, poultry, and fish; add various ingredients, such as stuffing and wraps; and place food products in decorative displays for promotional purposes.

Duties and Responsibilities

- Dividing carcasses into halves with a band saw
- Quartering the halves with a saw or knife
- Reducing the quarters into saleable or edible portions
- Grinding inexpensive cuts of meat and trimming
- Cleaning and cutting fish and poultry
- Preparing special meat products
- Corning, smoking, tenderizing, or preserving meat

OCCUPATION SPECIALTIES

Carvers

Carvers carve individual portions from roasts and poultry with carving knives and meat-slicing machines to obtain the greatest number of meat servings.

Meat Butchers

Meat Butchers cut, trim, bone, tie and grind meats to portion and prepare meat in cooking form.

Chicken & Fish Butchers

Chicken & Fish Butchers butcher and clean fowl, fish and shellfish preparatory to cooking. Where poultry cutting is increasingly done by machines, they are responsible for tasks, such as de-boning breast meat, that are too difficult for machines to perform with precision.

Deli Cutters-Slicers

Deli Cutters-Slicers cut delicatessen meats and cheeses with slicing machines and knives.

Meat Inspectors

Meat Inspectors inspect and grade meats for wholesale and retail businesses.

WORK ENVIRONMENT

Physical Environment

Meat cutters work in food-processing locations such as kitchens, walk-in refrigerators, and various sanitary environments.

Transferable Skills and Abilities

Interpersonal/Social Skills
- Cooperating with others
- Working as a member of a team

Organization & Management Skills
- Following instructions
- Making decisions

Research & Planning Skills
- Developing evaluation strategies

Technical Skills
- Working with machines, tools or other objects
- Working with your hands

Plant Environment

Meat cutters involved in initial meat processing generally work in either slaughterhouse facilities or industrial food-processing facilities.

Human Environment

Many meat cutters work either on their own, preparing cuts at their own pace, or as part of smaller teams of processors who work in concert with one another.

Technological Environment

Meat cutting and animal processing require an array of technologies and equipment, including knives, grinders, slicers, and conveyer belts.

EDUCATION, TRAINING, AND ADVANCEMENT

High School/Secondary

Meat cutters traditionally learn the trade through apprenticeships or on-the-job training. Entry-level positions in meat processing do not usually require more education than a high school diploma or GED certification. Exposure to culinary and industrial-arts programs in high school can lay some groundwork for a career in food processing. Chemistry and biology courses can provide elementary information regarding food-borne pathogens.

Suggested High School Subjects
- Applied Math
- Business Math
- English
- Food Service & Management

Famous First

The first federal meat inspection law was approved in 1890. It required the inspection of salted pork and bacon intended for export, as well as livestock.

Postsecondary

Postsecondary education is not required for most meat-cutting professions. However, course work in business management, culinary arts, or hospitality management may help those seeking managerial positions within the meat-processing industry.

Adult Job Seekers

Many adult job seekers transition to food-handling or -processing positions from previous roles in sanitation, food service, or other industrial processing positions. The daily work schedule for meat processors varies from employer to employer. Many large-scale processors run their operations night and day to keep up with demand. Retail meat cutters and specialty butchers traditionally work regular retail hours, including weekends and holidays, to meet customer demand.

Professional Certification and Licensure

Food-processing professionals may be required to obtain sanitation and safety-regulation certification, depending on the state in which they are located. Meat cutters who prepare meat to specific religious standards traditionally complete a certification program within a particular religious organization.

Additional Requirements

Meat cutting and industrial-grade food-service preparation requires strong hand-eye coordination and the ability to work with dangerous equipment in adherence to safety protocol. Workers must be able to work for long hours while wearing sanitation equipment, including gloves, masks, and safety goggles.

Fun Fact

It's estimated that in 2016, the typical American will eat 54.3 pounds of beef a year. That's down from about 94.1 pounds in 1976—which was one of the highest amounts in the last 50 years.

Source: http://www.nationalchickencouncil.org/about-the-industry/statistics/per-capita-consumption-of-poultry-and-livestock-1965-to-estimated-2012-in-pounds/

EARNINGS AND ADVANCEMENT

Earnings depend on the type, size and geographic location of the employer and the employee's experience and skill. Meat cutters employed by retail grocery stores are generally among the highest paid workers, while those in meatpacking plants are generally lower. Apprentice meat cutters earn a starting wage from fifty to seventy-five percent of a skilled meat cutter's pay.

Meat cutters had median annual earnings of $28,660 in 2014. The lowest ten percent earned less than $18,670, and the highest ten percent earned more than $45,920.

Meat cutters may receive paid vacations, holidays, and sick days; life and health insurance; and retirement benefits. These are usually paid by the employer.

Metropolitan Areas with the Highest
Employment Level in this Occupation

Metropolitan area	Employment	Employment per thousand jobs	Annual mean wage
Los Angeles-Long Beach-Glendale, CA	5,850	1.44	$26,870
Chicago-Joliet-Naperville, IL	5,010	1.33	$26,340
New York-White Plains-Wayne, NY-NJ	3,510	0.65	$39,570
Philadelphia, PA	2,750	1.48	$34,550
Atlanta-Sandy Springs-Marietta, GA	2,380	1.00	$27,760
Houston-Sugar Land-Baytown, TX	2,000	0.70	$25,330
San Diego-Carlsbad-San Marcos, CA	1,990	1.50	$28,920
Miami-Miami Beach-Kendall, FL	1,940	1.85	$26,590
Dallas-Plano-Irving, TX	1,930	0.86	$28,100
Santa Ana-Anaheim-Irvine, CA	1,860	1.25	$26,590

Source: Bureau of Labor Statistics

EMPLOYMENT AND OUTLOOK

There were about 140,000 meat cutters and butchers employed nationally in 2014. Employment is expected to grow about as fast as the average for all occupations through the year 2024, which means employment is projected to increase 3 percent to 7 percent. A growing population and the desire by consumers for ready-to-eat foods will create demand, but this demand will be somewhat offset by increased productivity at meat processing plants. Jobs will also be available each year because of the need to replace experienced workers who transfer to other occupations or retire.

Employment Trend, Projected 2014–24

Total, all occupations: 7%

Meat Cutters and Butchers: 5%

Food processing workers: 3%

Note: "All Occupations" includes all occupations in the U.S. Economy. Source: U.S. Bureau of Labor Statistics, Employment Projections Program

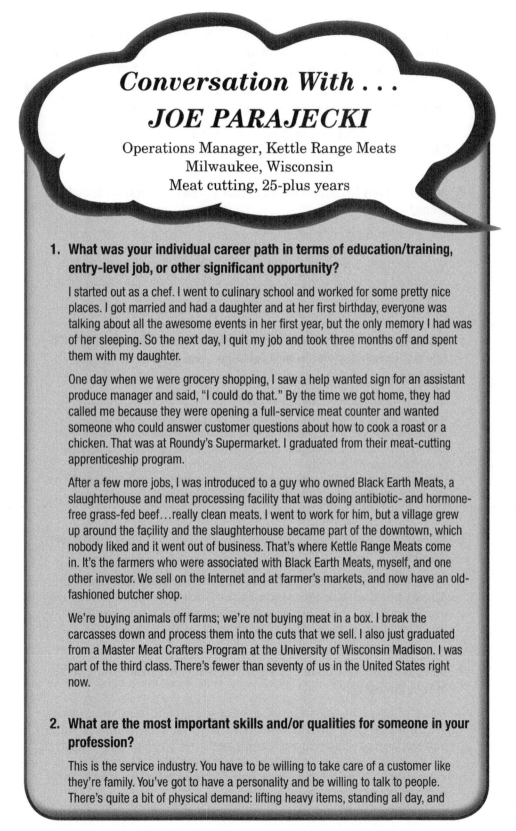

Conversation With . . .
JOE PARAJECKI

Operations Manager, Kettle Range Meats
Milwaukee, Wisconsin
Meat cutting, 25-plus years

1. What was your individual career path in terms of education/training, entry-level job, or other significant opportunity?

I started out as a chef. I went to culinary school and worked for some pretty nice places. I got married and had a daughter and at her first birthday, everyone was talking about all the awesome events in her first year, but the only memory I had was of her sleeping. So the next day, I quit my job and took three months off and spent them with my daughter.

One day when we were grocery shopping, I saw a help wanted sign for an assistant produce manager and said, "I could do that." By the time we got home, they had called me because they were opening a full-service meat counter and wanted someone who could answer customer questions about how to cook a roast or a chicken. That was at Roundy's Supermarket. I graduated from their meat-cutting apprenticeship program.

After a few more jobs, I was introduced to a guy who owned Black Earth Meats, a slaughterhouse and meat processing facility that was doing antibiotic- and hormone-free grass-fed beef…really clean meats. I went to work for him, but a village grew up around the facility and the slaughterhouse became part of the downtown, which nobody liked and it went out of business. That's where Kettle Range Meats come in. It's the farmers who were associated with Black Earth Meats, myself, and one other investor. We sell on the Internet and at farmer's markets, and now have an old-fashioned butcher shop.

We're buying animals off farms; we're not buying meat in a box. I break the carcasses down and process them into the cuts that we sell. I also just graduated from a Master Meat Crafters Program at the University of Wisconsin Madison. I was part of the third class. There's fewer than seventy of us in the United States right now.

2. What are the most important skills and/or qualities for someone in your profession?

This is the service industry. You have to be willing to take care of a customer like they're family. You've got to have a personality and be willing to talk to people. There's quite a bit of physical demand: lifting heavy items, standing all day, and working in the cold—it's between 32 and 38 degrees. There's also quite a bit of mental demand. In a lot of cases you're working with a sharp knife or a saw with a blade that's made to cut bone. If you get distracted, you're going to get hurt.

3. What do you wish you had known going into this profession?

I wish I had known that I was this good in this profession. I don't think I would have taken the culinary road. I just love meat cutting so much.

4. Are there many job opportunities in your profession? In what specific areas?

Yes, and the field is growing because we're seeing more and more small butcher shops, farmer's markets, and meat-share programs. People want that connection to the farm, to the butcher. There are jobs in grocery stores and meat processing plants. Most meat processing plants are in the Midwest states: Iowa, Illinois, Indiana. Wisconsin has a few.

5. How do you see your profession changing in the next five years? What role will technology play in those changes, and what skills will be required?

We're seeing computers come into play for things like inventory and temperature. But at the end of the day, it's the skill of the person. It's a lot of understanding muscle and how to cut that muscle, which a machine can't do. As people get more connected to their food, antibiotic- and hormone-free meat and humane handling of animals is coming into play. Now there's an resurgence of the old charcuterie products coming back. Everyone wants to make them, but you have to do it right or you can hurt somebody.

6. What do you enjoy most about your job? What do you enjoy least about your job?

The answer to both questions is people! I have great relationships with customers. But the Internet has made some people think they know everything. A customer will say, "I'm going to have a party and I want seventy-five hanging tenderloins." Well, there's only one to a cow, so how do I get you that?

7. Can you suggest a valuable "try this" for students considering a career in your profession?

Instead of being a bag boy in a grocery store, be a meat clerk. There are regulations that say you can't pick up a knife or work on anything that's got a motor until you're eighteen, but you can clean up and wrap the meat in the Styrofoam trays and put it in the display cases. That's typically where someone starts. You'll know from watching the guys and gals in the back room if this is something you want to do. If it is, they're going to open up the door and teach you.

MORE INFORMATION

American Association of Meat Processors
One Meating Place
Elizabethtown, PA 17022
717.367.1168
www.aamp.com

North American Meat Association
1970 Broadway, Suite 825
Oakland, CA 94612
510.763.1533
www.meatassociation.com

United Food & Commercial Workers International Union
1775 K Street, NW
Washington, DC 20006
202.223.3111
www.ufcw.org

John Pritchard/Editor

Metal/Plastic Working Machine Operator

Snapshot

Career Cluster: Manufacturing; Production

Interests: Machinery, working with your hands, working as part of a team

Earnings (Yearly Average): $32,130

Employment & Outlook: Decline Expected

OVERVIEW

Sphere of Work

Metal/plastic working machine operators work in all the manufacturing industries. They operate machines that create metal or plastic parts or materials in an industrial process that comprises cutting, shaping, and forming metal and plastic to manufacture the desired end products. Their work includes setting up the machines needed to carry out the process.

The products manufactured by metal/plastic working machine operators are essential for a modern industrial society. They are used for thousands of applications in engine building, consumer products, instruments, avionics, and automotive manufacture. Despite increasing computerized processes, human control of metal/plastic working machines is still essential, particularly when setting up the machines and monitoring their output.

Work Environment

The most common workplace for metal/plastic working machine operators is a factory. There, metal/plastic working machine operators work next to their machines, which are located in designated production areas or in tool rooms or job shops. This industrial setting includes some noise, and personal protective equipment must be worn. Adherence to safety standards is required.

Regular working hours correspond to the norm in the manufacturing industries, generally forty hours a week. However, overtime is common, and workers must be prepared for shift work that may include evenings, nights, weekends, and holidays.

Profile

Working Conditions: Work Indoors
Physical Strength: Medium Work
Education Needs: High School Diploma, On-The-Job Training, Apprenticeship
Licensure/Certification: Recommended
Opportunities For Experience: Internship, Apprenticeship, Part-Time Work
Holland Interest Score*: RCE

* See Appendix A

Occupation Interest

The occupation is appealing to people interested in working with industrial machines in factories. These people should be willing to work shifts and put in overtime when required.

There are few formal educational requirements, but there is strong emphasis on on-the-job training. A high school degree is not required but having a degree enhances the applicant's chances for initial employment. A willingness and the ability to learn new skills while working is essential for advancement in the position. Teamwork on the factory floor is also required.

A Day in the Life—Duties and Responsibilities

The working day of a metal/plastic working machine operator depends on work orders. Work varies depending on whether the worker sets up machines or operates; many skilled workers are able to perform both tasks.

Set up requires preparing the metal or plastic working machine for the desired production run. Work orders or blueprints contain instructions to set specific tolerances for product manufacture and to sequence machine operations.

Set up can entail installing specific dies in the machine. After set up, the setter performs trial runs. Here, a setter examines machine operations and watches for vibrations and the quality of the products manufactured. If necessary, the setter adjusts the speed or actions of the machine and may realign its processes. At the end of a specific production run, a setter may remove and change dies to set up the machine for its next operations.

Operating and tending a metal or plastic working machine often includes loading it with the materials for production. After starting the machine, the operator must constantly monitor its performance. The operator is responsible for controlling and adjusting the operations of the machine, aligning its operating speed or the specific work processes it performs. Operators are responsible for minor maintenance such as lubricating and cleaning their machines.

The operator must check and test the output of the machine. For flawed products, the operator should try to determine the causes and begin to troubleshoot the operations of the machine. Operators are expected to be able to fix minor problems of their machines and determine when to call in a mechanic.

Often, operators are responsible for ensuring correct transport of the manufactured products. Operators will document the work of their machines, generally in an electronic database. Both setters and operators are expected to leave their working area clean and tidy.

Duties and Responsibilities

- Reading blueprints and working orders to determine tooling instructions
- Positioning cutting tools and workpieces for correct operations
- Determining cutting speeds, feed rates, and cutting tools to be used
- Starting machines and controlling their operation
- Removing chips and controlling coolant systems
- Making minor adjustments or tool changes
- Performing routine machine maintenance
- Stacking or loading finished items in shipping containers or placing items on a conveyor system

OCCUPATION SPECIALTIES

Lathe Tenders

Lathe Tenders tend one or more previously set-up lathes such as turret lathes, engine lathes and chucking machines, to perform one or a series of repetitive operations such as turning, boring, threading or facing metal workpieces.

Milling-Machine Tenders

Milling-Machine Tenders set up and operate various types of milling machines to mill flat or curved surfaces on metal workpieces, such as machine, tool or die parts.

Extruding and Drawing Machine Operator

Extruding and Drawing Machine Operator set up or operate machines to extrude (pull out) thermoplastic or metal materials in the form of tubes, rods, hoses, wire, bars, or structural shapes.

Forging, Rolling, Cutting, Punching, or Drilling Machine Operators

These machine operators set up or operate machines that shape, form, cut, or drill metal or plastic parts.

Pourers and Casters

Pourers and Casters operate hand-controlled mechanisms to pour and regulate the flow of molten metal into molds to produce castings or ingots.

Model Makers

Model Makers set up and operate machines, such as milling and engraving machines to make working models of metal or plastic objects.

Patternmakers

Patternmakers lay out, machine, fit, and assemble castings and parts to metal or plastic foundry patterns and core molds.

WORK ENVIRONMENT

Physical Environment

The most common workplace for metal/plastic working machine operators is within a factory, an environment that includes noise, dirt, and some possible hazards from operating industrial machines. Appropriate personal protective equipment—such as safety glasses, earplugs, or steel-toed industrial boots—is to be worn. Sometimes wearing a respirator may be required to protect a worker from inhaling harmful from fumes.

Transferable Skills and Abilities

Organization & Management Skills
- Coordinating tasks
- Managing people/groups
- Paying attention to and handling details
- Performing routine work

Technical Skills
- Performing scientific, mathematical and technical work
- Working with machines, tools or other objects
- Working with your hands

Plant Environment

Most factories seek to minimize their workers' exposure to noise and dirt. They tend to be located in industrial parts of urban areas, although some can be found in a more suburban or remote setting.

Human Environment

Work in a factory entails daily contact with fellow workers, and most metal/plastic working machine operators work in teams. Setters may confer with colleagues about their tasks. There is a growing organizational tendency to build teams of operators who rotate among different machines.

Technological Environment

Metal/plastic working machines are complex industrial manufacturing equipment. A setter or operator should have a basic understanding of their operating technology and be able to manipulate and to control an advanced technical machine. Increasingly, setup, operations, and control are done digitally.

EDUCATION, TRAINING, AND ADVANCEMENT

High School/Secondary

While not required, a high school degree or GED certificate significantly increases an applicant's chances for employment in this occupation. This is especially true for obtaining a first job.

In high school, a student should take a group of classes with technical focus. Such classes may include blueprint reading, machining technology, metals technology, and industrial arts. Applied and shop mathematics, applied physics, and shop classes are also useful. A chemistry class provides understanding of the science behinds plastics. English and communication classes are helpful. Computer literacy is essential and can be gained from a course in computer science.

For an introduction to the field, summer work as a production assistant or a laborer in a factory with metal or plastic working operating machines is useful. It also provides early experience in the occupation. Experience can be gained also from internships organized by a high school or offered by companies in the manufacturing industries.

Suggested High School Subjects
- Applied Math
- Applied Physics
- Blueprint Reading
- English
- Industrial Arts

- Machining Technology
- Metals Technology
- Shop Math

Famous First

The first plastic household product was a water tumbler produced in 1945 by MIT chemist Earl S. Tupper. Tupper went on to market a line of leak-proof polyethylene containers sold under the Tupperware brand.

Postsecondary

This occupation does not require any postsecondary education. However, there are community colleges that offer training and certification programs in operating metal/plastic working machines.

There are eleven apprentice specialties recognized by the U.S. Department of Labor's Office of Apprenticeship for this occupation. These include multioperation-machine operator, spring coiling machine setter, extruder operator, heavy forger, or roll operator.

To advance in the field, individuals must gain a deeper knowledge of computerized machine operations, which can be gained from attending courses in computer-aided design (CAD), computer-aided manufacturing (CAM), or computer numerically controlled (CNC) machines.

Related College Majors
- Machine Technologist

Adult Job Seekers

A person who has worked as a metal/plastic working machine operator before and seeks to reenter the workforce in this occupation should not face major obstacles, especially if the time away from the occupation was used to gain new skills, such as learning about a computerized-machine-control-related program.

An adult job seeker without experience in the profession can obtain an entry-level position as long as they possess the physical stamina required, particularly to load and unload the machines. Prior experience can be gained by working as a production assistant or a laborer in the field.

Adult job seekers can approach companies and their factories or machine shops directly. Using the services of public employment and placement offices is another good option. Asking at local unions or pursuing want ads on the Internet or in print publications is also useful.

Professional Certification and Licensure

There are no licensing requirements. Workers can pursue professional certifications. As of 2013, the National Institute for Metalworking Skills offers fifty-two different skills certifications for members of this occupation. The Fabricators and Manufacturers Association International offers certification as a precision sheet metal operator (PSMO).

Additional Requirements

Many employers demand submission to random drug and alcohol testing. Working while intoxicated is prohibited. There are also certain medications that are prohibited when operating machinery. Physical strength and fitness is required to endure the physical stress of the work.

Fun Fact

Every now and then a line from a movie takes on life of its own. In the late 1960s and beyond, it was the advice given to a recent college graduate, in the movie "The Graduate": "I just want to say one word to you. Just one...Plastics!"

EARNINGS AND ADVANCEMENT

Earnings of metal and plastic working machine operators depend on the type, size, geographic location, and the extent of unionization of the employer, the type of machine operated, and the skill level of the individual. Metal and plastic working machine operators had medial annual earnings of $32,130 in 2014. The lowest ten percent earned less than $19,740, and the highest ten percent earned more than $57,780.

Metropolitan Areas with the Highest Employment Level in this Occupation

Metropolitan area	Employment	Employment per thousand jobs	Annual mean wage
Portland-Vancouver-Hillsboro, OR-WA	1,460	1.38	$27,530
Los Angeles-Long Beach-Glendale, CA	1,030	0.25	$37,560
Minneapolis-St. Paul-Bloomington, MN-WI	520	0.28	$40,310
Santa Ana-Anaheim-Irvine, CA	510	0.34	$33,920
Houston-Sugar Land-Baytown, TX	480	0.17	$40,960
Phoenix-Mesa-Glendale, AZ	350	0.19	$37,180
San Diego-Carlsbad-San Marcos, CA	350	0.27	$32,890
Warren-Troy-Farmington Hills, MI	330	0.29	$32,920
Cleveland-Elyria-Mentor, OH	310	0.31	$32,190
Dallas-Plano-Irving, TX	300	0.13	n/a

Source: Bureau of Labor Statistics

EMPLOYMENT AND OUTLOOK

Nationally, there were about 1 million metal and plastic working machine operators employed in 2014. Employment is expected to decline relative to all occupations through the year 2024, which means employment is projected to drop by 10 percent or more. The demand for metal and plastic working machine operators has been affected by increased automation and the growth of overseas production facilities.

Employment Trend, Projected 2014–24

Total, all occupations: 7%

Production occupations: -3%

Metal and plastic machine workers: -13%

Note: "All Occupations" includes all occupations in the U.S. Economy. Source: U.S. Bureau of Labor Statistics, Employment Projections Program

Related Occupations

- Apparel Worker
- Computer-Control Machine Tool Operator
- Precision Assembler
- Structural Metal Worker
- Welder

Conversation With . . .
JOHN KOCZERGA

Manufacturing Operations Manager
New England Plastics Corp.
Woburn, Massachusetts
Plastic manufacturing and fabrication, 40 years

1. What was your individual career path in terms of education/training, entry-level job, or other significant opportunity?

My dad was a machinist and I always liked mechanical things, so I also wanted to be a machinist. He urged me to go to a technical school rather than a regular high school. I had decided that if I didn't have a job as a machinist when I graduated, I would join the Air Force. As part of a co-op program at the technical high school I attended, I got my first production machinist job in 1976. I graduated a year later and stayed at that first machinist job until spring of 1982. That's when a friend got me to apply for a tool makers' job here at Northeast Plastics. I didn't want to do production work for the rest of my life, and decided to try building injection molds instead because the hourly wage was higher. I've been here ever since.

I started out doing secondary operations on molded plastic parts. When jobs permitted, I'd help make components for injection molds under the supervision of the shop manager or other tool makers. Eventually, I learned enough to design on a drafting board and build injection molds on my own. Examples of the types of parts we mold are medical, power supply components, automotive suspension parts, and so on. We used to do a lot of camera parts.

2. What are the most important skills and/or qualities for someone in your profession?

The ability to learn and retain information and the ability to focus on details. Toys such as model planes and cars come out of injection molds. They can be complicated, with many moving parts. It takes detailed planning to make different parts of the mold and have them all assemble and fit correctly. Some molds are daunting, so you take one piece at a time and eventually you create what I consider a piece of art.

Injection molds are called "tools" or "tooling"—it's a specific tool for a specific part. It's quite satisfying to take a raw piece of metal and turn it into a useful tool. Also, you really should have some manual machining background to be able program and set up the machine. If you're working simply as a machine operator, you load and unload work pieces into the machine and press the start button.

It seems everybody thinks you need a college education to survive these days. Well, not everyone is college material and some skills you won't learn in college. We still need a skilled manufacturing labor force in this country if the country is to survive. Just think about what would happen if we went to war with a country that manufactures parts for fighter jets. Good luck getting support.

3. What do you wish you had known going into this profession?

Math is critical to this profession. I wish I had understood it better earlier. Take school seriously.

4. Are there many job opportunities in your profession? In what specific areas?

Shops are often looking for entry-level and experienced mold makers or tool designers. Other jobs in injection molding are process techs, machine operators, inspectors, and more.

5. How do you see your profession changing in the next five years? What role will technology play in those changes, and what skills will be required?

We design molds and tooling on a computer aided design (CAD) program. We also use a computer aided machining (CAM) program to create cutter paths to machine contours and shapes, which is more complicated than CAD.

Reluctantly, we've had to use China to build some of our molds and tools because it's cheaper and allows us to compete. I've heard work is coming back from China, but I don't see it yet.

6. What do you enjoy most about your job? What do you enjoy least about your job?

What I enjoy most is the freedom to manage myself and to work on new things every day. I work in the shop and I design and quote. I love the challenge of a complicated part. Being a tool maker, every day you can be working on something different. Its hands-on, rather than all automatic machinery, and that's what I like. At some mold shops they have dedicated workers for different parts of the injection mold, which can get boring because you're at the same machine every day doing the same tasks.

What I enjoy least are very demanding customers who don't recognize your efforts.

7. Can you suggest a valuable "try this" for students considering a career in your profession?

Join a co-op program. If your school sponsors field trips to different shops, go along. Once or twice a year, we give engineering students tours of our shop and spend an hour or an hour and a half with them.

MORE INFORMATION

Association for Manufacturing Technology
7901 Westpark Drive
McLean, VA 22102
703.893.2900
www.amtonline.org

Fabricators and Manufactures Association International
833 Featherstone Road
Rockford, IL 61107
815.399.8700
www.fmanet.org

National Institute for Metalworking Skills
10565 Fairfax Boulevard, Suite 203
Fairfax, VA 22030
703.352.4971
www.nims-skills.org/web/nims/home

National Tooling and Machining Association
1357 Rockside Road
Cleveland, OH 44134
800.248.6862
www.ntma.org

Precision Machined Products Association
6700 West Snowville Road
Brecksville, OH 44141
440.526.0300
www.pmpa.org

Precision Metalforming Association
6363 Oak Tree Boulevard
Independence, OH 44131
216.901.8800
www.pma.org

Society of the Plastics Industry
1667 K Street, NW, Suite 1000
Washington, DC 20006
202.974.5200
www.plasticsindustry.org

Reinhart Lutz/Editor

Millwright

Snapshot

Career Cluster: Manufacturing
Interests: Machinery, working with your hands, working with a team
Earnings (Yearly Average): $50,460
Employment & Outlook: Faster than Average Growth Expected

OVERVIEW

Sphere of Work

Millwrights are skilled workers who are responsible for the layout, installation, and maintenance of mechanical equipment at factories, mills, power plants, and construction sites. Millwrights work closely with an assortment of machines, which they install, dismantle, repair, and move. They use a broad range of tools and vehicles to perform their job, including large power tools, small hand tools, and forklifts. They also work with managers to determine the best, most efficient location for a particular machine.

Work Environment

Millwrights work in a variety of locations, most commonly power plants, factories, and construction sites. These environments are typically dirty and noisy and contain many potential hazards, so millwrights have to be careful and closely follow safety standards. The machinery is dangerous as well. Millwrights sometimes have to perform their job in uncomfortable positions, such as kneeling, crouching, or bending.

Profile

Working Conditions: Work Indoors, Work both Indoors and Outdoors
Physical Strength: Heavy Work
Education Needs: On-The-Job Training, High School Diploma with Technical Education, Junior/Technical/Community College, Apprenticeship
Licensure/Certification: Usually Not Required
Opportunities For Experience: Apprenticeship, Military Service, Part-Time Work
Holland Interest Score*: RES

* See Appendix A

Occupation Interest

The millwright profession tends to attract highly skilled workers who enjoy using their hands outside of an office environment. Millwrights should enjoy collaborating with other workers to ensure a machine is handled correctly. They must also be critical thinkers with the ability to figure out repair issues on a variety of different machines and adapt to the different tasks involved. Millwrights enter the profession from an assortment of different backgrounds.

A Day in the Life—Duties and Responsibilities

A millwright's day-to-day duties and responsibilities vary depending on the job location and the type of equipment being worked on. Millwrights spend the majority of their time installing, dismantling, repairing, and moving a variety of machines in power plants, factories, and construction sites. Throughout the day, they communicate and collaborate with managers and other millwrights. They work closely with technical specifications and machinery blueprints to ensure jobs are performed correctly.

When a machine is in need of repairs, a millwright must first determine the source of the problem. He or she uses a variety of tools to replace defective parts or make necessary adjustments and alignments. After repairs and adjustments are performed, the millwright tests the machine and observes its functioning. When a site is installing a new machine, a millwright helps determine the best location for it in terms of efficiency and safety. If an old machine is being replaced, the millwright disassembles it to free up floor space for the replacement.

Before the new machine is installed, a millwright must assess whether steel beams need to be put in to support the machine. Forklifts and cranes are used frequently when installing new machines. Safety and clearance standards need to be followed during the entire installation and disassembling process. Protective clothing items such as boots, gloves, and hard hats are commonly worn. It is typical for a millwright to work under a contract, so they may only be at one location for a few days.

Duties and Responsibilities

- Reading blueprints and schematic drawings to determine work procedures
- Assembling and installing equipment such as shafting, conveyors, and tracks
- Constructing foundations for machines
- Aligning, assembling and securing machinery to foundations or other structures
- Dismantling machines
- Moving machinery and equipment
- Repairing, oiling and maintaining plant machinery and equipment

OCCUPATION SPECIALTIES

Automated Equipment Engineer-Technicians

Automated Equipment Engineer-Technicians install machinery and equipment used to emboss, die-cut, sore, fold and transfer paper or cardboard stock to paper or cardboard products.

Machinery Erectors

Machinery Erectors erect and test machinery and heavy equipment according to blueprints and specifications.

Manufacturer's Service Representatives

Manufacturer's Service Representatives install and repair machinery or equipment in the customer's establishment, following blueprint and manufacturer instructions and applying knowledge of mechanical, hydraulic and electrical machinery.

Maintenance Mechanics

Maintenance Mechanics repair and maintain, in accordance to diagrams, sketches, operations manuals and manufacturers' specifications, machinery and mechanical equipment such as engines, motors, pneumatic tools, conveyor systems and production machines and equipment.

Machine Assemblers

Machine Assemblers put together machines and equipment such as stokers, blowers and compression pumps according to customers' needs.

WORK ENVIRONMENT

Physical Environment

The immediate physical environment of a millwright varies depending on the job. The most common environments include factories, power plants, and constructions sites. These locations are typically noisy and dirty and pose hazards that can cause serious injury.

Transferable Skills and Abilities

Organization & Management Skills
- Following instructions
- Making decisions
- Paying attention to and handling details
- Performing duties which change frequently

Research & Planning Skills
- Developing evaluation strategies
- Using logical reasoning

Technical Skills
- Working with machines, tools or other objects
- Working with your hands

Plant Environment

Millwrights who are employed at factories, production and power plants, and mills are typically employed full time and are responsible for the inspection, installation, and maintenance of all machinery on-site.

Human Environment

Millwrights perform alongside other workers in the construction and manufacturing industries, including managers, machine operators, engineers, and other millwrights. Depending on the location, millwrights may work with professionals in a power plant or factory as well. Communication is essential for ensuring a job is done safely and correctly.

Technological Environment

Millwrights employ a variety of hand tools, including hammers, levels, and tools for welding and cutting. Measuring tools such as micrometers and lasers are used to precisely measure machine parts. For larger jobs, cranes, hoists, and forklifts may be used to move machine parts.

EDUCATION, TRAINING, AND ADVANCEMENT

High School/Secondary

There are no specific education requirements to become a millwright, but employers may require an applicant to have a high school diploma or an equivalent GED certificate. There are many basic and advanced high school courses that would benefit a student interested in the profession, including mathematics, mechanical drawing, and any courses related to mechanics. Some high schools have machine shops, where students can learn the fundamentals of basic machinery function and repair.

Suggested High School Subjects
- Applied Math
- Blueprint Reading
- Drafting
- Electricity & Electronics
- English
- Industrial Arts
- Machining Technology
- Mechanical Drawing
- Metals Technology
- Shop Math
- Shop Mechanics
- Welding
- Woodshop

Famous First

The first sawmill to run successfully on electricity was the Allis-Chalmers mill in Folsom, Calif., which in 1896 began producing lumber for the American River Land and Lumber Company.

Postsecondary

Millwrights are not typically required to have a college degree, but it can be useful to have a strong educational background in related subjects, such as mechanical and electrical engineering and mathematics. Many technical schools also offer programs in industrial maintenance; such programs generally feature both formal classroom instruction and hands-on training in an assortment of machine-related tasks, including blueprint reading, welding, and shop mathematics. These programs, which typically last from a few months to a year, provide students with a solid background in machine repair, industrial mechanics, and standard safety practices. In addition, technical schools sometimes offer job-placement programs, and they are also a great place to network with more experienced professionals in the industry. An employer is more likely to hire an individual who has completed a relevant program.

Related College Majors
- Heavy Equipment Maintenance & Repair

Adult Job Seekers

Those interested in the millwright profession who do not have any experience or education in the field or a related industry should enroll in a relevant program at a technical school or community college. Individuals seeking employment can also talk to a local union or contractor for guidance.

Professional Certification and Licensure

Certification and licensure is not usually required, but at the beginning of their careers, millwrights usually enter a formal apprenticeship program. These programs are usually sponsored by employers, local unions, contractors, or the state labor department. They generally last three to four years and include both formal technical instruction and on-the-job training from experienced millwrights. Apprentices need to have at least 144 hours of technical instruction and 2,000 hours of paid hands-on training. Once an apprentice has completed his or her program, he or she is considered to be fully qualified and able to perform tasks with less supervision. Throughout his or her career, a millwright will have to go through further training offered by representatives of machine manufacturers, professional trainers, or other experienced millwrights.

Additional Requirements

Millwrights need to possess a strong mechanical aptitude in order to use the variety of tools required for the job. They must also be physically fit and able to accurately read blueprints and other specifications.

Fun Fact

Today, millwrights construct and maintain machinery, but originally, they were carpenters who built mills—hence the name.

Source: http://www.millwrightemployers.org/whatisamillwright.html

EARNINGS AND ADVANCEMENT

Earnings and Advancement depend on the size and geographic location of the employer and the employee's years of experience. Median annual earnings of millwrights were $50,460 in 2014. The lowest ten percent earned less than $31,280, and the highest ten percent earned more than $74,540.

Millwrights may receive paid vacations, holidays, and sick days; life and health insurance; and retirement benefits. These are usually paid by the employer.

Metropolitan Areas with the Highest
Employment Level in this Occupation

Metropolitan area	Employment	Employment per thousand jobs	Annual mean wage
Houston-Sugar Land-Baytown, TX	1,410	0.50	$46,050
Indianapolis-Carmel, IN	1,060	1.13	$37,100
Warren-Troy-Farmington Hills, MI	880	0.77	$66,610
Los Angeles-Long Beach-Glendale, CA	730	0.18	$65,720
Birmingham-Hoover, AL	730	1.47	$43,410
Portland-Vancouver-Hillsboro, OR-WA	700	0.66	$51,940
Detroit-Livonia-Dearborn, MI	680	0.94	$64,640
Kansas City, MO-KS	630	0.63	$65,320
Atlanta-Sandy Springs-Marietta, GA	560	0.23	$46,750
St. Louis, MO-IL	480	0.37	$53,630

Source: Bureau of Labor Statistics

EMPLOYMENT AND OUTLOOK

There were approximately 41,000 millwrights employed nationally in 2014. Employment of millwrights is expected to grow much faster than the average for all occupations through the year 2024, which mean employment is expected to increase 15 percent or more. Millwrights will be needed to maintain and repair existing machinery and to dismantle and install new equipment. Job openings will also arise from the need to replace workers who retire or transfer to other occupations.

Employment Trend, Projected 2014–24

Millwrights and industrial machinery maintenance workers: 16%

Total, all occupations: 7%

Installation, maintenance, and repair occupations: 6%

Note: "All Occupations" includes all occupations in the U.S. Economy. Source: U.S. Bureau of Labor Statistics, Employment Projections Program

Related Occupations
- Boilermaker
- Computer-Control Machine Tool Operator
- Elevator Installer/Repairer
- Machinist
- Precision Assembler
- Riveter
- Sheet Metal Worker

Related Military Occupations
- Automotive & Heavy Equipment Mechanic
- Electronic Instrument Repairer
- Seaman
- Weapons Maintenance Technician

Conversation With . . .
ADAM EMERY

Millwright, Three Rivers Corporation
Midland, Michigan
Millwright, 6 years

1. What was your individual career path in terms of education/training, entry-level job, or other significant opportunity?

My high school was geared to industrial education—mechanical arts, metal shop, those kinds of things. I liked working with my hands and assumed I would be satisfied with a career in the construction trades. After I graduated from high school, I went to a trade school to learn to be a pipe fitter. I worked as a pipe fitter for a few years when I started noticing millwrights doing work that was more challenging, more technical, and something that I could do on a daily basis that was less mind-numbingly boring. As soon as I finished my pipe fitters journeyman ship, I returned to school to be a millwright. My paychecks come from Three Rivers Corporation but the work we do is at Dow Chemical plants. I report every day to a Dow person who tells me to go to this plant and fix certain things.

2. What are the most important skills and/or qualities for someone in your profession?

You need patience. You must be able to continually learn. It's not like pipefitting, where you learn the principles and can use them anywhere. You're going to consistently encounter new and evolving equipment. There's just too much for one guy to know. Also, it requires attention to detail because we're setting things to thousandths of an inch, whereas with pipefitting, we measure to eighths of an inch.

3. What do you wish you had known going into this profession?

I wish I had known about it before I started as a pipe fitter because I'd be further along in this trade. Nobody ever mentioned or explained what millwrights or pipe fitters were. To get the word out in high schools would be awesome. Also, you need to be ready for physical labor. There will be days when you have to work your butt off and you can't back down from that challenge.

4. Are there many job opportunities in your profession? In what specific areas?

There's a ton of opportunity in our area. All the seasoned guys are retiring; there aren't that many left. Dow is realizing that they have zero millwrights ready to go and that they have to bite the bullet and start paying for on-the-job training, letting younger guys work with the more senior millwrights. There's a skills gap right now. I haven't been able to learn what all the old guys who are retiring know. Generally speaking, millwrights work in the oil and gas industry, the auto industry, the petrochemical industry, and the chemical industry. Basically we handle material-handling equipment, so anywhere there's a conveyer belt or a drag crane, you're going to find a millwright or machine repairman.

5. How do you see your profession changing in the next five years? What role will technology play in those changes, and what skills will be required?

Companies are trying to bridge the gap between crafts to reduce costs and the number of people on staff. They want people who are multi-talented; they want us to have a little bit of pipe fitter background and a little bit of electrical background. This applies to the non-union companies, though. Unions would not like that at all. Increasingly, equipment is using a variable frequency drive (VFD), so electronics is coming in. An understanding of electrical theory and how AC/DC voltage works on an electric motor will continue to be very important for a millwright.

6. What do you enjoy most about your job? What do you enjoy least about your job?

What I enjoy most is the pay! But I like my job, too. The camaraderie between the guys helps the days go by. I feel respected. When I'm called to fix something, it means the plant mechanic couldn't fix it. So I get to come in and save the day. I like that high-pressure situation. I want to be the guy with the ball when the game's on the line.

What I enjoy least is the cold and the heat. A lot of our processes run at 110 degrees, and if you have to go in there and work, it's hot. Then all winter long, it'll be cold and you may be outside working.

7. Can you suggest a valuable "try this" for students considering a career in your profession?

If you like working with your hands and you want to be in high demand and have a feeling of accomplishment when you leave every day, a millwright might be what you want to be. To get into this, you would have to apprenticeship for millwrights.

MORE INFORMATION

Associated General Contractors of America
Director, Construction Education Services
2300 Wilson Boulevard, Suite 400
Arlington, VA 22201
703.548.3118
www.agc.org

International Union, UAW
Solidarity House
8000 East Jefferson Avenue
Detroit, MI 48214
313.926.5000
www.uaw.org

Precision Machined Products Association
6700 W. Snowville Road
Brecksville, OH 44141
404.526.0300
www.pmpa.org

United Brotherhood of Carpenters
101 Constitution Avenue, NW
Washington, DC 20001
202.546.6206
www.carpenters.org

United Brotherhood of Carpenters' Millwrights
6801 Placid Street
Las Vegas, NV 89119
702.938.1111
www.ubcmillwrights.com

United Steelworkers of America
Five Gateway Center
Pittsburgh, PA 15222
412.562.2400
www.usw.org

Patrick Cooper/Editor

Oil & Gas Drilling Operator

Snapshot

Career Cluster: Mining; Petroleum Production
Interests: Engineering and construction, welding, machine shop skills, supervising work with heavy machinery, outdoor working conditions
Earnings (Yearly Average): $53,160
Employment & Outlook: Average Growth Expected

OVERVIEW

Sphere of Work

Oil and gas drilling operators are responsible for maintaining and operating equipment used to excavate underground deposits of oil and natural gas. Oil and gas drilling can be considered part of the heavy-equipment industry, and the skills and training needed to operate drilling machines are similar to those used to operate heavy construction equipment.

Drilling operators, or drillers, perform a variety of tasks related to the operation of the drills. An operator may oversee and complete maintenance and routine checks to ensure that the system is working properly. He or she may also be responsible for keeping progress records and supervising peripheral staff members who help with the drilling operation. Primarily, a drilling operator is responsible for operating a drill and monitoring gauges that display how well the drill is functioning.

Profile

Working Conditions: Work Outdoors
Physical Strength: Heavy Work
Education Needs: On-The-Job Training, High School Diploma or G.E.D., High School Diploma with Technical Education
Licensure/Certification: Usually Not Required
Opportunities For Experience: Internship, Volunteer Work, Part-Time Work
Holland Interest Score*: REC, REI

* See Appendix A

Work Environment

Oil and gas drilling operators tend to work full time, and overtime hours are not uncommon. Drilling operations continue twenty-four hours a day, seven days a week, and drillers are needed for night, weekend, and holiday hours. Most oil and gas workers work for seven to fourteen days and then have an equal number of days off. Drilling operators work in a variety of environments, as drilling takes place in various locations on land and can also be conducted offshore. Oil workers often must contend with a variety of climatic and environmental hazards, including extreme heat, sunlight, rain, storms, and inclement ocean weather. Offshore drilling operations often need to be postponed when weather conditions become too hazardous.

Drillers are typically regarded as crew managers and supervise teams of general workers, known as roustabouts, and other peripheral personnel during operations. They in turn report to managers, who oversee multiple drilling crews and are responsible for maintaining the overall productivity of the operations.

Work on oil and gas rigs is physically demanding, and workers suffer a higher rate of physical injury than those in many other occupations. Much of the equipment used for oil and natural gas exploration can be hazardous to operate, and fatal injuries have occurred frequently in oil- and gas-harvesting environments. In addition, oil- and gas-rig machinery produces constant loud noises that can damage hearing, so employees must exercise proper precautions by using noise-dampening safety equipment.

Occupation Interest

Oil and gas drilling may appeal to somebody seeking profitable work that does not require an advanced degree. The industry also appeals to individuals who favor outdoor work environments and are interested in the operation of heavy machinery. Those interested in the field should be aware that oil and gas drilling operations require hard labor and pose a significant physical risk in terms of injury and fatigue.

A Day in the Life—Duties and Responsibilities

An oil or gas driller may begin a typical day by meeting with members of the previous drilling crew to discuss their progress and any difficulties encountered during the shift. Oil and gas drilling is accomplished with the use of large hydraulic, electric, or gas-powered drills that use various bits, or replaceable tips, to drill through rock, earth, and other obstacles. Drill machinery may break or become damaged during this process, and a drilling operator may begin his or her shift by determining whether the current equipment is working properly and replacing parts if necessary. Oil and gas drilling operators must also keep records of their daily activities, which may include logs of the cleaning and maintenance work performed by various subordinate employees. In addition, when a driller begins a shift, he or she may need to consult with one or more managers to review the day's progress and establish the guidelines for the new shift.

During a shift, the drilling crew must continually extend the drill and progress deeper into the sediment. This requires adding new sections, called joints, to the drill pipes, a process that involves contributions from many employees. As drilling progresses, rock and mud excavated from the hole need to be "floated" to the top and removed. Roustabouts do much of this work to ensure that the drilling remains on schedule.

During drilling, the drilling operator maintains a close watch on gauges that display variables affecting the drill, such as pressure. The drilling operator is responsible for detecting problems and deciding whether to stop drilling to address them. If a drill head breaks or cannot turn effectively, it may be necessary to retract part of the drill to address the problem. These types of issues can take hours to resolve, depending on the severity of the problem, and it is the drilling operator's responsibility to oversee the resolution of any mechanical issues that affect the drill during his or her shift.

Duties and Responsibilities

- Digging holes, setting forms, and mixing and pouring concrete into forms to make foundations for steel or wooden derricks
- Bolting together pump and engine parts and connecting tanks
- Setting and bolting the crown block to posts at the top of the derrick
- Connecting sections of drill pipe using various tools

OCCUPATION SPECIALTIES

Oil Pumpers

Oil Pumpers operate electric, diesel, gas or automated pumping equipment to pump and route petroleum products through pipelines at mainline or terminal stations.

Tool Pushers

Tool Pushers supervise and coordinate activities of workers who drill oil and gas wells at well sites.

Clean-Out Drillers

Clean-Out Drillers operate truck-mounted hoists equipped with derricks to clean out and restore old and damaged oil or gas wells.

Rotary Derrick Operators

Rotary Derrick Operators rig derrick equipment and operate pumps to circulate mud through drill holes.

Rotary Drillers

Rotary Drillers operate gasoline, diesel, electric or steam draw works to drill oil or gas wells.

Well Pullers

Well Pullers control powerhoisting equipment to pull casing, tubing and pumping rods from oil and gas wells for repair and to lower repaired equipment, testing devices and servicing tools into well.

Mud-Plant Operators

Mud-Plant Operators tend a machine that mixes mud for use in drilling oil and gas wells.

Oil-Well Service Operators

Oil-Well Service Operators control pumping and blending equipment to acidize, cement or fracture gas or oil wells and permeable rock formations.

WORK ENVIRONMENT

Physical Environment

The immediate physical environment of a drilling operator varies according to the location of the drilling operation. Land-based drilling operations take place in a variety of environments, ranging from deserts to snow-and-ice-covered areas. Many drilling operations take place on offshore drilling rigs, which present a unique set of obstacles, including contending with oceanic waves and weather patterns that can interfere with drilling operations.

A drilling rig is a complex operation that contains equipment used to evaluate and find oil or gas deposits, drill into various types of substrate, and harvest and collect oil or gas once a deposit has been reached. Some drilling rigs are small, portable workstations used to drill for deposits that are located fairly close to the surface. In other cases, large drilling platforms are needed to drill through thousands of feet of sediment. The type of drilling rig used depends on the nature of the sediment and the location of the oil or gas deposit being harvested.

Transferable Skills and Abilities

Organization & Management Skills
- Coordinating tasks
- Making decisions
- Managing people/groups
- Paying attention to and handling details
- Performing duties which change frequently
- Performing routine work

Research & Planning Skills
- Developing evaluation strategies

Technical Skills
- Working with machines, tools or other objects

Human Environment

Drilling rig operators are considered supervisory personnel and must manage a variety of subordinate workers during their shifts. This aspect of the job requires good communication skills and the ability to think critically while working. In addition, drilling operators answer to a team leader who is directly responsible for all operations involved in a specific drilling project. In general, employees of a rig operation function as a team to ensure safety and efficient operation. Drilling operators with more experience may be placed in charge of a larger number of subordinate employees and required to take on more of a leadership role in their company.

Technological Environment

Drilling rigs may use hydraulic, electrical, gas, or pneumatic power, and the types of pipes and drills used vary. A drilling operator may be trained specifically to handle one type of drilling apparatus, but those with experience in multiple types of drilling machines may have an advantage in finding employment. In addition, companies often develop new technology to enhance oil and gas exploration and harvesting operations, and drilling operators must typically remain aware of new technological advancements in their field.

EDUCATION, TRAINING, AND ADVANCEMENT

High School/Secondary

A high school education is not necessarily required to obtain work on an oil rig, but many employers prefer candidates to have completed high school or an equivalent program. High school students can prepare for a career in the oil industry by taking advantage of machine-shop classes, which teach the use of basic tools. Not all high schools offer shop programs, so students may need to seek this instruction through part-time work, volunteer or internship programs, or independent study.

Suggested High School Subjects
- Algebra
- Applied Math
- Blueprint Reading
- Electricity & Electronics
- English
- Geometry
- Industrial Arts
- Machining Technology
- Small Engine Repair
- Welding

Famous First

The first oil well drilled in the ocean was drilled in 1896 just off Summerland, Santa Barbara County, Calif. By 1910 the coastal region there was covered with oil derricks. Production largely ceased by 1940, and the derricks were eventually removed. In the 1950s, however, a large oil field was discovered several miles offshore. A blowout there in 1969 caused a major oil spill, which reached Santa Barbara and became a rallying point for environmentalists.

Postsecondary

Postsecondary education is generally not required, but aspiring oil and gas drilling operators may benefit from attending vocational training programs that teach basic skills such as welding and heavy-equipment operations. Drillers seeking to advance to higher-level positions may similarly benefit from further education.

Related College Majors
• Mining & Petroleum Technologies

Adult Job Seekers

Adults with experience in mechanics or the operation of heavy equipment may be able to transition to the position of drilling operator with on-the-job training. Oil companies often hire individuals with little direct experience and maintain training programs for those seeking work in various positions aboard drilling rigs. Those with experience working in offshore facilities may have an additional advantage in obtaining work with offshore drilling projects.

Professional Certification or Licensure

There are no required certifications or licenses for oil and gas drilling operators. However, employers generally require significant on-the-job training. Once hired by a drilling team, an employee must typically work under a supervisor for a period of time ranging from several weeks to several months before being allowed to handle drill operations independently. During this period, the employee will also be trained in managing subordinate personnel to ensure the completion of daily tasks.

Additional Requirements

Drilling operators must have physical strength and stamina, as the job often demands a certain amount of direct physical labor. They must also have excellent communication and interpersonal skills. Operators also benefit from good depth perception and coordination, as these qualities help workers avoid job-related injuries.

Fun Fact

When we think of oil in the U.S., we often think of Texas or Louisiana. But the potential uses of oil emerged farther north, in 1855, with the publication of Benjamin Silliman's "Report on Rock Oil, or Petroleum, from Venango County, Pennsylvania." Texas saw its first big gusher near Beaumont in 1901.

Source: http://www.pbs.org/wnet/extremeoil/history/1850.html

EARNINGS AND ADVANCEMENT

Median annual earnings of oil and gas drilling operators were $53,160 in 2014. The lowest ten percent earned less than $30,580, and the highest ten percent earned more than $93,660.

Oil and gas drilling operators may receive paid vacations, holidays, and sick days; life and health insurance; and retirement benefits. These are usually paid by the employer. Some employers also provide workers with hard hats, safety glasses, gloves, and safety shoes.

Metropolitan Areas with the Highest
Employment Level in this Occupation

Metropolitan area	Employment	Employment per thousand jobs	Annual mean wage
Houston-Sugar Land-Baytown, TX	4,320	1.52	$75,850
Midland, TX	800	9.13	n/a
Oklahoma City, OK	640	1.07	$61,390
Fort Worth-Arlington, TX	480	0.51	$73,630
Pittsburgh, PA	430	0.38	$49,870
Bakersfield-Delano, CA	420	1.42	$76,750
Lafayette, LA	380	2.41	$54,410
Tulsa, OK	350	0.82	$54,380
Corpus Christi, TX	340	1.83	$55,120
Denver-Aurora-Broomfield, CO	330	0.25	$62,200

Source: Bureau of Labor Statistics

EMPLOYMENT AND OUTLOOK

Nationally, there were approximately 80,000 oil and gas drilling operators employed in 2014. U.S. oil and gas drilling is heavily concentrated in Texas, Oklahoma, Louisiana, Kansas, California and Alaska. There is some drilling in Wyoming, North Dakota, New Mexico, Ohio, Montana, Colorado and Utah. Major offshore exploration and drilling occur off the coasts of Louisiana and Texas, southern California, Alaska and some along the Atlantic coast. Turnover is high in offshore drilling.

Employment of oil and gas drilling operators is expected to grow about the same as the average for all occupations through the year 2024, which means employment is projected to increase 3 percent to 9 percent. Long-term rising oil prices and the need to find new sources of oil and gas should allow for some job openings in oil and gas exploration and production activities.

Employment Trend, Projected 2014–24

Oil and gas drilling operators: 8%

Total, all occupations: 7%

Production occupations: -3%

Note: "All Occupations" includes all occupations in the U.S. Economy. Source: U.S. Bureau of Labor Statistics, Employment Projections Program

Related Occupations
- Construction Laborer
- Highway Maintenance Worker
- Roustabout

MORE INFORMATION

American Association of Drilling Engineers
P.O. Box 107
Houston, TX 77001
281.293.9800
www. aade.org

American Petroleum Institute
Communications Dept.
1220 L Street, NW
Washington, DC 20005-4070
202.682.8000
www.api.org

Association of Energy Services Professionals Intl.
15215 S. 48th Street, Suite 170
Phoenix, AZ 85044
480.704.5900
www.aesp.org

Independent Petroleum Association of America
1201 15th Street, NW, Suite 300
Washington, DC, 20005
202.857.4722
www.ipaa.org

International Association of Drilling Contractors
P.O. Box 4287
Houston, TX 77210-4287
713.292.1945
www.iadc.org

Micah Issitt/Editor

Operations Director

Snapshot

Career Cluster: Business Administration; Government & Public Service

Interests: Business operations, management, logistics, supervising others

Earnings (Yearly Average): $96,430

Employment & Outlook: Average Growth Expected

OVERVIEW

Sphere of Work

Operations directors are responsible for making strategic business decisions to ensure that their organizations run smoothly and profitably. They occupy the top tier of management and, as such, bear responsibility toward the owners and stakeholders for the organization's performance. Significantly compensated, they are expected to provide a corresponding level of leadership and direction to other managers, as well as to formulate and communicate high-level policy. In the non-profit and government sectors, they may have job titles such as chief or superintendent.

Work Environment

Operations directors usually spend most of their work day in office environments. Typically, they have their own office or office suite close to other members of an organization's top management team. Operations directors can expect to spend a fair amount of time traveling away from home if their organization is national or multinational. They are frequently expected to put in as many hours as required to fulfill their duties. As a result, many operations directors work sixty or more hours a week, including evenings, weekends, and holidays.

Profile

Working Conditions: Work Indoors
Physical Strength: Light Work
Education Needs: Bachelor's Degree, Master's Degree
Licensure/Certification: Usually Not Required
Physical Abilities Not Required: No Heavy Labor
Opportunities For Experience: Military Service, Part-Time Work
Holland Interest Score*: ESR

* See Appendix A

Occupation Interest

This occupation suits people who combine technical knowledge and abilities relevant to the industry they work in with sophisticated business and leadership skills and the desire and commitment needed to effectively run an organization. They must have the experience, foresight, and ability to develop an organization's strategic direction by taking into account the competitive environment, market opportunities and challenges, micro- and macroeconomics, sociopolitical factors, resource requirements, and operations. Strong analytical abilities and the capacity to set goals for short- and long-term planning are a must in this profession. This job usually requires long hours and a level of responsibility that may cause stress.

A Day in the Life—Duties and Responsibilities

An operations director's day may be dedicated to dealing with one issue or a wide variety of issues. It is likely, however, that a significant proportion of the day will be spent communicating with others, either one-on-one or in group meetings. The operations director is likely to schedule regular meetings with key staff and committees about issues such as budgets, financial results, sales forecasts, and special projects. He or she will meet regularly with the key staff who report to them. This may include, for example, the chief financial officer, human resources director, sales and marketing directors, and any other key staff. The operations director is likely to delegate duties as needed to his or her support staff, as well as task them with special projects, research, and analysis. Individuals in this position are additionally responsible for developing lower-level employees into future managers.

The organization's executives and directors may also be involved at a strategic level in special projects and initiatives. Depending on the type of organization, this may include, for example, crisis and reputation management, new product development and launches, mergers and acquisitions, site openings and closures, strategic operational and logistic changes, and policy development.

The operations director is responsible for reporting to the company's board of directors, owners, and investors. In the case of publicly listed companies, this includes shareholders. The operations director is responsible for ensuring that the company fulfills its legal and fiduciary responsibilities. In doing so, the operations director makes a personal guarantee to the company's board and shareholders that the information provided in official legal and financial reports is accurate and reliable

Duties and Responsibilities

- Setting general goals and policies in collaboration with other top executives and the board of directors
- Meeting with business and government leaders to discuss policy-related matters
- Directing the operations of firms and agencies
- Overseeing department managers and junior executives
- Achieving organizational goals quickly and economically

WORK ENVIRONMENT

Physical Environment

Operations directors usually work from their own offices, which tends to be pleasant and well-appointed. The operations director's physical environment will be influenced by the size and type of employer and the industry in which he or she operates.

Relevant Skills and Abilities

Communication Skills
- Speaking effectively
- Writing concisely

Interpersonal/Social Skills
- Asserting oneself
- Cooperating with others
- Motivating others

Organization & Management Skills
- Demonstrating leadership
- Making decisions

Research & Planning Skills
- Developing evaluation strategies
- Solving problems

Work Environment Skills
- Traveling

Human Environment

This role involves a great amount of interaction with others. Operations directors must possess advanced oral and written communication skills, including the ability to collaborate, negotiate, and resolve conflict. They must be able to conduct themselves with diplomacy and tact and interact confidently with powerful people.

Technological Environment

Daily operations may demand the use of standard office technologies, including computers, telephones, e-mail, photocopiers, and the Internet. Operations directors are usually supported by an executive secretary or administrative team who completes much of the more routine paperwork and requests. The technology used by someone in this position can vary depending on the industry the organization occupies

EDUCATION, TRAINING, AND ADVANCEMENT

High School/Secondary

High school students can best prepare for a career as an operations director by taking courses in applied communication subjects such as business writing as well as computer science. Foreign languages may also be beneficial. Courses that develop general business skills may include accounting, entrepreneurship, bookkeeping, business management, and applied mathematics. Administrative skills may be developed by taking subjects such as business computing and typing. Becoming involved in part-time administrative or clerical work after school or during the weekends builds people skills and is a helpful way to begin learning about business operations and management. Leadership experience can be developed through taking part in extracurricular activities.

Suggested High School Subjects
- Applied Communication
- College Preparatory
- Composition
- Computer Science
- English
- Entrepreneurship

Famous First

The first containerized shipping operation was launched in 1956 by Malcolm McLean of Maxton, North Carolina who developed a large shipping container that could be loaded with goods at the factory, carried by truck to a port facility, and then placed on a ship for transport. McLean's first container, Ideal X, left the port of Newark, New Jersey in April 1956. Today, containerized shipping is the industry standard worldwide and a multi-billion dollar business.

College/Postsecondary

In keeping with the level of responsibility of the position, most employers expect their operations directors to possess postsecondary qualifications. The minimum requirement is considered to be a bachelor's degree in business or another relevant field. A master's degree in business administration (MBA) is sometimes, but not always, considered to be a requirement. Because this position is extremely results-oriented, some individuals earn more advanced degrees or certifications, while others advance as a result of proving their abilities through on-the-job experience.

Related College Majors

- Business Administration & Management
- Enterprise Management & Operation
- Entrepreneurship
- Finance
- Non-Profit Management & Operation
- Retailing & Wholesaling Operations

Adult Job Seekers

Adults seeking a career as an operations director should emphasize any prior management experience or advanced knowledge of the core competencies of business management, such as financial management, human resource management, operations, and sales and marketing. Adult job seekers may need to supplement their current skill set by taking classes in relevant areas. Candidates should keep in mind that many companies promote their existing managers into top executive positions. Networking, job searching, and interviewing are, therefore, critical, and this should include registering with executive recruitment agencies.

Professional Certification and Licensure

There are no formal professional certifications or licensing requirements for operations directors, but professional associations offer operations directors certifications and some industry authorities require staff to hold special licenses. The American Management Association (AMA) and National Management Association (NMA) provide certificate programs in a range of specialty areas, as well as general management.

Additional Requirements

The workload and pressures placed on operations directors are often relentless or intense, so these individuals should be highly motivated, confident, and able to thrive under pressure. Work/life balance may be difficult to achieve or maintain in such a demanding and responsible role, which often requires a great commitment of time and energy.

Fun Fact

To move or not to move for a job: are you willing? Many careers have been advanced by a move but it's important to make sure that moving is for you. That's because moving was found to be more stressful than having a baby or getting a new job.

Source: Nov. 30, 2012 My Move Consumer Insights Study by MyMove.com.

EARNINGS AND ADVANCEMENT

Operations directors' earnings depend on the level of managerial responsibility, length of service, and type, size and geographic location of the firm. Salaries in manufacturing and finance are generally higher than in state and local government.

Median annual earnings of operations directors were $96,430 in 2013. The lowest ten percent earned less than $50,000, and the highest ten percent earned well over $175,000.

Operations directors are paid vacations, holidays, and sick days; life and health insurance; and retirement benefits. These are paid by the employer. They may also receive the use of company aircraft and cars, expense allowances and stock options.

Metropolitan Areas with the Highest
Employment Level in This Occupation

Metropolitan area	Employment	Employment per thousand jobs	Hourly mean wage
New York-White Plains-Wayne, NY-NJ	81,500	15.55	$77.74
Los Angeles-Long Beach-Glendale, CA	69,290	17.43	$61.50
Chicago-Joliet-Naperville, IL	63,250	17.09	$52.40
Washington-Arlington-Alexandria, DC-VA-MD-WV	51,760	21.86	$68.59
Atlanta-Sandy Springs-Marietta, GA	50,480	21.87	$57.36
Houston-Sugar Land-Baytown, TX	47,220	17.12	$63.07
Dallas-Plano-Irving, TX	37,270	17.34	$63.07
Boston-Cambridge-Quincy, MA	34,020	19.45	$67.32
Phoenix-Mesa-Glendale, AZ	28,210	15.83	$52.02
Santa Ana-Anaheim-Irvine, CA	28,000	19.28	$62.99

Source: Bureau of Labor Statistics.

EMPLOYMENT AND OUTLOOK

Operations directors held about 2 million jobs nationally in 2012. Employment is most concentrated in business services, retail stores, financial institutions, educational institutions, hospitals and the government. Employment is expected to grow as fast as the average for all occupations through the year 2022, which means employment is projected to increase 9 percent to 15 percent. Demand for jobs is expected to increase in the financial services and health services industry but expected to decline in many manufacturing industries.

Employment Trend, Projected 2012–22

Operations Directors and General Managers: 12%

Total, All Occupations: 11%

Top Executives: 11%

Note: "All Occupations" includes all occupations in the U.S. Economy. Source: U.S. Bureau of Labor Statistics, Employment Projections Program.

Related Occupations
- City Manager
- Computer & Information Systems Manager
- Education Administrator
- Financial Manager
- Human Resources Specialist/ Manager
- Information Technology Project Manager
- Management Consultant
- Medical & Health Services Manager
- Public Administrator
- Public Relations Specialist
- Retail Store Sales Manager

Related Military Occupations
- Executive Officer
- Operations Officer

Conversation With . . .
MIKE KARR

Vice President of Operations
SEKISUI SPI, 2 years
Operations Manager field, 15 years

1. What was your individual career path in terms of education/training, entry-level job, or other significant opportunity?

I never dreamed of "working in a factory" when I left high school but after a few years of working odd jobs and attending community college classes, I needed money. A friend got me into his company that made automotive aftermarket products. Planning to only stay the summer, I was there 13.5 years. I started looking around and determined better ways to do some of the processes. Management recognized this and asked me to go back to school and move into a supervisor role. From there I kept moving up while earning an Associate's Degree in Business Administration. Over time, the combination of knowing production and office operations opened up opportunity. I continued to move up and earned a BBA through an accelerated college program. As my network grew, I gained other opportunities that included running an aerosol packaging plant and doing sales for another company. I am now the VP of Operations for this company and responsible for two facilities, one in Bloomsburg, Pennsylvania and the other in Holland, Michigan.

2. What are the most important skills and/or qualities for someone in your profession?

The ability to provide accurate and timely information along with solutions has been the key to my success. That and the ability to deal with all the challenges that managing people brings by staying consistent, fair, and direct. Like any success in business, keeping current, studying and understanding you scope of responsibility, and acting decisively are keys. I've always been able to look at processes and systems and ask "Is there a better way to do that?" to make decisions when others did not want the responsibility, to develop employees and teams and keep them focused on our goals, and to maintain a strong focus on the "numbers," sometimes called Key Performance Indicators, or KPIs.

I've also been willing to move to take on new challenges, and to counter my shortfalls by hiring experts in the areas where my skills are weak.

3. What do you wish you had known going into this profession?

You will work long hours. The more responsibility you take on, the more you never really get away from the job. If you run a 24/7 plant, there is no true down time because you have to be able to deal with emergencies — or at least put the systems in place to deal with emergencies — and that's critical when it comes to employee safety. Somebody getting hurt or worse is the worst position an Operations Manager can be in, both personally and professionally. You are responsible for all that goes on, and you have to embrace that responsibility or else get out of this profession.

4. Are there many job opportunities in your profession? In what specific areas?

Opportunities for Operations Managers are often in service industries, and often low paying. Opportunities to run large manufacturing plants are not plentiful, and you need a good network and much experience to succeed. However, I strongly believe that if you want to do this and put the time in to learn, you will find a company that needs your skills.

5. How do you see your profession changing in the next five years? What role will technology play in those changes, and what skills will be required?

Like many positions, technology — including social media — requires a person to constantly evolve. How you train, how you buy equipment, types and changes in equipment, utilities, asset management, trucking and overall logistics are just some of the areas that change quickly. Something like 3D printing could change an industry within a couple of years. An Operations Manager always has to look ahead or be blind-sided by market and technology changes.

6. What do you like most about your job? What do you like least about your job?

I enjoy setting direction and being involved with employees on attaining goals. I enjoy when people are making a living because everyone has success. I like shaping the strategy and the planning involved. The least enjoyable part of my job is my constant concern about employee safety. I train constantly and try to limit risks; my goal has always been to send everyone home intact, the same way they came in. When that does not happen, it can make the job miserable

7. Can you suggest a valuable "try this" for students considering a career in your profession?

Work in a factory for a summer and see the processes. Also, I would think most any Operations Manager would be willing to sit with you and explain the path needed to gain the required knowledge and experience. It is not a job someone could do right out of college. You should have some level of college, even just basic business management, and then work in production, shipping, scheduling, quality, HR, and maybe even customer service. Use what you learn to grow your skills and experience.

SELECTED SCHOOLS

Many colleges and universities, especially those with business schools, offer programs in business administration and operations management. The student can also gain initial training through a technical or community college. For advanced positions, a master's of business administration (MBA) with a concentration in operations is usually expected. Below are listed some of the more prominent graduate institutions in this field.

Carnegie Mellon University
Tepper School of Business
500 Forbes Avenue
Pittsburgh, PA 15213
412.268.2268
tepper.cmu.edu

Columbia University
Columbia Business School
3022 Broadway
Manhattan, NY 10027
212.854.5553
www8.gsb.columbia.edu

Harvard University
Harvard Business School
Soldiers Field
Boston, MA 02163
617.495.6000
www.hbs.edu

Indiana University, Bloomington
Kelley School of Business
1309 E. 10th Street
Bloomington, IN 47405
812.855.8100
kelley.iu.edu

Massachusetts Institute of Technology
Sloan School of Management
50 Memorial Drive
Cambridge, MA 02142
617.253.2659
mitsloan.mit.edu

Northwestern University
Kellogg School of Management
2169 Campus Drive
Evanston, IL 60208
847.467.7000
www.kellogg.northwestern.edu

Purdue University
Krannert School of Management
403 W. State Street
West Lafayette, IN 47907
765.496.4343
www.krannert.purdue.edu

Stanford University
Stanford Graduate School of Business
655 Knight Way
Stanford, CA 94305
650.723.2146
www.gsb.stanford.edu

University of Michigan, Ann Arbor
Ross School of Business
701 Tappan Avenue
Ann Arbor, MI 48109
734.763.5796
michiganross.umich.edu

University of Pennsylvania
The Wharton School
1 College Hall
Philadelphia, PA 19104
215.898.6376
www.whatron.upenn.edu

MORE INFORMATION

American Management Association
1601 Broadway
New York, NY 10019
212.568.8100
www.amanet.org

National Management Association
2210 Arbor Boulevard
Dayton, OH 45439
937.294.0421
www.nma1.org

Business and Professional Women's Foundation
1718 M Street NW, #148
Washington, DC 20036
202.293.1100
www.bpwfoundation.org

Kylie Hughes/Editor

Painting/Coating Machine Operator

Snapshot

Career Cluster: Manufacturing; Production

Interests: Painting, doing detail work, performing physically demanding work

Earnings (Yearly Average): $31,460

Employment & Outlook: Slower than Average Growth Expected

OVERVIEW

Sphere of Work

Painting and coating machine operators use industrial machines to paint or coat a variety of objects, from vehicles and home appliances to jewelry and other personal accessories. Painting and coating machines are even used to apply coatings of color and other substances to certain consumables. The operation of painting and coating machines requires specific on-the-job training, and most workers learn their trade through apprenticeships. Automotive painting is one of the most prominent subcategories within the larger painting and coating industry, and many of the organizations that exist to assist painting and coating specialists focus on workers in the automotive industry.

Work Environment

Painting and coating machine operators usually work full time during regular business hours. Some large companies operate on extended production schedules that require employees to work weekend, evening, or night hours. Workers may at times be asked to work overtime to adjust to increased production needs.

In many cases, painting and coating machine operators work in teams, with each individual painting or coating a different part of the eventual product. At times, painting and coating specialists may work alongside individuals involved in other facets of the manufacturing process. Automotive painting specialists, for instance, may work alongside others who specialize in auto restoration and repair. In addition, painting and coating workers typically work under plant or factory managers who may oversee many different parts of the manufacturing operation. In some cases, painting and coating machine operators may interact with marketing, sales, or customer-service personnel.

As many paints and coatings produce toxic fumes, painting and coating machine operators tend to work in specially ventilated rooms and use safety equipment to avoid injury. Workers risk exposure to toxic chemicals and may also spend long hours standing or in other positions that can cause strain or injury. The Clean Air Act of 1990 places restrictions on permissible levels of emissions, and workers using painting or coating machines must comply with company procedures for keeping emissions below regulation levels.

Profile

Working Conditions: Work Indoors
Physical Strength: Medium Work
Education Needs: No High School Diploma, On-The-Job Training, High School Diploma or G.E.D., High School Diploma with Technical Education, Apprenticeship
Licensure/Certification: Recommended
Opportunities For Experience: Part-Time Work
Holland Interest Score*: CRE

* See Appendix A

Occupation Interest

Those seeking work in the painting and coating industry should be detail oriented and comfortable with performing difficult, physically demanding work. The occupation appeals to those who do not wish to pursue advanced education and prefer to learn through apprenticeships or on-the-job training. Individuals interested in automobile restoration or repair may be drawn to the specialized field of automotive painting and coating.

A Day in the Life—Duties and Responsibilities

A typical day for a painting or coating machine operator will differ depending on the industry in which he or she works and the types of painting and coating processes being used. Most painting and coating workers begin by setting up their painting machines, which may include preparing or mixing paint, calibrating nozzles and other machine parts, and arranging work stations for the day's activities.

Different types of painting and coating machines and processes require different basic activities. For instance, dipping machines apply paint or coating to objects by dipping the objects into vats of liquid. An individual operating such a machine may mount objects to be painted on the machine and use controls to dip them into a liquid mixture of paint or another coating. Workers operating spray machines use nozzles to spray paint or other coatings onto objects. Spray machines may be entirely automated, or they may involve a combination of automated and manual functions. Individuals working with these machines may need to spend time mixing or preparing paints or coatings.

Painting and coating machine operators working with spray guns typically work in specially outfitted spray rooms or in general workshop areas that have been fitted with ventilation equipment. Goggles and ventilation masks are typically worn to avoid injury and exposure to toxic chemicals. Spray gun operators work on a variety of different objects, including auto parts, instruments, furniture, appliances, and jewelry. The facilities and type of spray gun used will differ depending on the object being coated. In addition, different types of paint or coating are used for different applications. Powder coating, for instance, involves applying a thin layer of powdered paint, which can then be heated to form a skin similar to that created by liquid paint.

Machines used for applying paint or coating must be periodically serviced, cleaned, and adjusted for optimal performance. In some cases, peripheral staff members handle equipment maintenance, while in other cases, the workers who operate the machines are also responsible for maintenance and adjustment.

Duties and Responsibilities

- Cleaning items before coating them
- Figuring areas to be coated and the amount of solution or paint to be mixed
- Making sure the solution or paint is the right consistency
- Adjusting spray gun nozzles and other controls so the coating will be applied evenly

OCCUPATION SPECIALTIES

Foam Gun Operators

Foam Gun Operators spray reinforced plastic products, such as shower stalls, bathtubs and automobile parts with a mixture of resins and activators (foam), using a foam gun.

Airbrush Painters

Airbrush Painters coat, decorate, glaze, retouch and tint articles such as fishing lures, toys, pottery, artificial flowers, greeting cards and household appliances using airbrushes.

Spray Painters I

Spray Painters I spray the surfaces of machines, manufactured products or working areas with protective or decorative material, such as paint, enamel, glaze, gel-coat or lacquer using a spray gun.

Spray Painting Machine Operators

Spray Painting Machine Operators tend the spray-painting machines that automatically apply lettering, diagrams or designs on products, such as speedometer faces, automobile steering-wheel hubs and radio or television control knobs. They remove the product from the machine and examine the coating for smears, runs, incomplete painting or other flaws.

Spray Painters II

Spray Painters II perform the duties described under Spray Painters I, except that their job involves coating a surface that does not have a need for a finished appearance. They spray manufactured articles on assembly lines or travel to work sites to spray materials such as waterproofing, adhesive, foam or paint onto the surfaces of articles.

Spray Gun Stripers

Spray Gun Stripers paint decorative stripes on manufactured articles, using spray guns and templates. They also touch up stripes and may paint stripes or spiral designs on articles such as bisque ware or wheels as they revolve on a turntable.

Stainers

Stainers stain furniture using a brush, pad, sponge or spray gun or by dipping parts or frames into a vat of stain by hand and wiping off the excess.

WORK ENVIRONMENT

Physical Environment

Painting and coating machine operators generally work in factory environments or in workshops, depending on the type of business. Spray-gun operators may work in spray booths or spray rooms within larger workshops. Painting and coating rooms are well ventilated and are typically outfitted with a variety of safety equipment, such as emergency showers and eye-flushing stations for when a worker's skin or eyes have come into contact with dangerous chemicals.

Plant Environment

Painting and coating are essential steps in many large-scale manufacturing processes, and many painting and coating machine operators work in manufacturing plants or factories alongside workers handling other parts of the manufacturing process. In automotive factories, for instance, they are part of a larger process that involves the construction and assembly of various automotive parts.

Transferable Skills and Abilities

Organization & Management Skills
- Paying attention to and handling details
- Performing routine work

Technical Skills
- Working with machines, tools or other objects
- Working with your hands

Human Environment

Painting and coating machine operators generally work under the supervision of department or plant managers who oversee the work of multiple employees involved in the manufacturing process. Successful painting and coating specialists work well with others and are adept at taking instruction from managers and supervisors. Some painting and coating machine operators may have the opportunity to transition into management roles by becoming supervisors within their organizations.

Technological Environment

Technology used in painting and coating processes varies depending on the scope of the business. In some small shops and companies, workers use handheld paint guns and coating machines to complete their work. In larger manufacturing environments, workers may use paint machines connected to automated systems. Technological innovation in the painting and coating field has come largely in the form of new paints and coatings designed to conform to modern environmental and safety standards. New paints use fewer toxic and environmentally harmful chemicals, thereby providing a safer work environment for painting and coating workers.

EDUCATION, TRAINING, AND ADVANCEMENT

High School/Secondary

Most companies that hire painting and coating machine operators require candidates to have completed high school or an equivalent program. High school students can prepare to enter the field by taking classes in basic mathematics, chemistry, and physics, which enable them to perform basic measurements or calculations while on the job. Some high schools offer classes in basic home maintenance, construction, and other types of workshop activities, which can be helpful for those seeking work in the painting and coating industry.

Suggested High School Subjects
- Auto Collision Technology
- Auto Service Technology
- English
- Metals Technology
- Shop Math

Famous First

The first manufacturer to specialize in varnish was Christian Schrack, a carriage maker who opened a varnish production shop in Philadelphia in 1815. Before then furniture was commonly finished with oil or shellac.

Postsecondary

A four-year degree from a college or university is generally not required, but machine operators may benefit from completing a technical or vocational program that specifically trains students to use a variety of manufacturing and construction equipment, including painting and coating machines. Automotive painting specialists often attend classes in which they are instructed in special techniques used for automotive painting.

Most painting and coating machine operators learn the trade on the job, working under experienced operators until they are considered able to operate the machinery on their own. Training may last from several weeks to more than a year, depending on the type of painting and coating work required. For instance, individuals who work in factories and operate painting and coating machinery as part of a production line may require far less training than individuals who perform hands-on painting of intricate or specialized items.

Adult Job Seekers

Adults with backgrounds in factory and manufacturing work can often transition to painting or coating machine operation through on-the-job training. Candidates with previous painting or repair experience will have an advantage in seeking employment. Those interested in working in automotive painting, instrument painting, or other highly specialized areas of the painting and coating industry will often need to undergo longer periods of training.

Professional Certification and Licensure

There are no national licensing or certification requirements for painting and coating machine operators, but some employers may be more likely to hire individuals who have obtained certification in various related skills. Automotive painting workers are typically the only painting and coating workers who regularly seek professional certification before beginning their careers. The National Institute for Automotive Service Excellence offers a training and testing program that provides proof of a trainee's skill level in automobile painting and refinishing. Painting and coating machine operators should consult credible professional associations within the field and follow professional debate as to the relevancy and value of any certification program.

Additional Requirements

Painting and coating machine operators should be in relatively good physical condition, as a typical day on the job may require a worker to spend long hours standing in place or bending or crouching into positions that can cause muscular and nervous strain. In addition, color vision is generally required for those working in painting and coating, as workers must be able to see colors to evaluate the quality of the paint coating. The operation of some painting and spraying machines also requires significant hand-eye coordination and mechanical ability.

Fun Fact

Greek philosopher Plato discovered that mixing two paint colors produces a third.
Source: https://www.arlingtonartscenter.org/blog/five-fun-facts-about-paint/

EARNINGS AND ADVANCEMENT

Earnings of painting and coating machine operators depend on the geographic location and extent of unionization of the employer and the type of industry. Manufacturing painters may be paid an hourly or piecework rate. Many automotive painters employed by dealerships and independent repair shops receive a commission based on the labor cost charged to the customer. Under this method, earnings depend largely on the amount of work done and how fast it is completed.

Painting and coating machine operators had median annual earnings of $31,460 in 2014. The lowest ten percent earned less than $18,960, and the highest ten percent earned more than $45,150.

Painting and coating machine operators may receive paid vacations, holidays, and sick days; life and health insurance; and retirement benefits. These are usually paid by the employer.

Metropolitan Areas with the Highest
Employment Level in this Occupation

Metropolitan area	Employment	Employment per thousand jobs	Annual mean wage
Chicago-Joliet-Naperville, IL	450	0.12	$32,810
Riverside-San Bernardino-Ontario, CA	440	0.35	$27,780
Los Angeles-Long Beach-Glendale, CA	400	0.10	$37,390
Minneapolis-St. Paul-Bloomington, MN-WI	330	0.18	$29,950
New York-White Plains-Wayne, NY-NJ	270	0.05	$36,310
Houston-Sugar Land-Baytown, TX	260	0.09	$30,710
Portland-Vancouver-Hillsboro, OR-WA	240	0.23	$29,080
Dallas-Plano-Irving, TX	240	0.11	$23,850
Atlanta-Sandy Springs-Marietta, GA	230	0.10	$33,100
Miami-Miami Beach-Kendall, FL	220	0.21	$35,700

Source: Bureau of Labor Statistics

EMPLOYMENT AND OUTLOOK

There were approximately 98,000 painting and coating machine operators employed nationally in 2014. Employment of painting and coating machine operators is expected to grow slower than the average for all occupations through the year 2024, which means employment is projected to increase 0 percent to 3 percent. The number of goods requiring painting or coating is increasing, but job growth will be affected by improvements in the automation of paint and coating applications that will raise worker productivity. For example, painting and coating machine operators will be able to coat goods more rapidly as they use sophisticated industrial machinery that moves and aims spray guns more efficiently.

Employment Trend, Projected 2014–24

Total, all occupations: 7%

Painting and coating workers: 1%

Production occupations: -3%

Note: "All Occupations" includes all occupations in the U.S. Economy. Source: U.S. Bureau of Labor Statistics, Employment Projections Program

Related Occupations
- Automotive Body Repairer
- Sign Painter & Letterer

MORE INFORMATION

American Coatings Association
1500 Rhode Island Avenue NW
Washington, DC 20005
202.462.6272
www.paint.org

**National Automotive Technicians
Education Foundation**
101 Blue Seal Drive SE, Suite 101
Leesburg, VA 20175
703.669.6650
www.natef.org

**National Institute for Automotive
Service Excellence**
101 Blue Seal Drive, SE, Suite 101
Leesburg, VA 20175
703.669.6600
www.ase.com

Micah Issitt/Editor

Power Plant Operator

Snapshot

Career Cluster: Energy Production & Distribution

Interests: Power transmission and distribution, power plant mechanics, electronics, electricity, equipment repair

Earnings (Yearly Average): $70,070

Employment & Outlook: Decline Expected

OVERVIEW

Sphere of Work

Power plant operators are responsible for controlling the various processes leading to the generation of electrical power from fossil, nuclear, or renewable fuels. They work for power companies, which can be either public or private corporations.

Power plants must provide a reliable supply of electrical energy, prevent accidents, and optimize output. Power plant operators are responsible for monitoring, inspecting, adjusting, and sometimes repairing the instruments and equipment used to generate power.

Work Environment

Work takes place primarily in a control room that regulates the operations of a power plant. Inspection and maintenance of plant equipment takes operators inside the power plant, which can be located in an urban, suburban, or rural area. Hydroelectric and some nuclear power plants are primarily located in rural areas.

Power plants operate continuously, and shift work, including nights, weekends, and holidays, is required. Power plant operators work with colleagues in the control room and with various other workers in the plant. They also interact with superiors who give specific instructions on operational details, including possible plant shutdowns for maintenance or other contingencies.

Profile

Working Conditions: Work Indoors
Physical Strength: Light Work
Education Needs: On-The-Job Training, High School Diploma or G.E.D., High School Diploma with Technical Education, Junior/Technical/Community College
Licensure/Certification: Required
Opportunities For Experience: Apprenticeship, Military Service
Holland Interest Score*: RES

* See Appendix A

Occupation Interest

A power plant operator should be interested in the technical and mechanical aspects of power plant operations and willing to accept shift work. Interest in guiding complex technical processes and a willingness to serve the community and industry are good foundations for a successful career in this field. Pride in one's work, attention to detail, and a dedication to service are key factors for success.

A Day in the Life—Duties and Responsibilities

Power plant operators begin their shift by being briefed on the status of the plant and any inspections or maintenance measures that are scheduled. Shifts are typically eight to twelve hours long. Throughout their shift, power plant operators monitor all data concerning the actions of their plant to ensure smooth operations and intervene in case of disturbances.

Key work includes controlling the functionality of all plant equipment, namely the boilers, turbines, generators, and reactors of the plant. The power plant operator is responsible for ensuring the plant's delivery of power into the electricity grid at a set voltage and a given electricity flow. To monitor, control, and regulate operations, the operator checks charts, meters, and gauges. Individual plant equipment is checked constantly for status and any indication of possible problems or malfunctions that require intervention.

The responsibilities of the senior power plant operator include ordering the starting and stopping of central equipment such as turbines, generators, or nuclear reactors. A senior operator is also responsible for ensuring the safety of the power plant's operations and the staff's adherence to proper safety and occupational health regulations. Junior power plant operators may be asked to personally perform equipment checks and clean, lubricate, maintain, and repair equipment. All operators participate in emergency drills.

At the end of a shift, a power plant operator will have logged key information about operations performed during the shift. Any key findings will be reported to supervisors. The plant operator communicates regularly with power-systems operators involved in the efficient running of the main power plant.

Duties and Responsibilities

- Regulating equipment according to data provided by recording and indicating instruments and/or computers
- Monitoring gauges to determine the effect of generator loading on other power equipment
- Monitoring computer-operated equipment
- Adjusting controls to regulate the flow of power between generating stations and substations
- Noting malfunctions of equipment, instruments or controls

OCCUPATION SPECIALTIES

Motor-Room Controllers

Motor-Room Controllers control generation and distribution of electrical power from power station to plant facilities and maintain equipment.

Load Dispatchers

Load Dispatchers coordinate personnel in generating stations, substations and lines of electric power stations.

Hydroelectric-Station Operators

Hydroelectric-Station Operators control electrical generating units and mechanical and hydraulic equipment at hydroelectric generating stations.

Power-Reactor Operators

Power-Reactor Operators control nuclear reactors that produce steam to generate electricity and coordinate auxiliary equipment operation.

Substation Operators

Substation Operators control current convertors, voltage transformers and circuit breakers to regulate electricity flow through substations and over distribution lines.

Generator Switchboard Operators

Generator Switchboard Operators control central electric generating plant switchboards to distribute and regulate power.

Switchboard Operators

Switchboard Operators control converters, rectifiers, transformers and generators to direct, distribute and maintain power to chemical processing equipment.

Turbine Operators

Turbine Operators control steam-driven turbogenerators in electric or nuclear power generating stations.

Switchboard Operator Assistants

Switchboard Operator Assistants compile gauge readings and perform other tasks as directed by the switchboard operator in an electric-generating plant. They clean and oil mechanical and electrical equipment and report malfunctions and may assist in tests to diagnose the cause of equipment malfunction.

WORK ENVIRONMENT

Transferable Skills and Abilities

Communication Skills
- Speaking effectively
- Writing concisely

Interpersonal/Social Skills
- Being able to work independently
- Working as a member of a team

Organization & Management Skills
- Demonstrating leadership
- Making decisions
- Paying attention to and handling details
- Performing routine work

Research & Planning Skills
- Developing evaluation strategies
- Using logical reasoning

Technical Skills
- Working with machines, tools or other objects
- Working with your hands

Physical Environment

The senior plant operator will rarely leave the control room, except when accompanying special inspections or supervising plant equipment. The control room is where all plant operators perform most of their work, unless they are sent to attend to equipment. Generally, work is done in a secured environment, and operators sit or stand throughout their shift. Although not particularly strenuous, the job of a power plant operator requires constant attention.

Plant Environment

Power plants are classified by the source of their fuel. Fossil fuels such as coal and gas are the most common, and nuclear power plants are the most secured.

Hydroelectric power plants are situated at dams, generally in rural locations. Some micropower plants can be controlled remotely.

Human Environment

In larger power plants, especially nuclear plants, power plant operators tend to work in teams that are supervised by a senior operator. Power plant operators need to communicate effectively among themselves and with plant staff and management. Shift work is inevitable at all levels of seniority.

Technological Environment

Power plant operators work in complex technical environments with digitalized control systems. At the junior level, operators work with such tools as are required to perform equipment repair and maintenance.

EDUCATION, TRAINING, AND ADVANCEMENT

High School/Secondary

Entry-level power plant operators must have a high school diploma or a GED certificate. High school students should take mathematics and science classes, preferably at the advanced placement (AP) level. Mathematics classes should cover algebra, trigonometry, geometry, and applied mathematics. In the sciences, classes in electricity and electronics, machining technology, applied physics, computer science, and general science are strongly recommended. Students with an interest in hydroelectric power plants should study geology. Courses in chemistry and biology are also useful. Shop classes provide skills needed at the entry level. Good English skills are essential.

Suggested High School Subjects
- Algebra
- Applied Math
- Applied Physics

- Biology
- Electricity & Electronics
- English
- Geometry
- Machining Technology
- Mathematics
- Science
- Shop Mechanics

Famous First

The first power transmission installation using alternating current was set up by Westinghouse Electric and Manufacturing Company in Telluride, Colo., in 1890. The generator was a 100-horsepower, 3,000-volt unit driven by water power, and the transmission line was three miles long. A motor at the end of the line was able to be started as a result of the successful transmission.

Postsecondary

Power plant operators must undergo several years of on-the-job training and receive technical instruction at a power plant before being entrusted with full plant operations. This training can begin right after high school or after some further vocational and technical education. An associate's degree from a community college, especially in the field of electricity, electronics, or mathematics, will enhance chances of initial employment; such a degree can also be pursued after training. Operators with a bachelor's or associate's degree will have greater opportunities for advancement. Many senior power plant operators have a bachelor's degree in one of the physical sciences or in engineering.

There are three formal apprenticeships recognized by the United States Department of Labor: power plant operator, hydroelectric station operator, and turbine operator. A person interested in nuclear power plant operations can also receive practical training as part of the U.S. Navy on board ships with nuclear reactors.

Adult Job Seekers

People who have worked in a related field are more apt to be offered an entry-level position. Previous work in the power industry or with other utilities is helpful, as is experience in any area of a power plant or a power transmission and distribution network.

Professional Certification and Licensure

Many power companies require that applicants pass the Plant Operator (POSS) and the Power Plant Maintenance (MASS) exams offered by the Edison Electric Institute.

All nuclear power plant operators must have a current license issued by the United States Nuclear Regulatory Commission (NRC). In addition to training and experience requirements and a medical exam, applicants must pass the NRC licensing exam. Every year, a specific plant-operating exam must be passed. Medical exams are due every two years, and the license must be renewed every six years.

Licensing requirements for nonnuclear power plant operators vary from state to state and generally depend on the specific job duties performed. Many experienced power plant operators seek a state license as a firefighter or even an electrical engineer.

Additional Requirements

Random drug and alcohol testing is nationally required of all nuclear power plant operators. Respective rules vary at different companies for nonnuclear power plant operators.

Fun Fact

Seventy-five percent of electricity that powers home electronics in the average home is used while the products are turned off. It's called "idle power."

Source: https://www.blackhillscorp.com/blog/peak/2013/06/03/7-fun-facts-you-didn%E2%80%99t-know-about-energy#.VvV8W3p0eJc

EARNINGS AND ADVANCEMENT

Earnings in the electric utility industry are relatively high, although the salaries of power plant operators vary by the location of the employer and the employee's experience. When a utility system has power plants of different sizes, newer power plant operators begin at smaller stations and are promoted to larger stations as openings become available.

Median annual earnings of power plant operators were $70,070 in 2014. The lowest ten percent earned less than $44,130, and the highest ten percent earned more than $94,060.

Power plant operators may receive paid vacations, holidays, and sick days; life and health insurance; and retirement benefits. These are usually paid by the employer.

Metropolitan Areas with the Highest
Employment Level in this Occupation

Metropolitan area	Employment	Employment per thousand jobs	Annual mean wage
Los Angeles-Long Beach-Glendale, CA	1,220	0.30	$86,130
New York-White Plains-Wayne, NY-NJ	1,020	0.19	$77,120
Houston-Sugar Land-Baytown, TX	970	0.34	$65,350
Atlanta-Sandy Springs-Marietta, GA	620	0.26	$63,200
Cincinnati-Middletown, OH-KY-IN	540	0.53	$69,090
Philadelphia, PA	530	0.28	$70,600
Kansas City, MO-KS	490	0.48	$73,310
Birmingham-Hoover, AL	480	0.96	$58,190
Riverside-San Bernardino-Ontario, CA	460	0.37	$66,350
St. Louis, MO-IL	440	0.34	$72,910

Source: Bureau of Labor Statistics

EMPLOYMENT AND OUTLOOK

Power plant operators held about 50,000 jobs nationally in 2014. Employment of power plant operators is expected to decline through the year 2024, owing to a continued emphasis on cost reduction and automation.

Employment Trend, Projected 2014–24

Total, all occupations: 7%

Plant and system operators (all types): 0%

Power plant operators, distributors, and dispatchers: -6%

Note: "All Occupations" includes all occupations in the U.S. Economy. Source: U.S. Bureau of Labor Statistics, Employment Projections Program

Related Occupations

- Chemical Equipment Operator
- Stationary Engineer
- Water Treatment Plant Operator

Related Military Occupations

- Power Plant Operator

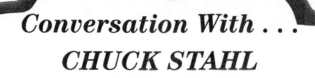

Conversation With . . .
CHUCK STAHL

Fuel Handling Operations Second Line Supervisor
Dominion Resources
Mount Storm Power Station, West Virginia
Power industry, 35 years

1. What was your individual career path in terms of education/training, entry-level job, or other significant opportunity?

I earned a high school diploma, then an associate's degree in business and economics from Potomac State College, a junior college that's part of West Virginia University. I was hired as an entry-level employee by Dominion Resources at their Mount Storm Power Station and I've stayed because I was raising my family nearby in Maryland. I moved up the ranks.

A company such as Dominion offers multiple opportunities. I'm responsible for the people and the processes involved in receiving fuel for the power station, which is coal or any liquid fuel we receive. It's a 24/7 process. Thirty-three people report to me. Each day, those people receive the coal that comes by truck or train, from the stockpile inventory, or other locations, and are responsible for getting it into the power station. Then they are responsible for removing fly ash, bottom ash or gypsum—combustion byproducts—and disposing of them safely.

Extreme heat, extreme cold, excessive rain or snow and ice—these folks are outside dealing with that. In addition, they work around rotating equipment and energized electrical equipment, often in high temperatures, inside the power station and other buildings.

Every day, our job revolves around keeping our employees safe and maintaining environmental compliance. The United States Occupational Safety and Health Administration (OSHA) has jurisdiction over our power station and we strive to exceed their regulations. The federal Environmental Protection Agency (EPA) and the West Virginia Department of Environmental Protection regulate us on the environmental side, and we strive to exceed those compliance regulations as well.

I also deal with our suppliers and the truck and train entities that transport our fuel. I'm on call 24/7.

2. What are the most important skills and/or qualities for someone in your profession?

Anyone who comes to work needs to communicate with their coworkers and be part of a team to work together for the common goal. In our case, that means making sure everyone stays safe throughout the course of the day as well as making sure we comply with environmental regulations, as well as generating electricity for our customers in an efficient manner that keeps rates at a reasonable level.

As a supervisor, I have to be patient and willing to listen to somebody else's opinion, and also able to communicate my idea in a professional manner. You have to treat people with respect, even if somebody's having a bad day.

Processes within the power station have changed because of environmental regulations and likely will be ever-evolving as time passes, so you also have to be able to adapt to change. A mechanical aptitude is helpful, as is an awareness of business practices.

3. What do you wish you had known going into this profession?

I didn't have any clue what was involved in the generation of electricity but I have to believe the average person who doesn't work within the industry is in the same boat. Still, I wish I'd had the foresight to prepare myself for that. Now, technical schools and some colleges offer programs that prepare people for power generation careers.

4. Are there many job opportunities in your profession? In what specific areas?

I see a lot of opportunities for technical-engineering careers in our industry, as well as on the IT/cybersecurity side. Everything is computer-controlled and data is captured electronically and that's not going to decrease.

5. How do you see your profession changing in the next five years? What role will technology play in those changes, and what skills will be required?

We're going to need electricity but the shift is away from coal to other fuels—right now that's natural gas—and to other means of generating electricity such as wind and solar and whatever other new technology that might come out.

6. What do you enjoy most about your job? What do you enjoy least about your job?

I enjoy the interaction with people, whether here at the power station, within the company, or vendors. I've been part of our hiring process for ten years and therefore meet our new employees before they are employees. The process is difficult but it's rewarding.

The most difficult part of my job is, at times, dealing with difficult people issues that come up. We try to do the best we can as a management team to resolve those issues.

7. Can you suggest a valuable "try this" for students considering a career in your profession?

Internships are the best way for anyone to understand what's going on inside the power station. They're available for positions like engineering, and I've heard that they are also now available for eight weeks in summer for the actual power plant operations.

MORE INFORMATION

American Public Power Association
1875 Connecticut Avenue NW
Suite 1200
Washington, DC 20009-5715
202.467.2900
www.publicpower.org

Center for Energy Workforce Development
701 Pennsylvania Avenue NW
3rd Floor
Washington, DC 20004-2696
202.638.5802
www.cewd.org

Edison Electric Institute
701 Pennsylvania Avenue, NW
Washington, DC 20004-2696
202.508.5000
www.eei.org

International Brotherhood of Electrical Workers
900 Seventh Street, NW
Washington, DC 20001
202.833.7000
www.ibew.org

Nuclear Energy Institute
1201 F Street NW, Suite 1100
Washington, DC 20004-1218
202.739.8000
www.nei.org

Utility Workers Union of America
815 16th Street, NW
Washington, DC 20006
202.974.8200
webmaster@uwua.net
www.uwua.net

U.S. Nuclear Regulatory Commission
Washington, DC 20555-0001
800.368.5642
www.nrc.gov

R. C. Lutz/Editor

Precision Assembler

Snapshot

Career Cluster: Manufacturing; Production

Interests: Mechanical systems, industrial processes and production, mechanics, electrical components, computer science

Earnings (Yearly Average): $30,062

Employment & Outlook: Slower than Average Growth Expected

OVERVIEW

Sphere of Work

Precision assemblers are responsible for assembling a wide range of finished products, many of which include detailed components requiring multistage assembly. They produce components or goods with intricate parts, such as products used in aerospace and automotive manufacturing, weapons systems, electronics, radios, and some elements of computer systems. Precision assemblers work on a wide variety of products in varying subfields, assembling electrical and mechanical components for industrial, agricultural, and military use.

Work Environment

Virtually all precision assemblers work in facilities that produce some sort of durable product. Since they work with such a large variety of materials, the work may require long periods of standing or sitting and may take place in hot, cramped factories or vast aerospace and automotive production plants. Precision assemblers who work on radio and computer assemblages tend to work in brightly lit, quiet spaces that are temperature and dust controlled, while those in transportation production often come into contact with grease, oil, and industrial chemicals and may work in facilities with high noise levels.

Profile

Working Conditions: Work Indoors
Physical Strength: Medium Work
Education Needs: On-The-Job Training, High School Diploma with Technical Education
Licensure/Certification: Usually Not Required
Opportunities For Experience: Part-Time Work
Holland Interest Score*: CRE, CRS, CSR, RCE

* See Appendix A

Occupation Interest

Individuals drawn to the profession of precision assembler tend to enjoy detailed work. They are able to work on fairly complex projects quickly without sacrificing quality. They are often involved in preparing materials for other stages in manufacturing, such as welding or soldering, and so must have a working knowledge of other stages in the process. Precision assemblers often work with cutting-edge technology and should have an interest in mechanical systems and industrial processes. These positions are often filled by lower-level factory employees who demonstrate an aptitude for complex work.

A Day in the Life—Duties and Responsibilities

The daily duties of precision assemblers vary according to the type of goods they are producing and the materials with which they are working. Some work on electrical systems and components that produce radio and computer equipment; these workers spend most of their day fitting small components together into finished products, using specialized instruments, or working on the components themselves. Others work on machines such as turbines and engines used in aerospace and automotive manufacturing. Precision assemblers build the mechanical components and systems used in oil and natural-gas production, food packaging, industrial agriculture, and paper and printing. They may be responsible for producing specific parts of automobiles or aircraft, such as landing gear or wing sections, and so work with large, heavy materials and components. Precision assemblers who work with weapons systems, such as missiles and drone aircraft, may work in or interact directly with a military environment.

Some experienced precision assemblers work directly with engineers and technicians to design and implement specific instructions or create test patterns and prototypes. They may supervise the work of other assemblers on a project, or they may be involved in product development and advise engineers about how to best use a production facility. Assemblers need to be able to read blueprints and computer-generated instructions and to use precision tools

Duties and Responsibilities

- Interpreting blueprints and engineering specifications
- Positioning parts in their proper places
- Putting parts together by using precision measuring tools
- Lubricating moving parts
- Using machines for making fittings or fastening operations on the assembly line
- Putting together sub-assemblies to make units
- Connecting electrical wiring

OCCUPATION SPECIALTIES

Electromechanical Assemblers

Electromechanical Assemblers prepare and test devices such as tape drives and magnetic drums. They also examine parts for surface defects.

Machine Builders

Machine Builders analyze blueprint assembly instructions and manuals to construct, assemble or rebuild engines and turbines.

Aircraft Power Plant Assemblers

Aircraft Power Plant Assemblers analyze blueprints and other materials to put together and install parts of airplanes such as wings or landing gear.

Electronics Assemblers

Electronics Assemblers assemble electronics equipment, such as missile control systems, radio and test equipment, and computers.

WORK ENVIRONMENT

Physical Environment

Precision assemblers work in a variety of environments, depending on the type of product they are assembling. Virtually all work is performed indoors in a factory or industrial plant facility, however. Assemblers may need to stand and maintain focus for long periods of time. They generally work forty hours per week, and several daily shifts are common.

Relevant Skills and Abilities

Organization & Management Skills
- Making decisions
- Managing time
- Meeting goals and deadlines
- Performing routine work

Research & Planning Skills
- Developing evaluation strategies

Technical Skills
- Performing scientific, mathematical and technical work
- Working with machines, tools or other objects
- Working with your hands

Plant Environment

Plants may be noisy, and assemblers may need to use safety equipment to reduce damage to hearing. These facilities can be hot and cramped. Workers may run the risk of coming into contact with industrial chemicals.

Human Environment

Precision assemblers must be comfortable following detailed directions exactly while working with minimal supervision. They tend to be experienced employees and, as such, may mentor and train colleagues. They may work with engineers and technicians to refine or test designs, so they should be comfortable in a collaborative environment.

Technological Environment

Precision assemblers must be able to read blueprints and computer-generated designs and instructions. They should be familiar with all production stages of the item or system they are producing, which may mean a working knowledge of highly advanced robotic assemblers. They use highly calibrated tools and must be able to work with industrial-management software.

EDUCATION, TRAINING, AND ADVANCEMENT

High School/Secondary

Students interested in a career as a precision assembler should have a strong background in mechanics, math, and shop and a strong interest in industrial production. Drafting, model making, and computer science are also useful skills. Students may wish to take courses relevant to the specific goods they wish to produce, such as radio and computer technology or automotive repair.

Suggested High School Subjects
- Blueprint Reading
- Drafting
- English
- Machining Technology
- Metals Technology
- Shop Math
- Shop Mechanics
- Welding

Famous First

The first communications satellite was Echo I, a 26-inch sphere launched via rocket from Cape Canaveral, Fla., in 1960. Once in orbit, the satellite conveyed a message sent from Goldstone, Calif., to a Bell Telephone laboratory in Holmdel, NJ.

Postsecondary

Some precision engineers require more advanced training than others. For example, an electronics assembler may be required to have a technical degree or equivalent military training. Most technical colleges offer degrees that are relevant to precision assemblers, from automotive technology to electrical-systems training.

Related College Majors
- Machine Technologist

Adult Job Seekers

Adults interested in a career as a precision assembler can benefit from the in-house training and internal promotions common to industrial plants. Many companies offer classroom training for lower-level assemblers who have shown aptitude for precision work. Career training is also available in the military.

Most precision assemblers are members of labor unions such as the United Steelworkers, the International Brotherhood of Electrical Workers, and the United Automobile, Aerospace and Agricultural Implement Workers of America. Most of these unions require dues and offer training and advocacy.

Professional Certification and Licensure

No certification or licensure is necessary to become a precision assembler. Because of the detailed work required, however, some companies may test for vision and color sensitivity.

Additional Requirements

Precision assemblers must be able to focus on a repetitive but complex task for long periods of time and be very responsive to time pressures. They should have excellent hearing and vision and be able to stand or sit for most of the day. Though precision assemblers tend to work on their component alone, they must have a good understanding of the manufacturing process in general. They are highly skilled workers who enjoy detailed and fast-paced work.

Fun Fact

In the U.S., the majority of manufacturing plants – more than 80,000 --employ four or fewer people.
Source: http://manufacturingfacts.org/chart55.html

EARNINGS AND ADVANCEMENT

Earnings depend on the type and union affiliation of the employer and the level of skill required to do the job. Some precision assemblers are paid incentive or piecework rates. Precision assemblers had median annual earnings of $30,062 in 2014.

Precision assemblers may receive paid vacations, holidays, and sick days; life and health insurance; and retirement benefits. These are usually paid by the employer. Employers may also provide supplemental unemployment benefits, dental insurance, uniforms and tools.

EMPLOYMENT AND OUTLOOK

There were approximately 1 million precision assemblers employed nationally in 2014. Manufacturing industries employ over 75 percent of precision assemblers. Employment of precision assemblers is expected to grow slower than the average for all occupations through the year 2024, which means employment is projected to increase 0 percent to 5 percent. This is a result of the increased use of more efficient automation and outsourcing, which is the practice of moving assembly operations to countries with lower labor costs. Since this is such a large occupation, job openings will arise from the need to replace precision assemblers who retire or leave the occupation for other reasons.

Related Occupations
- Bindery Worker
- Electromechanical Equipment Assembler
- Machinist
- Metal/Plastic Working Machine Operator
- Millwright

Conversation With . . .
MARILYN GONZALEZ

MRB Operator, Sypris Electronics
Tampa, FL
Precision manufacturing field, 15 years

1. WWhat was your individual career path in terms of education/training, entry-level job, or other significant opportunity?

I'm originally from New York but graduated from high school in Aguadilla, Puerto Rico. After high school, I first moved to Ohio, then to Tampa looking for a new, independent life. I worked in retail for a year, then worked for a collections agency that unfortunately went out of business within a year.

One of my girlfriends told me that her husband's company was hiring. I applied for a soldering position here with no previous experience, and within days I was hired for the job. With the confidence I had in myself, I was able to pass standard certification training required by the federal government, known as the IPC-610, J-STD, NASA 8739 .1.2.3 and .4 soldering classes, to build government and space products. Once I completed my training, I moved into a mechanical position for about six months, then started soldering until I was offered a lead position in 2010.

For four years, I was in charge of a group that performed mechanical and soldering functions. Then I was offered the material repair board (MRB) position, which is the position I currently hold. Only two people in our company do this work; I specialize in delicate repairs to circuit boards. To me, this is an art. I feel I have to make my product as pretty as possible. Sometimes even I ask myself, "If it was a painting, would it sell?"

2. What are the most important skills and/or qualities for someone in your profession?

The ability to maintain creativity and patience while adapting to consistent change is important. Working in electronics, some things are very difficult but with practice, experience, and time, things get easier. For instance, on a circuit card, you might have a tiny micro-trace and you can't find a compatible trace. So, I've actually had to form a new micro-trace and attach it so it looks as original as possible.

3. What do you wish you had known going into this profession?

I wish I had known how entertaining and interesting electronics can be. I would have been motivated to continue my education. I didn't know how many opportunities electronics offered.

4. Are there many job opportunities in your profession? In what specific areas?

Yes, but without a degree opportunities are limited. With a degree, more doors will open, in areas like mechanical, industrial, and design engineering.

5. How do you see your profession changing in the next five years? What role will technology play in those changes, and what skills will be required?

Every day, technology is changing; I have lived it within my company. We've shifted from larger component parts to tiny, little micro parts. New equipment and new machinery arrives and new skills are required to operate them. It's hard to tell what skills will be required, but you must be willing to adapt and be open to changes.

6. What do you enjoy most about your job? What do you enjoy least about your job?

I enjoy working both independently and with my engineering team on new modifications and designs. I least enjoy working long hours, because overtime keeps me away from my son.

7. Can you suggest a valuable "try this" for students considering a career in your profession?

Take one of your old electronic devices apart or purchase a soldering kit to get an understanding of how components are mounted or soldered on a circuit card assembly.

MORE INFORMATION

**Fabricators & Manufacturers
Association, International**
833 Featherstone Road
Rockford, IL 61107
888.394.4362
www.fmanet.org

**International Brotherhood of
Electrical Workers**
900 Seventh Street, NW
Washington, DC 20001
202.833.7000
www.ibew.org

International Union, UAW
Solidarity House
8000 East Jefferson Avenue
Detroit, MI 48214
313.926.5000
www.uaw.org

Bethany Groff/Editor

Printing Machine Operator

Snapshot

Career Cluster: Media & Communications; Production

Interests: Lithography, printing technology, graphic design, fine arts, computers

Earnings (Yearly Average): $35,100

Employment & Outlook: Decline Expected

OVERVIEW

Sphere of Work

Printing machine operators, also known as printing machine technicians or pressmen, perform a wide range of functions related to operating, preparing, and maintaining a printing machine. Printing machines are commonly referred to as presses. Operators work in a variety of industries and on a variety of press types, including letter and letterset presses, flexographic presses, and offset lithograph presses. Depending on the size of the press, some operators may work with a team.

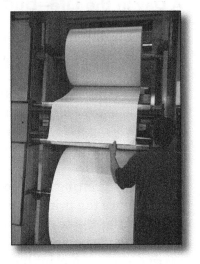

Work Environment

Operators perform their duties in a range of different locations, which are determined by the type of press they work with. For example, bigger presses, like those used in newspaper printing, are located in large rooms usually inside the headquarters of the newspaper. These larger presses are very loud and move at a very fast speed. Typically, the atmosphere is very much like that of an assembly line, with tasks being repeated in a certain order on a printing machine.

Profile

Working Conditions: Work Indoors
Physical Strength: Medium Work
Education Needs: On-The-Job Training, High School Diploma with Technical Education, Apprenticeship
Licensure/Certification: Recommended
Opportunities For Experience: Apprenticeship, Military Service, Part-Time Work
Holland Interest Score*: CRE, RSC

* See Appendix A

Occupation Interest

Printing machine operators need to be physically capable of performing their duties, which include working on various mechanical parts while bending, kneeling, and reaching. This profession tends to interest people who enjoy working with their hands and do not mind getting dirty. Since they need to be in frequent communication with other operators and supervisors, printing machine operators need to have strong communication skills.

A Day in the Life—Duties and Responsibilities

During the day, an operator will collaborate heavily with his or her coworkers and supervisors to ensure that printing jobs are done correctly. When something malfunctions on a press, an operator must perform maintenance quickly and accurately to ensure that deadlines are not jeopardized. The duties of the day vary by the type of printing machine being used, but there are some basic tasks that every printing machine operator goes through regardless of the press.

Before any printing can begin, a printing machine operator must first prepare the printing plate. Printing plates are the devices that transfer the text or images to be printed. Plates are applied directly to the paper via the press or through an intermediate image carrier, such as a print blanket, which is used in offset printing or offset lithography. Regardless of the printing process being used, an operator must constantly monitor the process. He or she will take care of any paper jams and pressure problems, clean the press, and refill any inkwells that are running low.

Printing machine operators in the newspaper business commonly use offset lithography printing. This high-speed process involves transferring ink from a high-capacity ink duct to the actual paper through a series of rollers and cylinders. Operators check the ink and the paper often for quality and any problems that need to be fixed quickly

Duties and Responsibilities

- Securing printing plates and adjusting the tolerances
- Cleaning and resetting rollers
- Adjusting control margins and ink flow
- Running proofs and making adjustments on the press
- Starting the press and monitoring its operation
- Cleaning ink fountains; removing, cleaning, and storing the plates
- Watching for problems or stoppages and correcting them quickly

OCCUPATION SPECIALTIES

Rotogravure-Press Operators

Rotogravure-Press Operators set up and operate rotary-type presses that print by gravure processes.

Web-Press Operators

Web-Press Operators set up and operate rotary presses that use rolls of paper (called webs).

Offset-Press Operators

Offset-Press Operators set up and operate offset printing presses.

Engraving-Press Operators

Engraving-Press Operators set up and operate presses that engrave decorative designs or lettering.

Platen-Press Operators

Platen-Press Operators make ready and operate platen-type printing presses to produce printed material. They make sure there is an even distribution of ink and readjust the presses during the time it is running to obtain a specified color registration.

Cylinder Press Operators

Cylinder Press Operators make ready and operate cylinder-type presses and insure that they operate smoothly.

WORK ENVIRONMENT

Transferable Skills and Abilities

Organization & Management Skills
- Making decisions
- Paying attention to and handling details
- Performing routine work

Research & Planning Skills
- Developing evaluation strategies

Technical Skills
- Performing scientific, mathematical and technical work
- Working with machines, tools or other objects
- Working with your hands

Physical Environment

Printing machine operators predominantly work in a printing room with other operators. The size and condition of this room varies depending on the company and the size of the printing machine. Larger machines move very fast and can create a noisy environment.

Human Environment

Operating a printing machine requires a lot of collaboration.

Operators work under deadlines, so they need to work together to make sure the printing job is done quickly and accurately. They also interact with supervisors and sometimes with clients who have requested a printing job.

Technological Environment

Printing machine operators work with a broad range of technologies, including handheld tools, such as wrenches and screwdrivers, and large printing-machine parts, such as rollers, ink ducts, and different paper stock. Safety gear, including gloves, goggles, and boots, must be worn when operating larger presses.

EDUCATION, TRAINING, AND ADVANCEMENT

High School/Secondary

Typically, a printing machine operator must have a high school diploma or the equivalent. There are several basic high school courses that would greatly benefit someone interested in a profession as a printing machine operator, including mathematics, mechanical drawing, and computers.

Suggested High School Subjects
- English
- Graphic Communications
- Industrial Arts
- Journalism
- Machining Technology
- Mechanical Drawing
- Shop Math
- Trade/Industrial Education

Famous First

The first printer who was a woman was Dinah Nuthead of Annapolis, Md, who obtained a license to print in 1696 in order to continue the printing business run by her late husband, William Nuthead.

Postsecondary

Although most employers do not require a printing machine operator to have an education beyond high school, there are many applicable courses offered at community colleges and vocational and technical schools for those interested in the industry. These schools typically offer a wide range of courses that provide formal classroom instruction and hands-on experience. Employers are more likely to hire someone who has completed a related course.

Graphic-design courses and any courses related to computers would also benefit a potential printing machine operator. Some schools offer graphic-design courses specifically for students who plan on pursuing a profession in printing and design. As technology in the printing industry continues to develop, more computer-based printing machines are being put into use. An individual interested in keeping up with this kind of technology would benefit greatly from a strong background in computers.

Related College Majors
- Graphic & Printing Equipment Operation, General

Adult Job Seekers

An individual without any experience in the printing industry should consider a technical or vocational school that offers relevant courses. Job seekers can also contact local printing unions for advice on how to get started in the industry. When an individual is hired, he or she usually starts as an assistant to more experienced workers. As a worker gains more experience and training, he or she will be promoted to the role of operator.

Professional Certification and Licensure

While no specific certification or licensure exists for printing machine operators, they are encouraged to seek out further training through either their company, their union, or the manufacturers of printing-machine technology. Printing technology is constantly developing and becoming more computerized, so operators who keep up with this technology are more likely to be promoted and further their career in the industry.

Additional Requirements

A printing machine operator must have a desire to be trained and to learn more about the industry. Because operators work in collaboration with others, they should have great communication skills and be able to work under deadlines as part of a team. They must also possess great attention to detail.

Fun Fact

At $2,700 per gallon (if sold retail), black printer ink is one of the world's most expensive liquids.
Source: http://www.sepialine.com/2013/10/02/20-unusual-printing-facts-youve-heard/

EARNINGS AND ADVANCEMENT

Earnings depend on the type of press being run and the area of the country in which the work is located. Median annual earnings of printing machine operators were $35,100 in 2014.

Printing machine operators may receive paid vacations, holidays, and sick days; life and health insurance; and retirement benefits. These are usually paid by the employer.

Metropolitan Areas with the Highest
Employment Level in this Occupation

Metropolitan area	Employment	Employment per thousand jobs	Annual mean wage
Chicago-Joliet-Naperville, IL	7,010	1.87	$40,360
Los Angeles-Long Beach-Glendale, CA	5,360	1.32	$35,900
New York-White Plains-Wayne, NY-NJ	5,280	0.98	$42,870
Minneapolis-St. Paul-Bloomington, MN-WI	3,620	1.98	$42,020
Atlanta-Sandy Springs-Marietta, GA	3,320	1.39	$37,750
Dallas-Plano-Irving, TX	2,590	1.16	$38,670
Washington-Arlington-Alexandria, DC-VA-MD-WV	2,530	1.06	$51,000
Cincinnati-Middletown, OH-KY-IN	2,470	2.44	$36,880
Santa Ana-Anaheim-Irvine, CA	2,290	1.54	$35,410
Kansas City, MO-KS	2,280	2.27	$40,820

Source: Bureau of Labor Statistics

EMPLOYMENT AND OUTLOOK

Printing machine operators held about 150,000 jobs nationally in 2014. Employment is expected to decline through the year 2024. Employment will dip because of increasing automation in the printing industry and because of the outsourcing of some production to foreign countries.

Related Occupations

- Desktop Publisher
- Photoengraver & Lithographer
- Prepress Technician

Related Military Occupations

- Printing Specialist

Conversation With . . .
PAUL STRACK

President, Custom XM
North Little Rock, Arkansas
Printing, 26 years

1. What was your individual career path in terms of education/training, entry-level job, or other significant opportunity?

I graduated with an accounting degree from Christian Brothers University in Memphis, became a Certified Public Accountant and practiced in public accounting for five years in Little Rock at Arthur Young & Company (now merged into Ernst & Young) before joining my family's printing company. I liked the people, as well as the opportunity to someday own the business. I started in sales because my previous work in auditing also was people-oriented.

Although print remains important, the printing business has been dramatically impacted by the digital revolution. Our company, now fifty years old, has evolved into a company that specializes in printing, advertising, and marketing/communications.

Though print has declined, certain sectors—such as health-related industries, higher education, and non-profits—still have a strong need for print. Think about the brochures and sales or recruiting pieces these industries use to reach out to potential patients, students, or donors. Statistics show that for non-profit fundraising, people still respond to the printed piece. The traditional method of people putting checks in the mail remains the leading way non-profits receive donations, even though online giving is growing.

Health clubs use print: You sign a contract on a two- or three-part form. Direct mail and sales-related pieces such as brochures are strong. We also print signs, banners, window graphics, and wall graphics. Things that are read are retained better, and people like the touch and feel of print.

2. What are the most important skills and/or qualities for someone in your profession?

This is a relationship business in terms of gaining and retaining clients, so you need people skills. You must communicate well. You need to be technologically savvy and able to manage clients' campaigns as well as your own business outreach via social media. You need to be detail-oriented. We're still a manufacturer and virtually every job that comes in here is a custom job with a due date and specifications such as quantity, type of finishing, and details such as does it fold, does it cut, does it patch?

You need to be flexible and have the ability to adapt because our profession changes constantly. We still have a pressman, who would be hard to replace given his rare and unique skill set, but we don't have a lot of large presses anymore. Every piece of equipment we have, even if it's mechanical, has a computer front end.

Organizational skills and patience are a must. Creativity is a plus. Someone who is forward thinking will do well.

3. What do you wish you had known going into this profession?

I wish had better foreseen the changes that technology would have on our industry. The Internet and digital technology had a significant impact that caught many of us off guard. Fortunately, we have been able to adapt.

4. Are there many job opportunities in your profession? In what specific areas?

Sales opportunities will always be in abundance. Creative design—for print, and more importantly, for digital (email, web design and more)—will continue to grow.

5. How do you see your profession changing in the next five years, what role will technology play in those changes, and what skills will be required?

I honestly wish I had the answer to that question. Our industry seems to change so much from year to year. Digital marketing will continue to change in our industry and we will continue to find ways to keep print relevant. Mail order catalogs, for instance, continue to have success because they go out to people after they look at something online. The marriage of print and online is very effective when done well.

6. What do you enjoy most about your job? What do you enjoy least about your job?

I enjoy the challenge of change. I have learned much about digital marketing over the past few years – email marketing, landing page development, analytics, and more. It's interesting, but it is tough at times.

As a business owner, I least like hiring and terminating team members when required. It's never an enjoyable process.

7. Can you suggest a valuable "try this" for students considering a career in your profession?

If you're interested in design, create an ad, business card, or brochure. If you're interested in advertising, create a campaign: an email or social media campaign for a product or an idea.

If you're interested in operating equipment, ask to shadow a press operator or equipment operator for a day. Assist in loading paper and ask questions.

MORE INFORMATION

Association for Suppliers of Printing, Publishing, and Converting Technologies
1899 Preston White Drive
Reston, VA 20191
703.264.7200
www.npes.org

Graphic Arts Education and Research Foundation
1899 Preston White Drive
Reston, VA 20191
866.381.9839
www.gaerf.org

Graphic Arts Technical Foundation
200 Deer Run Road
Sewickley, PA 15143
412.741.6860
www.printing.org

Graphic Communications International Union
International Brotherhood of Teamsters
25 Louisiana Avenue, NW
Washington, DC 20001
202.624.6800
www.teamster.org/content/graphics-communications

National Association for Printing Leadership
One Meadowlands Plaza, Suite 1511
East Rutherford, NJ 07073
800.642.6275
www.napl.org

NPES
1899 Preston White Drive
Reston, VA 20191-4367
703.264.7200
www.npes.org

Printing Industries of America
200 Deer Run Road
Sewickley, PA 15143
800.910.4283
www.printing.org

Printing, Publishing & Media Workers
Sector of the Communication Workers of America
501 E. Third Street, NW
Washington, DC 20001-2797
www.cwa-ppmws.org

Patrick Cooper/Editor

Production Coordinator

Snapshot

Career Cluster: Manufacturing; Production
Interests: Business management, manufacturing, industrial processing, quality control, facility supervision
Earnings (Yearly Average): $45,670
Employment & Outlook: Slower than Average Growth Expected

OVERVIEW

Sphere of Work

Production coordinators oversee the efficiency and productivity of goods at manufacturing and industrial processing facilities. They are also known as manufacturing supervisors, plant supervisors, and production managers. The production coordinator is traditionally a management level position. A coordinator's primary responsibility is to ensure that production, processing, or manufacturing work orders are met in a cost efficient and timely manner. They also ensure that products are created according to quality specifications, customer expectations, and with respect to worker safety.

Work Environment

Production coordinators are employed in all facets of industrial manufacturing and processing. They work in processing facilities and manufacturing complexes that produce such goods as fabricated metal, textiles, transportation equipment, chemicals, computers, and electronic products. Production coordinators in the agricultural, livestock, and food processing industries may be required to work outdoors and in inclement conditions, depending on their particular realm of industry.

Profile

Working Conditions: Work Indoors
Physical Strength: Light Work
Education Needs: Junior/
   Technical/Community College
Licensure/Certification: Required
Opportunities For Experience: Part-
   Time Work
Holland Interest Score*: ESR

* See Appendix A

Occupation Interest

Professionals who are drawn to a career as a production coordinator are traditionally team players who possess the ability to explicate instructions and complex systems in an informed but easily understandable manner. Production coordinators are also often innately sensitive to the potential for problems, both within systems and in relationships and workers. They possess a keen ability to handle situations and relationships in a manner that is beneficial to organizational productivity.

A Day in the Life—Duties and Responsibilities

Production coordinators have numerous daily responsibilities that are made more complex by the fact that they are traditionally the sole senior representative of a production branch within a particular company or organization.

Production coordinators must stay in constant contact with both their supervisors, co-coordinators, and team of subordinates, keeping them informed of success and failures in the production processes, suggesting arenas for improvement, and ensuring that all necessary equipment maintenance and facility upkeep is completed.

In addition to routinely monitoring the production processes, its materials, procedures, and surroundings, production coordinators are also responsible for making sure each process is undertaken in the most efficient and productive way. It is the responsibility of production managers to suggest improvements to processes. These changes are done through systematic changes, the inclusion of new or updated equipment, or through eliminating steps coordinators deem unnecessary or redundant.

Production coordinators work closely with account management and sales teams to ensure that clients are satisfied with the goods and services they order. Similarly, they are often the key point of contact for outside vendors who sell supplies and ingredients to manufacturing facilities. They also oversee plant safety and quality control and ensure all production systems and related equipment is operating within the specifications of local, state, and federal regulations.

Duties and Responsibilities

- Distributing work orders to departments
- Contacting sellers to verify shipment of goods on promised shipping dates
- Revising schedules according to work order specifications, priorities, and availability of workers and equipment
- Compiling production records
- Establishing completion dates for material
- Keeping inventory
- Communicating with transportation companies to prevent delays in transit

OCCUPATION SPECIALTIES

Material Coordinators

Material Coordinators coordinate and expedite the flow of material, parts and assemblies within or between departments in accordance with production and shipping schedules or department priorities.

Customer Service Coordinators

Customer Service Coordinators coordinate the production of printed materials, prepress or printing services with customers' requirements, and confer with customers throughout job production to keep them informed of the status of the job. They determine the materials to be used for the job, plan and draw the layout of the job, and route the materials to the proper work areas.

Production Clerks

Production Clerks compile data from customers' orders, production estimates, and perpetual (continuing) inventory to prepare production schedules, records and reports.

WORK ENVIRONMENT

Physical Environment

Production coordinators work primarily in industrial and manufacturing facilities. However, the position is required in any workflow that results in an end product, including publishing, agriculture, food services, and communications.

Transferable Skills and Abilities

Communication Skills
- Speaking effectively
- Writing concisely

Interpersonal/Social Skills
- Cooperating with others
- Working as a member of a team

Organization & Management Skills
- Coordinating tasks
- Making decisions
- Managing people/groups
- Paying attention to and handling details
- Performing duties which change frequently

Research & Planning Skills
- Analyzing information
- Developing evaluation strategies

Technical Skills
- Working with machines, tools or other objects

Human Environment

Strong collaboration and management skills are required of all production coordinator positions. Production coordinators are required to direct and motivate their staff on a daily basis and often act as the point person in production departments to other senior management staff.

Technological Environment

The technological parameters of each production coordinator position vary from industry to industry. However, familiarity with basic technological and mechanical processes is required.

EDUCATION, TRAINING, AND ADVANCEMENT

High School/Secondary

High school students can best prepare for a career as a production coordinator by engaging in coursework such as algebra, calculus, geometry, trigonometry, physics, rhetorical communication, and computer science. Advanced placement classes in these subjects are especially recommended. Drafting, industrial arts, and creative arts classes can also serve as important precursors related to systems design.

Participation in team sports, student government, and other intramural or extra-curricular activities can also lay the groundwork for future leadership positions.

Suggested High School Subjects
- Bookkeeping
- Business
- English
- Mathematics

Famous First

The first bar code and scanner were invented in 1949, but it wasn't until 1961 that bar codes came into use in commerce. Their first use there was in tracking railroad cars on the Boston & Maine line. Later, bar codes were used primarily in retail settings. In recent years, they have made their way back to logistics, as managers track the flow of materials and goods from one point to another using scanning technology.

Postsecondary

Postsecondary education is not traditionally a requirement for production coordinator vacancies, which often place more emphasis on the professional experience of candidates, particularly their experience in supervisory or management roles within their specific trade or industry. Nonetheless, applicants seeking production coordinator roles within specific industries benefit tremendously from the skills and experience gained by completing a certification program or bachelor's degree.

Related College Majors
- Operations Management & Supervision

Adult Job Seekers

Production coordinators are often required to work lengthy hours in addition to late night and weekend shifts. They may be required to be on-call and may be called into work during emergencies or as substitutes for absent employees. Depending on their particular industry, production coordinators often possess experience as production employees.

Professional Certification and Licensure

Certification and licensure for production coordinators is contingent on their particular realm of industry. Facilities supervisors and managers may also be required to possess annually updated certification issued by organizations such as the Occupational Safety and Health Administration.

Additional Requirements

Production coordinators play a major role in the morale of an organization, regardless of its size or output. As such, they must possess the ability to motivate staff members, many of whom have jobs that may be repetitive or physically demanding. It is the task of production coordinators to maintain a positive morale among the production workforce so that productivity and profits can be maximized.

Fun Fact

If U.S. manufacturing was its own country, it would be the world's 10th-largest economy, based on a 2012 report.

Source: http://www.themanufacturinginstitute.org/Research/Facts-About-Manufacturing/~/media/A9EEE900EAF04B2892177207D9FF23C9.ashx

EARNINGS AND ADVANCEMENT

Earnings of production coordinators depend on type and size of the employer and the individual's experience and level of responsibility. Median annual earnings for production coordinators were $45,670 in 2014. In addition to salary, production coordinators usually receive bonuses based on job performance.

Production coordinators may receive paid vacations, holidays, and sick days; life and health insurance; and retirement benefits. These are usually paid by the employer.

Metropolitan Areas with the Highest Employment Level in this Occupation

Metropolitan area	Employment	Employment per thousand jobs	Annual mean wage
Los Angeles-Long Beach-Glendale, CA	13,620	3.36	$47,910
New York-White Plains-Wayne, NY-NJ	11,990	2.22	$52,090
Houston-Sugar Land-Baytown, TX	9,470	3.33	$52,310
Chicago-Joliet-Naperville, IL	7,790	2.08	$47,690
Dallas-Plano-Irving, TX	6,370	2.85	$48,100
Phoenix-Mesa-Glendale, AZ	5,680	3.11	$44,490
Atlanta-Sandy Springs-Marietta, GA	5,500	2.30	$45,950
Seattle-Bellevue-Everett, WA	5,280	3.54	$51,530
Santa Ana-Anaheim-Irvine, CA	5,160	3.47	$51,970
Philadelphia, PA	4,720	2.53	$52,450

Source: Bureau of Labor Statistics

EMPLOYMENT AND OUTLOOK

Nationally, there were approximately 250,000 production coordinators employed in 2014. Employment is expected to grow slower than the average for all occupations through the year 2024, which means employment is projected to increase 0 percent to 5 percent. As more pressure is put on companies to manufacture and deliver their products more quickly and efficiently, the need for production coordinators will grow. However, the expected employment decline in manufacturing will limit the overall growth of this occupation.

Employment Trend, Projected 2014–24

Total, all occupations: 7%

Production coordinators: 3%

Material recording, scheduling, dispatching, and distributing workers: -1%

Note: "All Occupations" includes all occupations in the U.S. Economy. Source: U.S. Bureau of Labor Statistics, Employment Projections Program

Related Occupations

- Cost Estimator
- Dispatcher
- Operations Research Analyst
- Purchasing Agent
- Transportation Manager

MORE INFORMATION

**APICS, The Educational Society
for Resource Management**
8430 W. Bryn Mawr Avenue
Suite 1000
Chicago, IL 60631
800.444.2742
service@apicshq.org
www.apics.org

**Military Operations Research
Society**
1703 N. Beauregard Street, Suite 450
Alexandria, VA 22311
703.933.9070
www.mors.org

**Professional Construction
Estimators Association**
P.O. Box 680336
Charlotte, NC 28216
877.521.7232
www.pcea.org

John Pritchard/Editor

Quality Control Inspector

Snapshot

Career Cluster: Manufacturing; Production

Interests: Testing and inspecting, analysis, manufacturing processes, production processes, industrial engineering

Earnings (Yearly Average): $35,330

Employment & Outlook: Slower than Average Growth Expected

OVERVIEW

Sphere of Work

Quality control inspectors evaluate products and materials for errors and defects to ensure that they meet the manufacturer's specifications. Quality inspectors play a crucial role in automated manufacturing systems, providing firsthand, human intervention in an otherwise highly mechanized process. In addition to removing all defective products prior to resale, quality control inspectors may also be responsible for recommending changes to production processes in order to prevent further errors and disruptions to the work flow.

Work Environment

The majority of quality control inspectors work in manufacturing facilities. They test and inspect the parts that will be assembled into manufactured and salable items or the completed products themselves, depending on their particular industry of employment. For example, some inspectors may be responsible for evaluating materials such as lumber or petroleum products, while others may be responsible for testing electronic equipment, automobiles, or furniture prior to their sale. The mode of inspection varies from position to position as well. Some quality control inspectors may conduct stress tests or other analyses on the actual physical parts, while others may monitor various kinds of production data.

Profile

Working Conditions: Work Indoors
Physical Strength: Light Work
Education Needs: On-The-Job Training, High School Diploma or G.E.D., Junior/Technical/Community College
Licensure/Certification: Required
Opportunities For Experience: Part-Time Work
Holland Interest Score*: REI

* See Appendix A

Occupation Interest

Quality control typically attracts individuals who thrive in tasks related to deductive reasoning and who are perceptive to errors and problems in continuity and production. Quality inspectors also possess a keen eye for detail and the ability to spot discrepancies in both the products and processes. The position of quality inspector attracts people of all ages and from a variety of professional and educational backgrounds.

A Day in the Life—Duties and Responsibilities

Quality control inspectors must be familiar with all aspects of the products and manufacturing processes they inspect. Some quality control inspectors travel between several different facilities, inspecting the same processes and goods on a rotating basis. Some quality control inspectors may be required to review new production specifications frequently, depending on how often their employing organization changes their product line or production methods.

Inspection of materials and goods is the main duty of quality control inspectors. Inspectors may either survey each manufactured item or take frequent samples of the manufactured goods to gauge the quality of its construction and adherence to specifications. Reoccurring errors on production lines are often the result of malfunctioning equipment.

Quality control inspectors have the final say in the rejection of items they deem to be poor quality or unsuitable for sale. Inspectors must record data to track how much inventory was lost and detail the cause.

Inspectors are customarily required to report their findings to other members of an organization's staff. The frequency and form of these presentations varies from industry to industry. Manufacturers of artisan and specialty products may review quality control findings for every single production run, while companies and factories that assemble or create a large volume of product may only require weekly to bimonthly reporting, depending on the frequency of errors.

Duties and Responsibilities

- Conducting visual and physical examinations of products
- Testing products and recording results
- Comparing results of tests and examinations to determine if the products meet the standards set by the manufacturer
- Making reports and recommendations based on test results

OCCUPATION SPECIALTIES

Quality Control Technicians

Quality Control Technicians test and inspect products at various stages of production to determine and maintain the quality of the products. They make recommendations for modifications to the products and set up destructive or nondestructive tests to measure the performance or life of a product.

General Inspectors

General Inspectors inspect materials and products, such as sheet stock, auto body or engine parts, dental instruments, machine shop parts and metal castings for conformance to specifications. They compare the product with a parts list or with a sample model of the product to insure that the piece was assembled correctly.

WORK ENVIRONMENT

Physical Environment

The work environment for quality control inspectors varies from industrial and manufacturing settings to administrative settings.

Transferable Skills and Abilities

Interpersonal/Social Skills
- Cooperating with others
- Working as a member of a team

Organization & Management Skills
- Paying attention to and handling details

Research & Planning Skills
- Analyzing information

Technical Skills
- Performing scientific, mathematical and technical work
- Understanding which technology is appropriate for a task
- Working with data or numbers

Work Environment Skills
- Working in a factory setting
- Working in a laboratory setting

Plant Environment

Quality control inspectors work primarily in industrial settings, such as factories and production plants, where they can review the completed products as well as the equipment and processes used. Quality control inspectors employed by the pharmaceutical industry may also work in laboratory settings where they test and evaluate the safety of medications.

Human Environment

Quality control inspectors do not typically interact with coworkers extensively on a daily basis, as their primary focus is placed on the production process and the systems related to it. Their occasional presentation of findings and suggestions for improvement do, however, require extensive and clear communication with plant managers and industrial engineers.

Technological Environment

Quality inspectors utilize a variety of different use technologies, ranging from data-tracking tools to desktop-publishing software. The production technologies and equipment used in the manufacturing process vary in complexity according to an inspector's realm of industry.

EDUCATION, TRAINING, AND ADVANCEMENT

High School/Secondary

High school students can prepare for a career as a quality control inspector with course work in engineering, algebra, calculus, geometry, physics, and introductory computer science. Drafting, mapping, and traditional art classes can also serve as important precursors for careers related to industrial design. English composition course work prepares students for many of the reporting elements of the role.

Suggested High School Subjects
- Applied Communication
- Applied Math
- Biology
- Business Law
- Business Math
- Computer Science
- English
- Foods & Nutrition
- Foreign Languages
- Geometry
- Government
- Trade/Industrial Education

Famous First

The first business owner to be convicted for importing unsafe toys was Steve Thai of Los Angeles, who was convicted in 2002 after his company, Super Rambo, imported toy vehicles and play robots that had removable parts capable of choking a small child, in violation of U.S. consumer protection laws. He was fined $20,000 and given three years' probation.

Postsecondary

Job openings for quality control inspectors in supply, mechanical, and manufacturing industries do not traditionally require postsecondary education. However, a college degree may be required for inspectors working in more complex industries such as medical and pharmaceutical labs, digital engineering, and food processing. While some colleges offer degree and certificate programs in quality control management, they are rare. Aspiring quality control inspectors interested in these fields should consider earning a degree in food sciences and technology or industrial engineering.

Related College Majors
- Food Sciences & Technology
- Industrial/Manufacturing Technology

Adult Job Seekers

Individuals with extensive professional experience can often transition to the field without difficulty, particularly since the intricacies of most quality control positions are learned through on-the-job training. Quality control inspectors traditionally work normal business hours, although those employed by large manufacturers who are in constant production may be required to work nights, weekends, and holidays.

Professional Certification and Licensure

State and national certification and licensure may be required of quality control inspectors depending on their particular industry or area of employment. Valid certification and licensure is typically required for individuals working in quality control in the food processing, pharmaceutical, and electronics industries, given the potential hazards of the components involved. Rules and regulations vary by state.

Additional Requirements

Successful quality control inspectors are self-motivated individuals who do not mind repetitive tasks. Inspectors are also detail-oriented problem-solvers who are able to actively monitor all aspects of the manufacturing process to spot errors or deficiencies and to recommend improvements.

Fun Fact

With Baby Boomers retiring, more manufacturers are struggling to find qualified applicants for open positions, according to data from the American Society for Quality's 2016 Manufacturing Outlook Survey.

Source: http://www.asq.org/media-room/press-releases/2015/20151218-asq-outlook-survey.html

EARNINGS AND ADVANCEMENT

The typical promotion of quality control inspectors is to a supervisory position. Education and continued training provides greater advancement opportunities. Earnings of quality control inspectors depend on the type and geographic location of the employer and the duties required of the employee. Median annual earnings of quality control inspectors were $35,330 in 2014. The lowest ten percent earned less than $20,820, and the highest ten percent earned more than $60,440.

Quality control inspectors may receive paid vacations, holidays, and sick days; life and health insurance; and retirement benefits. These are usually paid by the employer.

Metropolitan Areas with the Highest
Employment Level in this Occupation

Metropolitan area	Employment	Employment per thousand jobs	Annual mean wage
Houston-Sugar Land-Baytown, TX	15,440	5.43	$42,220
Los Angeles-Long Beach-Glendale, CA	15,170	3.74	$39,900
Chicago-Joliet-Naperville, IL	12,200	3.25	$36,590
Warren-Troy-Farmington Hills, MI	8,230	7.19	$36,030
Seattle-Bellevue-Everett, WA	7,350	4.93	$57,900
Santa Ana-Anaheim-Irvine, CA	7,180	4.84	$39,550
Dallas-Plano-Irving, TX	7,100	3.17	$38,310
Atlanta-Sandy Springs-Marietta, GA	6,610	2.77	$35,240
New York-White Plains-Wayne, NY-NJ	6,150	1.14	$37,850
Phoenix-Mesa-Glendale, AZ	6,130	3.36	$42,820

Source: Bureau of Labor Statistics

EMPLOYMENT AND OUTLOOK

Inspectors, testers, sorters, samplers, and weighers, of which quality control inspectors are a part, held about 5000,000 jobs nationally in 2014. Employment is expected to grow slower than the average for all occupations through the year 2024, which means employment is projected to remain flat. This absence of growth is primarily due to the increased use of automated inspections and the moving of quality control duties from inspectors to production workers.

Employment Trend, Projected 2014–24

Total, all occupations: 7%

Quality control and other production inspectors: 0%

Production occupations: -3%

Note: "All Occupations" includes all occupations in the U.S. Economy. Source: U.S. Bureau of Labor Statistics, Employment Projections Program

Related Occupations
- Construction & Building Inspector
- Inspector & Compliance Officer
- Inspector & Tester
- Nuclear Quality Control Inspector

Conversation With . . .
DR. ERIC A. HAYLER

Chair-elect of American Society of Quality
Lean Six Sigma Master Black Belt
BMW Manufacturing Co., LLC, South Carolina
Quality control field, 12 years

1. What was your individual career path in terms of education/training, entry-level job, or other significant opportunity?

I went to college to study physics, then changed to chemistry and earned my bachelor's, masters, and PhD in chemistry, all at Rutgers University. I did my post-doc at Brookhaven National Laboratory, then spent eight years in mining as a chemist for the J.M. Huber Corp. I transitioned to BMW seventeen years ago, and worked as their laboratory manager for five years. During that time I became involved with the company's Lean Six Sigma program, a method of continuous improvement, then made my jump into the quality field, which includes a number of areas: quality control, quality management, auditing, and continuous improvement.

Six Sigma started in the 1980s at Motorola; companies such as DuPont were early adopters. In the last ten to fifteen years, it's been combined with the Lean principles that were perfected at Toyota. The result is a statistics-based program to improve quality and efficiency throughout an organization; in our case, from the process of building a car to human resources to our recruiting or purchasing departments.

My background as a chemist is a natural fit with the quality profession. In the mining industry, I solved problems with chemical analysis and created test methods. I measured things and monitored how processes were running.

At BMW, imagine we were to have an issue with how a car's dashboard and trim and body fit together. We'd go back and say: What are the specifications? Does everything meet the specs? We follow a five-part process to define, measure, analyze, improve, and control. We get at the root cause of problem, act to take care of it, and take actions so the improvements are sustained.

Quality also includes the ISO management standards, a basic set of standards that third-party auditors review.

2. What are the most important skills and/or qualities for someone in your profession?

You need analytical thinking ability to solve problems; have attention to detail; and be open-minded and willing to do something different. In order to do something better and more efficiently, you have to do something different and be willing to try things and take feedback.

You also need the ability to work with others on a team, including team-leading skills, using business relationships, and influencing other people.

3. What do you wish you had known going into this profession?

How important it is to get buy-in from other people. I came up with a lot of great ideas for my first Six Sigma project, but I did so without making sure everyone was onboard. As a result, some of my ideas weren't sustainable.

4. Are there many job opportunities in your profession? In what specific areas?

There's demand for quality professionals in many fields, including automotive, aerospace, software, construction, food and drug, biomedical, human development, and chemical.

5. How do you see your profession changing in the next five years, what role will technology play in those changes, and what skills will be required?

Quality as a profession is relatively mature in manufacturing, in much the same way that safety is everyone's job. The tendency in manufacturing is for something like quality to be decentralized and embedded throughout the organization. The health care and service sectors have been rapidly adopting quality, and it's gaining a foothold in education, and somewhat in government.

6. What do you enjoy most about your job? What do you enjoy least about your job?

The same thing: teaching. I love to create and foster a culture of quality and continuous improvement and the best way I can do that is by talking with people and showing how this will work to influence their behavior. But I don't like teaching the same things over and over.

7. Can you suggest a valuable "try this" for students considering a career in your profession?

Go where some sort of service or business is going on, like the Department of Motor Vehicles, a busy restaurant, or a deli counter. Stand there for 10 minutes, observe, and write down all the things you can think of to do it better. How could you make that process run more smoothly? What kind of waste do you see going on?

MORE INFORMATION

American Society for Quality
P.O. Box 3005
Milwaukee, WI 53201-3005
800.248.1946
www.asq.org

Society of Quality Assurance
154 Hansen Road, Suite 201
Charlottesville, VA 22911
434.297.4772
www.sqa.org

John Pritchard/Editor

Robotics Technician

Snapshot

Career Cluster: Engineering; Manufacturing; Maintenance & Repair; Technology

Interests: Robotics technology, engineering, computer science, electrical systems, machinery

Earnings (Yearly Average): $54,160

Employment & Outlook: Slower than Average Growth Expected

OVERVIEW

Sphere of Work

Robotics technicians, also known as electromechanical technicians, build and repair robots and mechanical devices in a manufacturing setting. Drawing on their knowledge of electrical and computer systems, robotics technicians develop efficient robots and keep them in good working order. Some technicians assist at all levels of a robot's conception, production, and installation. Others are experts when it comes to the machines they are assigned to maintain.

Technicians install new systems and replace old ones. Some robotics

technicians work closely with engineers in development and design. Others spend their time inspecting sites and making repairs. Robotics technicians read and interpret manuals and instructions, but they also think critically to find solutions to unusual or difficult problems with machines.

Work Environment

Most robotics technicians work in factories or similar manufacturing settings. Using a number of technologies, ranging from sophisticated computer programs to hand tools, technicians test machines and look for problems. A technician's work can be dangerous, so it is important for technicians to take proper safety precautions and follow correct procedures.

Profile

Working Conditions: Work Indoors
Physical Strength: Light Work
Education Needs:
  Technical/Community College
Licensure/Certification:
  Recommended
Physical Abilities Not Required: No
  Heavy Labor
Opportunities For Experience:
  Internship
Holland Interest Score*: REC

* See Appendix A

Occupation Interest

A robotics technician should be interested in engineering. He or she should enjoy taking machines apart and putting them back together again. Technicians are meticulous, and they always double-check their work. A robotics technician plays an important role within the larger framework of a factory operation.

A Day in the Life—Duties and Responsibilities

Every day is different for robotics technicians. Their responsibilities include building and installing new robotic devices, replacing old or outdated parts and machines, testing robot performance, troubleshooting problems within a system, maintaining inventories of necessary parts and tools, and programming computers.

There are generally two types of robotics technicians: those who work with engineers to design and assemble robots and those who maintain and repair those robots. The first type thinks creatively to find a way for machines to simulate the work of humans. Robot manipulators, or robots that simulate the work of arms or hands, are common in industrial settings, particularly when the work is repetitive or performed in a dangerous environment. Technicians work with engineers to develop machines like manipulators that perform a very specialized task within the larger framework of the factory or plant.

The second kind of robotics technician monitors the use of these machines. After the robot has been tested and installed, a technician routinely inspects it for missing or malfunctioning parts. This work is largely preventative, as a broken or worn-down machine can stall production across the plant. When a machine does break down, robotics technicians have the knowledge and skill to repair them.

Technicians typically work a regular forty-hour week, though sometimes companies schedule repairs of robotic equipment during weekends or holidays. In this event, a technician might have to work overtime.

Duties and Responsibilities

- Assisting engineers in designing and applying robot systems
- Inspecting electronic components prior to robot assembly
- Inspecting and testing robots for defects after assembly
- Installing robots or robot systems at users' sites
- Providing start-up assistance to users, including fine tuning performance and accuracy of robots
- Training other technicians and skilled workers to operate, program, repair, and service robots
- Keeping records of test procedures and results

WORK ENVIRONMENT

Physical Environment

Robotics technicians work in factories, plants, and other industrial settings.

Plant Environment

The plants and factories in which robotics technicians work are often dirty and loud. Technicians are often required to wear protective gear when performing their job. Working with large machines can be dangerous, so people must follow strict safety precautions.

Relevant Skills and Abilities

Communication Skills
- Speaking effectively
- Writing concisely

Organization & Management Skills
- Paying attention to and handling details

Research & Planning Skills
- Analyzing information
- Developing evaluation strategies
- Using logical reasoning

Technical Skills
- Applying the technology to a task
- Performing scientific, mathematical and technical work
- Working with machines, tools or other objects
- Working with your hands

Human Environment

Most robotics technicians work in teams that include other technicians, technologists, engineers, and machine operators. A robotics technician rarely works alone. Even minor repairs require assistance from or interaction with others.

Technological Environment

A robotics technician must be familiar with a range of technologies. In terms of computers and computer programming, most technicians use computer-aided design (CAD) software and industrial control software programs.

EDUCATION, TRAINING, AND ADVANCEMENT

High School/Secondary

Aspiring robotics technicians should enroll in courses focusing on mathematics, physics, computer science, and English. Shop classes and extracurricular activities related to robotics or simple machinery are also valuable. A robotics technician is familiar with various kinds of machines and understands why and how those machines work. They are comfortable using the scientific method and solving equations. They are also adept at reading manuals and diagrams and are able to explain complex instructions with ease. A job as a robotics technician requires a high school diploma or equivalent.

Suggested High School Subjects
- Algebra
- Applied Math
- Applied Physics
- Blueprint Reading
- Computer Science
- Electricity & Electronics
- English
- Geometry
- Machining Technology
- Mathematics

Famous First

The first Robot Olympics was the ROBOlympics (later renamed RoboGames) held in San Francisco in March 2004. Under the sponsorship of the Robotics Society of America, participants entered their robots in 31 events, including sumo, soccer, combat, and wrestling. The games have been held annually since then.

College/Postsecondary

Most robotics technician jobs require only two years of postsecondary training, culminating in an associate's degree or certificate. Community colleges and technical schools offer degree programs in electromechanics, robotics technology, industrial maintenance, and computer-integrated manufacturing. Many of these programs are accredited by the Accreditation Board for Engineering and Technology (ABET) and include courses in trigonometry, algebra, science, and engineering specializations.

Similar fields of study, including electrical engineering technology and mechanical engineering technology, are available in four-year bachelor's degree programs, but most robotics technicians do not pursue this career path. Students who earn a bachelor's degree are much more likely to pursue a career as an engineering technologist.

Related College Majors
- Robotics Technology

Adult Job Seekers

Robotics technicians draw upon a number of transferrable skills, including those of an electrician, mechanic, and computer programmer. Adults who already work as industrial machine operators or simply work in a factory setting might pursue work as a robotics technician. However, they will most likely need to return to school to acquire the proper training; it is unusual for a robotics technician to learn his or her trade completely on the job, though many complete internships.

Professional Certification and Licensure

Robotics technicians are not required to seek certification or licensure in their field, but it is recommended. Some companies offers a number of certifications tailored to different careers in and principles of robotics. For example, one can take certification tests in categories such as application lifecycle management, business planning and alignment, complex and embedded systems, design and development, and enterprise modernization. Local robotics societies also offer workshops and seminars for professional development.

Additional Requirements

Robotics technicians must be efficient and precise. They should work well with others, appreciate the needs of organizations, and be able to execute their job in the fulfillment of those needs. They enjoy working with their hands but are also adept at working with computers. Technicians must be able to think both analytically and creatively. The creation and maintenance of robotic systems requires technicians to draw upon all of their talents and knowledge. Due to the noisy conditions common in factories and plants, it is important that robotics technicians be able to focus on their work despite distractions.

Fun Facts

One of the earliest uses of the word "robot" was in the 1920s play, *Rossum's Universal Robots*, by Czech writer Karel Capek. It comes from the Slavonic word "robota," which means servitude, drudgery, or forced labor. In the play, robots, which are produced to do the work humans prefer not to, eventually rise up in revolt.

Source: sciencefriday.com/segment/04/22/2011/science-diction-the-origin-of-the-word-robot.html

HERB, the home butler robot, has been developed at Pittsburgh's Carnegie Mellon University's Robotics Institute to help people live independently at home. His name stands for "home exploring robot butler."

Sources: https://www.yahoo.com/katiecouric/meet-herb-your-robot-butler-205850797.html and http://www.cmu.edu/herb-robot/

EARNINGS AND ADVANCEMENT

Earnings of robotics technicians depend on the type and size of the employer and the individual's education, experience and job responsibilities. Mean annual earnings of robotics technicians were $54,160 in 2013. The lowest ten percent earned less than $33,490, and the highest ten percent earned more than $80,070.

Robotics technicians may receive paid vacations, holidays, and sick days; life and health insurance; and retirement benefits. These are usually paid by the employer. Some employers have profit-sharing and/or tuition reimbursement plans and also reimburse job-related travel expenses.

Metropolitan Areas with the Highest Employment Level in this Occupation

Metropolitan area	Employment [1]	Employment per thousand jobs	Hourly mean wage
San Jose-Sunnyvale-Santa Clara, CA	690	0.75	$25.11
Boston-Cambridge-Quincy, MA	670	0.38	$28.94
Phoenix-Mesa-Glendale, AZ	590	0.33	$24.77
Santa Ana-Anaheim-Irvine, CA	440	0.31	$22.10
Los Angeles-Long Beach-Glendale, CA	360	0.09	$26.67
San Diego-Carlsbad-San Marcos, CA	330	0.25	$28.42
Baltimore-Towson, MD	290	0.23	$32.47
Atlanta-Sandy Springs-Marietta, GA	290	0.13	$27.60
Chicago-Joliet-Naperville, IL	270	0.07	$32.01
Oklahoma City, OK	270	0.45	$18.53

[1]Does not include self-employed. Source: Bureau of Labor Statistics

EMPLOYMENT AND OUTLOOK

Nationally, there were approximately 17,500 electro-mechanical technicians, of which robotics technicians are a part, employed in 2012. Employment is expected to grow slower than the average for all occupations through the year 2022, which means employment is projected to increase 1 percent to 7 percent. Many job openings will result from the need to replace robotics technicians who transfer to other occupations or retire.

Employment Trend, Projected 2012–22

Total, All Occupations: 11%

Robotics Technicians: 4%

Engineering Technicians (All): 1%

Note: "All Occupations" includes all occupations in the U.S. Economy. Source: U.S. Bureau of Labor Statistics, Employment Projections Program

Related Occupations
- Computer Service Technician
- Computer-Control Machine Tool Operator
- Computer-Control Tool Programmer
- Electrical & Electronics Engineer
- Electrician
- Electromechanical Equipment Assembler
- Engineering Technician

Conversation With . . .
PAUL CARUSO

Robotics Technician
iRobot Corporation, Bedford, MA
Electronics & Robotics Professional, 33 years

1. What was your individual career path in terms of education/training, entry-level job, or other significant opportunity?

After graduating from James Madison High School in New York, I went on to earn a two-year degree from The College of Staten Island in electrical engineering and a one-year certificate in electronic technology at the PSI Institute. In the past, I worked as a technician for Tandy Corporation. I was a field technician for Circuit City for almost seven years, before going to work for iRobot in 2006. Today, I'm a Senior Quality Engineering Technician with iRobot Corporation.

2. What are the most important skills and/or qualities for someone in your profession?

This position requires a lot of troubleshooting. Working in robotics, it's important to take a methodical approach to solving a problem—starting at one point and working step-by step until you solve the issue. That requires patience.

3. What do you wish you had known going into this profession?

If I had known what I know now, I would have continued with my studies to get my bachelor's degree, plus take other classes along the way to broaden my knowledge in areas outside of electronics and electrical engineering.

4. Are there many job opportunities in your profession? In what specif-ic areas?

Yes, there are many opportunities in robotics, including video conferencing/remote presence; medical electronics and telemedicine (which is the remote delivery of clinical information and health care services via the Internet or satellite, etc.); home and elderly independent-living robotics; and many more.

Robotics technicians often find themselves working for a robotics company, such as iRobot, in a diagnostic lab environment. Since robots are such complicated machines, special parts and tools are required to service them that are not always accessible away from the lab. As robots become more pervasive in society, there will be a need for technicians to travel into the field for troubleshooting, updates, and repairs—particularly for larger robots installed in hospitals, manufacturing plants, and elderly care facilities that are not easily transportable.

5. How do you see your profession changing in the next five years? What role will technology play in those changes, and what skills will be required?

Constant breakthroughs in technology mean we will see advances in robotics that were impossible to consider only a few years ago. You will soon be able to buy cars that drive themselves. There will be robots working together to clean the house and ambidextrous robots helping the elderly with daily tasks. This will create a need for more technical people to design and maintain these robots. We will need people with mechanical, software and electrical engineering degrees who can work together to solve complicated problems.

6. What do you enjoy most about your job? What do you enjoy least about your job?

I truly enjoy working with my hands. And there's great satisfaction that comes with solving a difficult problem in a way that will help improve the quality of the product. What I don't enjoy? Of course, there's always paperwork involved with any job, which isn't quite as exciting.

7. Can you suggest a valuable "try this" for students considering a ca-reer in your profession?

I suggest that students attend electronic trade shows, where they can walk the show floor and get a glimpse at the latest technology hitting markets. Not only is it a great way to see cutting-edge technology, but it's also a great way to make connections with companies that may be hiring or seeking internship candidates. Internships are critical to breaking into a career in robotics.

SELECTED SCHOOLS

Many technical and community colleges offer programs in or related to robotics technology. Commercial trade schools are also an option. Students are advised to consult with their school guidance counselor or research area post-secondary schools to find the right program.

MORE INFORMATION

American Society for Engineering Education
1818 N Street NW, Suite 600
Washington, DC 20036-2479
202.331.3500
www.asee.org

Association for Unmanned Vehicle Systems International
2700 S. Quincy Street, Suite 400
Arlington, VA 22206
703.845.9671
www.auvsi.org

Institute of Electrical and Electronics Engineers
3 Park Avenue, 17th Floor
New York, NY 10016-5997
212.419.7900
www.ieee.org

National Robotics Training Center
1951 Pisgah Road
P.O. Box 100549
Florence, SC 29501-0549
800.228.5745
www.nrtcenter.com

Technology Student Association
1914 Association Drive
Reston, VA 20191-1540
703.860.9000
www.tsaweb.org

Molly Hagan/Editor

Textile Machine Operator

Snapshot

Career Cluster: Manufacturing; Production
Interests: Machinery, machine maintenance and repair, inspection, quality control, manufacturing
Earnings (Yearly Average): $27,270
Employment & Outlook: Decline Expected

OVERVIEW

Sphere of Work

Textile machine operators control equipment that produces textiles for a range of products, including clothes, tires, and roofing material. They are in charge of tending to the equipment and ensuring everything is working correctly. Workers load, start, control, stop, and clean the machinery. They inspect the textiles produced by the machines for quality control. It is a physical job that requires great attention to detail and the ability to perform several physically demanding tasks.

Work Environment

Commonly, a textile machine operator works in a textile mill. Many of these facilities are well ventilated and use climate control to counter the heat generated by the machines. The machines create a noisy environment, so workers usually wear ear protection and protective clothing. If the machine operator is around any chemical compounds used to treat textiles, such as bleach, protective breathing equipment may also be required.

Profile

Working Conditions: Work Indoors
Physical Strength: Medium Work
Education Needs: On-The-Job Training, High School Diploma or G.E.D., High School Diploma with Technical Education
Licensure/Certification: Usually Not Required
Opportunities For Experience: Part-Time Work
Holland Interest Score*: RCE, RIE

* See Appendix A

Occupation Interest

The physical demands of working as a textile machine operator require an individual to be in good shape. It is also important for a worker to be mindful of his or her surroundings, since the machines work at high speeds and can easily injure a person. Textile machine operators are collaborative people who enjoy working with others to create a quality product. Workers with a variety of backgrounds enter the field, but a strong knowledge of machinery is preferred.

A Day in the Life—Duties and Responsibilities

Different machines and textile products call for different tasks. Before loading the machine with either natural or synthetic fibers, an operator inspects the machine to guarantee it is working properly. Some workers will first run the machine without any fibers in it to see that it functions smoothly. This kind of inspection is done regularly throughout the day, particularly during shift changes. Fibers are then inspected and cleaned of any foreign matter through processes called carding and combing.

There are several kinds of carding machines used to treat fiber, including drum carders and cottage carders. These machines straighten, clean, and disentangle fibers. Since these machines operate at high speeds, an operator must be careful not to get limbs or clothing stuck in any of the moving parts. Once cleaned and straightened, the fibers are drawn into a substance called a sliver that is then loaded onto spinning machines. These machines create yarn, which is then either woven, tufted, or bonded through heat or chemicals, depending on the desired final product. Whatever the product may be, the final step is finishing the textile. This is done through dying and sometimes treating the textiles with protective products.

During all of these processes, textile machine operators monitor the various automated machines and textiles. They work together to report and repair any malfunctions in the machinery. They are in charge of setting the timing on the machinery and threading the yarn onto harnesses. As the yarn is run through the different machines, an operator has to monitor its progress for quality control.

Duties and Responsibilities

- **Maintaining and adjusting machinery**
- **Adjusting rates of functioning**
- **Repairing breaks in fiber**
- **Monitoring supplies of yarn**
- **Controlling colors and patterns for textiles**

OCCUPATION SPECIALTIES

Extruder Operators

Extruder Operators set up and run machines that extrude and color manmade fibers for textiles.

Dye Reel Operators

Dye Reel Operators tend machines that bleach or dye cloth in rope form and machine-sew pieces together.

Bleachers

Bleachers tend machines that dye or bleach yarn wound on beams, tubes or spring coils.

WORK ENVIRONMENT

Physical Environment

A manufacturing setup in a textile mill is the most common environment. Operators labor in close quarters with other workers.

Plant Environment

Because of the airborne materials produced by fibers and chemicals, textile mills are well ventilated. The machinery generates a lot of noise. Workers have to be careful not to injure themselves on the machines.

Human Environment

Working with textile machinery requires a lot of collaboration. Operators interact with each other to produce quality products and to ensure the machines are working properly. They must often report to supervisors, who oversee production.

Technological Environment

Operators use heavy, automated machinery to produce textiles. These include spinning mules, ring spinners, and weaving machines. Small hand tools such as wrenches and screwdrivers are used to make repairs. Safety equipment such as work boots, gloves, and masks are often mandatory.

Transferable Skills and Abilities

Interpersonal/Social Skills
- Being able to work independently

Organization & Management Skills
- Following instructions
- Paying attention to and handling details
- Performing routine work

Technical Skills
- Using technology to process information
- Working with machines, tools or other objects

EDUCATION, TRAINING, AND ADVANCEMENT

High School/Secondary

Many textile companies require their entry-level workers to have a high school diploma or the equivalent. There are some basic courses offered at high schools that would benefit someone interested in becoming a textile machine operator, including mathematics, mechanical drawing, and any machine-related course.

Suggested High School Subjects
- Clothing & Textiles
- English
- Industrial Arts
- Machining Technology
- Shop Math
- Shop Mechanics

Famous First

The first textile machine capable of operating efficiently in an industrial setting was manufactured in 1786 by Hugh Orr with the help of Robert and Alexander Barr in their shop in Bridgewater, Mass. In November 1786 the Senate granted them a financial reward of £200 for their work, followed by six tickets in the land lottery of the time.

Postsecondary

Although most textile companies do not require an applicant to have a college education, there are several technical schools and community colleges that provide training relevant to the profession. Some schools offer programs in machine and electrical repair. These programs provide students with formal classroom instruction as well as hands-on training. Any courses concerning machinery repair and maintenance would be beneficial to a potential operator. It would also be helpful to take some computer-related courses to build knowledge of new technologies.

Related College Majors

* Industrial/Manufacturing Technology

Adult Job Seekers

Those considering employment as a textile machine operator should research the average income and job outlook of the profession. Textile machine operators commonly work forty hours a week, but large orders can sometimes require overtime. Individuals should think about this type of schedule and be sure it works with their personal and family life.

Those with no manufacturing or machinery background should look into a training program at a community college or technical school, as employers are more likely to hire someone who has completed such a program. These schools sometimes offer job-placement programs, and textile companies will look to them for prospective new hires. Such schools also offer a great opportunity for networking.

Professional Certification and Licensure

Some textile trade associations and other related groups offer training programs for textile machine operators. Workers can take online courses through the American Association of Textile Colorists and Chemists that cover textile fundamentals and the finishing process. Textile mills will also provide on-the-job training. The length of the training process varies depending on the complexity of the machine and the tasks the worker will be performing. As the training progresses, an operator will learn how to prepare, load, operate, and perform preventative maintenance on the machines.

There are some textile-machine manufacturers who provide on-site training workshops. Sometimes these manufacturers will even send out a representative to textile mills for training. Manufacturer Karl Mayer, for example, provides regional training schools around the globe that offer specialized courses on different textile machines. The courses cover practical application of the machines, pattern preparation, assembly and disassembly of parts, and other related areas. Some companies may require an individual to take a training course in order to be considered for promotions.

Additional Requirements

Being a textile machine operator is physically demanding. It requires long periods of time standing, kneeling, bending, and sometimes climbing. Applicants should be in great physical shape and possess a lot of stamina and manual dexterity. An operator needs to be aware of his or her surroundings at all times because the machines can cause severe injuries. If an operator is hoping to advance in the profession, he or she should be open to learning new skills. Operators who show interest in taking on further responsibilities are more likely to be promoted to supervisor, instructor, or other higher-paying positions.

Fun Fact

Textile Merchants and Weavers have their own saint: St. Anthony Mary Claret, the son of a weaver born in Salient, in Catalonia, Spain, in 1807. He served as archbishop of Santiago de Cuba, and died in a Cistercian monastery in France, in 1870.

Source: http://www.catholic.org/saints/saint.php?saint_id=1452

EARNINGS AND ADVANCEMENT

Textile machine operators advance by receiving training and working with less need for supervision. Earnings depend on the type of mill and the individual's skill, speed and accuracy. Median annual earnings of textile machine operators were $27,270 in 2014.

Textile machine operators may receive paid vacations, holidays, and sick days; life and health insurance; and retirement benefits. These are usually paid by the employer. Most companies also operate stores in which employees may buy products made by the company at discount prices.

Metropolitan Areas with the Highest
Employment Level in this Occupation

Metropolitan area	Employment	Employment per thousand jobs	Annual mean wage
Dalton, GA	1,730	26.87	$26,490
Los Angeles-Long Beach-Glendale, CA	1,080	0.27	$24,080
Atlanta-Sandy Springs-Marietta, GA	900	0.38	$31,100
Greenville-Mauldin-Easley, SC	850	2.76	$28,940
Greensboro-High Point, NC	660	1.89	$26,430
Hickory-Lenoir-Morganton, NC	620	4.33	$25,740
Chattanooga, TN-GA	620	2.70	$32,210
Anderson, SC	550	9.03	$29,730
Spartanburg, SC	530	4.22	$30,080
Charlotte-Gastonia-Rock Hill, NC-SC	480	0.53	$28,610

Source: Bureau of Labor Statistics

EMPLOYMENT AND OUTLOOK

There were about 70,000 textile machine operators employed nationally in 2014. Employment is expected to decline through the year 2024. Automation and textile products imported from other countries will reduce the need for workers. Most openings will occur to replace workers who retire or leave the occupation.

Related Occupations

- Apparel Worker
- Bindery Worker
- Computer-Control Machine Tool Operator
- Laundry/Dry Cleaning Machine Operator
- Shoemaker & Repairer
- Upholsterer

Conversation With . . .
JOE DICESARE

Footwear Materials Developer, Nike, Inc.
Beaverton, Oregon
Materials development profession, 2 years

1. What was your individual career path in terms of education/training, entry-level job, or other significant opportunity?

Whether putting together LEGO® bricks in elementary school or solving complex math problems in high school and college, I've always had an interest in solving problems. This naturally led me down the path of accelerated math and science education. Originally, I planned to become a civil engineer and I knew North Carolina State University offered many engineering programs.

A high school advisor told me about an amazing opportunity, a Centennial Scholarship to NCSU's College of Textiles. That meant I had to become a textile engineer, but the scholarship included enrichment funds for career development. I went to an open house where a professor told me that the College of Textile's classes are small—for example, fifteen people, instead of maybe one hundred in some civil engineering classes. Coming from a small high school, that was a selling point. I realized the professors were genuinely interested in my well-being. So, I went through the process, was awarded a Centennial Scholarship, and majored in textile engineering. The scholarship put me in the spotlight as a leader in and out of the classroom and allowed me to grow my network of connections. It kept pressure on me to keep performing at a high level.

During junior year, I started looking at companies that would combine my passion for materials and engineering with my love of sports, so I applied to Nike, Adidas, Under Armour, Columbia, and Patagonia. I even used part of my scholarship's enrichment funds to visit companies on the West Coast and met with alumni who worked at these companies.

I applied for several internships, but Nike picked me to be a material operations intern in summer 2013. This was a major turning point. I treated every day there as if it were an interview, and made it clear to my manager that I would like to return for a full-time position after my senior year. I stayed in touch with him, and they hired me soon after graduation.

As a footwear materials developer, I work to manage our materials strategy. I work for our Global Football Office—soccer, in the U.S. I work on materials strategies, building a toolbox of materials that are tested and proven. I look at their performance and cost.

2. What are the most important skills and/or qualities for someone in your profession?

My textile engineering degree allows me to work with material vendors to develop materials that are suitable for footwear applications. I still use my textile knowledge in terms of my understanding of how certain materials act and how they are made.

You also need "soft skills," such as being able to communicate effectively and to work within a team. Personal skills—like being someone who's pleasant to work with—are a huge benefit, especially going into an entry-level position.

3. What do you wish you had known going into this profession?

My major was very focused on the molecular level of fibers and fabrics, but did not cover how materials could be applied to footwear applications. I would have liked more information on that.

4. Are there many job opportunities in your profession? In what specific areas?

Yes, there are opportunities for entry level positions involving all different material types, even outside of textiles. As a footwear material developer, I work across many functions including design, development, engineering, costing, and marketing.

5. How do you see your profession changing in the next five years, what role will technology play in those changes, and what skills will be required?

I see an increased emphasis on material development in my particular area, and an increased emphasis on how we work with material vendors.

6. What do you enjoy most about your job? What do you enjoy least about your job?

I enjoy the collaboration. Working with people to achieve a common goal is one of my favorite things to do. Whether training together in sports, or trying to implement a new material at work, knowing that bright and motivated people are around me is a great feeling.

Nike is an enormous place. I'm constantly meeting new people who have different backgrounds and skill sets. This is great, but it can be difficult when I'm looking for the right person to reach out to for a specific need.

7. Can you suggest a valuable "try this" for students considering a career in your profession?

Someone who is interested in the sports performance field should go to a sporting event and talk to some of the players. Ask why they bought the shoes they are wearing and what they do or don't like about them. Having a base understanding of what the consumer wants is essential. In my position, I always keep in mind how a material I am developing will benefit the consumer.

MORE INFORMATION

American Association of Textile Chemists and Colorists
P.O. Box 12215
Research Triangle Park, NC 27709
919.549.8141
www.aatcc.org

American Textile Machinery Association
201 Park Washington Court
Falls Church, VA 22046
703.538.1789
www.atmanet.org

American Textile Manufacturers Institute
Communications Division
1130 Connecticut Avenue, NW
Suite 1200
Washington, DC 20036-3954
202.862.0500
www.textileweb.com

National Textile Association Industry
6 Beacon Street, Suite 1125
Boston, MA 02108
617.542.8220
www.nationaltextile.org

Union of Needletrades, Industrial and Textile Employees
275 7th Avenue
New York, NY 10001-6708
212.265.7000
www.uniteunion.org

Patrick Cooper/Editor

Tool & Die Maker

Snapshot

Career Cluster: Manufacturing

Interests: Machinery, engineering, mechanical drawing, drafting, computer science, mathematics

Earnings (Yearly Average): $48,890

Employment & Outlook: Decline Expected

OVERVIEW

Sphere of Work

Tool and die makers produce an assortment of precision metal parts, tools, fixtures, and other instruments. Metal forms, known as dies, are also produced. These items are produced using computerized and mechanically controlled machines. Makers analyze specifications and schematics for what they are producing, set up the machines needed for production, and then operate the machines. They also perform repairs on the instruments they produce.

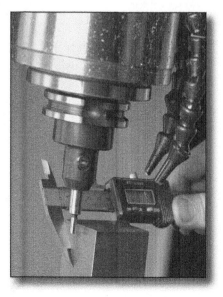

Work Environment

Tool and die makers work in machine shops and other manufacturing environments that are well ventilated. They frequently work with tools and machinery that can present a variety of hazards. Because of this, makers are required to follow various safety precautions, including wearing safety gear such as helmets and goggles, which help protect them from extreme heat and metal shards. Tool and die makers collaborate with other workers to ensure tools and die are produced quickly and accurately.

Profile

Working Conditions: Work Indoors
Physical Strength: Medium Work
Education Needs: On-The-Job Training, High School Diploma with Technical Education, Junior/Technical/Community College, Apprenticeship
Licensure/Certification: Recommended
Opportunities For Experience: Apprenticeship
Holland Interest Score*: RIE

* See Appendix A

Occupation Interest

Being a tool and die maker requires great attention to design specifics, an understanding of schematics, and the ability to collaborate with others. The job attracts people who are very detail oriented and enjoy working with their hands. Tool and die makers have a strong knowledge of a variety of machinery, allowing them to produce and repair a broad range of items. Their work is dynamic and involves solving new problems on a daily basis.

A Day in the Life—Duties and Responsibilities

Tool and die makers, like others in the machinery industry, are detail-oriented people with a strong knowledge of how things work. Their day-to-day responsibilities can vary depending on the product being made or repaired. The time it takes to complete a job also depends on what is being produced.

The work of a tool and die maker begins with analyzing blueprints, schematics, or other drawings created by engineers. Makers rely heavily on computers for these drawings. They use computer-aided design (CAD) and computer-aided manufacturing (CAM) programs to assess a job. Once the job is assessed, a maker will set up the machinery needed to manufacture the tools and dies. The machinery and tools used in production vary, but they are typically manual, automatic, or computer numerical control (CNC) machines or tools. Makers use these computer programs to create blueprints for tools and dies.

After the parts for the tool or die have been cut, a maker will file or grind them as necessary so that new manufactured parts fit together smoothly. Tools and dies are inspected for dimensional accuracy and defects. Toolmakers then test the tool produced to ensure quality. Tool and die makers produce a variety of tools and other metal forms. They can also create metal molds for use in die-casting composite materials and plastics.

Duties and Responsibilities

- Visualizing the final product from blueprints, sketches, models, or written specifications
- Determining the type of stock, layout, machining, and assembly operations needed to complete the job
- Setting up and operating machine tools
- Using hand tools to smooth and finish the workpiece
- Using precision measuring instruments to check for proper dimensions of the workpiece

OCCUPATION SPECIALTIES

Stamping Die Makers

Stamping Die Makers lay out, fit, assemble and finish metal castings to make and repair stamping dies.

Die Sinkers

Die Sinkers lay out, machine and finish impression cavities in die blocks to produce forging dies.

Mold Makers

Mold Makers lay out, machine, fit, assemble and finish metal parts to make and repair dies for diecasting of metal products.

Tool Makers

Tool Makers analyze specifications, lay out stock and operate machine tools to fabricate or repair cutting tools and other machine tools.

Bench and Stamping Die Makers

Bench and Stamping Die Makers lay out, fit and assemble casting and metal parts to make and repair stamping dies.

Die Finishers

Die Finishers grind, file, sand and polish surfaces of metalworking die members to specified shapes and smoothness and inspect dies for model conformity.

WORK ENVIRONMENT

Physical Environment

Machine shops and other manufacturing settings are the primary locations where tool and die makers perform their work. When using computers for design and manufacturing processes, some tool and die makers work in a more office-like environment.

Plant Environment

Tool and die makers generally work in manufacturing environments that are filled with heavy machinery. These shops present many hazards, so makers must be constantly aware of their surroundings and follow safety standards.

Transferable Skills and Abilities

Interpersonal/Social Skills
- Being patient

Organization & Management Skills
- Following instructions
- Paying attention to and handling details

Technical Skills
- Performing scientific, mathematical and technical work
- Working with machines, tools or other objects

Human Environment

Tool and die makers collaborate regularly with colleagues and supervisors in the shop. They also communicate with clients and manufacturers.

Technological Environment

Tool and die makers use a wide range of technologies, including small hand tools, such as wrenches and screwdrivers, and large, automated machinery for cutting metal. They use CAM and CAD programs and CNC machines for metal design and manufacturing.

EDUCATION, TRAINING, AND ADVANCEMENT

High School/Secondary

Most employers of tool and die makers require that applicants have a high school diploma or the equivalent. Several basic high school courses can provide a strong background in mathematics and computer science, which are crucial to the field. Math courses such as trigonometry and geometry should be considered. Students interested in tool and die making can also benefit from drafting, mechanical drawing, and engineering courses. Many high schools offer shop classes that provide students with experience in basic machinery, and some of these shops also provide metalworking instruction.

Suggested High School Subjects
- Algebra
- Applied Math
- Applied Physics
- Blueprint Reading
- Drafting
- English

- Geometry
- Industrial Arts
- Machining Technology
- Mechanical Drawing
- Metals Technology
- Physics
- Shop Mechanics
- Trigonometry
- Welding

Famous First

The first pneumatic hammer was made by Charles Brady King of Detroit, Mich., in 1890. The hammer was exhibited at the World's Columbian Exposition in Chicago in 1893. The following year, King received a patent on the hammer. By 1896, King was making some of the first automobiles.

Postsecondary

Many employers require a tool and die maker to have a bachelor's degree in a relevant field, such as mathematics or engineering. Several advanced positions require a postsecondary degree. Colleges and universities offer many degree programs beneficial to those interested in the field, including applied calculus, advanced computer science, physics, and mechanical engineering.

Many technical and vocational schools offer programs related to tool and die making. These training programs can last from several weeks to several months, and the schools often provide students with certification and help them find entry-level positions in the industry upon completion.

Those who do not receive training through a technical or vocational school will commonly receive training through an apprenticeship program. Apprenticeships can last four to five years. Some combine on-the-job hours with formal classroom instruction. In some circumstances, apprentices can obtain program sponsorships from local unions or manufacturers.

Related College Majors
- Tool & Die Making/Technology

Adult Job Seekers

An individual with no experience in the field should consider enrolling in a technical or vocational school that offers a relevant training or certification program. An employer is much more likely to hire someone who has completed a training program or earned a degree in a related field. Additionally, vocational schools are a great place for individuals interested in tool and die making to network with more experienced people in the field. Many schools offer job-placement programs. People new to the field should be prepared for years of on-the-job training and always be open for more instruction.

Professional Certification and Licensure

There are several certification programs offered for tool and die makers. Certification is offered through training facilities, state apprenticeship boards, and schools. Becoming certified helps a tool and die maker find employment. In addition, certification can lead to opportunities for advancement and higher pay. To become certified, tool and die makers have to demonstrate their skills and knowledge and take a written exam.

Additional Requirements

Tool and die makers need to be very detail oriented in order to follow specifications correctly. The use of CAD and CAM programs requires strong math and computer skills. Stamina and physical health is also required, as tool and die makers often work long hours.

Fun Fact

Tool and die makers used tools and dies (a kind of industrial cookie cutter) to cut metals. But they also use a process called "stamping" to punch products through sheet metal. Think of a door hinge, which might use three steps to punch holes and bend the edge.

Source: http://oldnorthwestterritory.northwestquarterly.com/2014/08/tool-die-the-secret-to-creating-almost-anything/"

EARNINGS AND ADVANCEMENT

Earnings of tool and die makers depend on the size, geographic location, and union affiliation of the employer, and the employee's training, skill and experience. In 2014, tool and die makers had median annual earnings of $48,890. The lowest ten percent earned less than $31,310, and the highest ten percent earned more than $72,120.

Tool and die makers may receive paid vacations, holidays, and sick days; life and health insurance; and retirement benefits. These are usually paid by the employer.

Metropolitan Areas with the Highest Employment Level in this Occupation

Metropolitan area	Employment	Employment per thousand jobs	Annual mean wage
Warren-Troy-Farmington Hills, MI	4,700	4.10	$52,910
Chicago-Joliet-Naperville, IL	4,330	1.15	$50,800
Cleveland-Elyria-Mentor, OH	2,560	2.53	$56,300
Grand Rapids-Wyoming, MI	1,900	4.66	$50,280
Milwaukee-Waukesha-West Allis, WI	1,740	2.12	$50,540
Detroit-Livonia-Dearborn, MI	1,500	2.09	$59,770
Los Angeles-Long Beach-Glendale, CA	1,170	0.29	$52,150
St. Louis, MO-IL	980	0.75	$49,020
Minneapolis-St. Paul-Bloomington, MN-WI	970	0.53	$56,720
Nashville-Davidson--Murfreesboro--Franklin, TN	910	1.12	$48,720

Source: Bureau of Labor Statistics

EMPLOYMENT AND OUTLOOK

There were approximately 78,000 tool and die makers employed nationally in 2014. Employment of tool and die makers is expected to decline through the year 2024.This is primarily due to increases in automation, such as computer-controlled machine tools and computer-aided design, that have made workers more efficient.

Related Occupations

- Computer-Control Machine Tool Operator
- Machinist
- Photoengraver & Lithographer

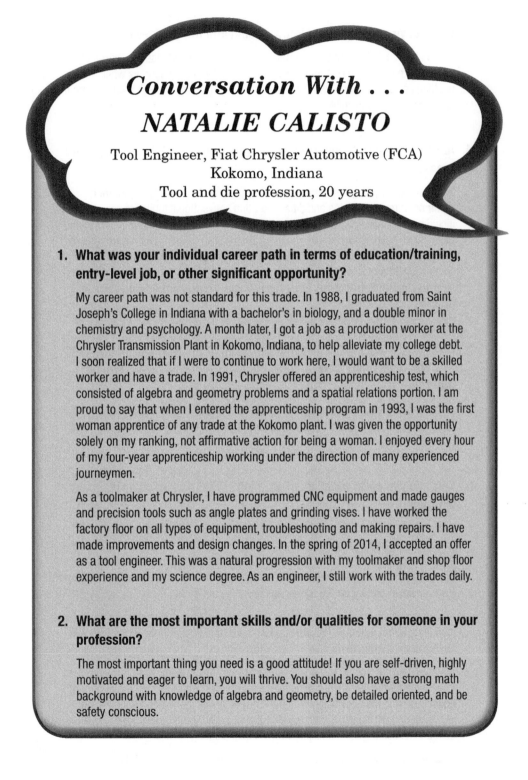

Conversation With . . .
NATALIE CALISTO

Tool Engineer, Fiat Chrysler Automotive (FCA)
Kokomo, Indiana
Tool and die profession, 20 years

1. What was your individual career path in terms of education/training, entry-level job, or other significant opportunity?

My career path was not standard for this trade. In 1988, I graduated from Saint Joseph's College in Indiana with a bachelor's in biology, and a double minor in chemistry and psychology. A month later, I got a job as a production worker at the Chrysler Transmission Plant in Kokomo, Indiana, to help alleviate my college debt. I soon realized that if I were to continue to work here, I would want to be a skilled worker and have a trade. In 1991, Chrysler offered an apprenticeship test, which consisted of algebra and geometry problems and a spatial relations portion. I am proud to say that when I entered the apprenticeship program in 1993, I was the first woman apprentice of any trade at the Kokomo plant. I was given the opportunity solely on my ranking, not affirmative action for being a woman. I enjoyed every hour of my four-year apprenticeship working under the direction of many experienced journeymen.

As a toolmaker at Chrysler, I have programmed CNC equipment and made gauges and precision tools such as angle plates and grinding vises. I have worked the factory floor on all types of equipment, troubleshooting and making repairs. I have made improvements and design changes. In the spring of 2014, I accepted an offer as a tool engineer. This was a natural progression with my toolmaker and shop floor experience and my science degree. As an engineer, I still work with the trades daily.

2. What are the most important skills and/or qualities for someone in your profession?

The most important thing you need is a good attitude! If you are self-driven, highly motivated and eager to learn, you will thrive. You should also have a strong math background with knowledge of algebra and geometry, be detailed oriented, and be safety conscious.

3. What do you wish you had known going into this profession?

I wish I had basic hydraulic, electrical, and pneumatic knowledge. It's extremely important to be able to understand and control these energy sources when you're working on equipment so that you won't get hurt. Your safety must always come first and it is your responsibility.

4. Are there many job opportunities in your profession? In what specific areas?

There are many job opportunities, including CNC machinist and programmer; repairing or revising molds and dies; operating conventional toolroom equipment including electric discharge machining (EDM), lathes and grinders; and performing bench work such as layout and gauge calibration. At FCA, tool and die workers also troubleshoot and repair equipment on the factory floor. You can choose to work in a small shop, in a medical device corporation or a larger factory, like the automotive industry. Tool and die workers also are needed in the aerospace field and in the military.

5. How do you see your profession changing in the next five years? What role will technology play in those changes, and what skills will be required?

In the next five years, technology will definitely change the profession. New equipment like 3D printers, laser cutters and machining centers will require programming skills.

6. What do you enjoy most about your job? What do you enjoy least about your job?

What I enjoy most about being a tool and die worker is how fulfilling it is. To read a blueprint, plan your project, and transform a block of steel into a usable machine detail with accurate print dimensions is very cool and satisfying. It's exciting to witness this transformation and it is a form of artwork. I feel like an artist when I put the completed project on the "done" bench.

As you gain experience, you gain confidence and speed. I also enjoy how much there is to learn about material, tooling, speeds, feeds, and securing the workpiece. I'm still exposed to something new almost every day.

However, this does come at a price. The thing I least enjoy is the factory environment. I love nature, fresh air and sunshine. Factories are loud with the mechanical hum of equipment, and the air is heavy with the smell of oil and lubricants. There are few windows, and we stand on concrete eight hours a day. Safety is a concern: I'm always aware that I could sustain an injury from a fall or a cut.

7. Can you suggest a valuable "try this" for students considering a career in your profession?

To discover if this occupation is right for you, take any high school or technical school shop course that uses bandsaws, mills, lathes or grinders. Many schools have a robotics team, which would offer design and programming opportunities. Take courses in AutoCAD, blueprint reading, "Machinery's Handbook," or drafting. An internship with a smaller tool and die shop would be invaluable. For entertainment, watch the show "How It's Made" on the Science Channel. It gives great insight into factory automation and quite often shows toolmakers at work on various equipment.

MORE INFORMATION

Association for Manufacturing Technology
7901 Westpark Drive
McLean, VA 22102
703.893.2900
www.amtonline.org

Fabricators & Manufacturers Association International
833 Featherstone Road
Rockford, IL 61107
815.399.8700
www.fmanet.org

National Institute for Metalworking Skills
10565 Fairfax Boulevard, Suite 203
Fairfax, VA 22030
703.352.4991
www.nims-skills.org

National Tooling and Machining Association
1357 Rockside Road
Cleveland, OH 44134
800.248.6862
www.ntma.org

Precision Metalforming Association
6363 Oak Tree Boulevard
Independence, OH 44131
216.901.8800
www.pma.org

Patrick Cooper/Editor

Transportation & Distribution Manager

Snapshot

Career Cluster: Business Administration; Manufacturing; Warehousing, Transportation and Distribution

Interests: Logistics, supply chain management, warehousing and distribution, customer service

Earnings (Yearly Average): $85,400

Employment & Outlook: Average Growth Expected

OVERVIEW

Sphere of Work

Transportation and distribution managers create, organize, and oversee the transport services of companies that manufacture and distribute products. The main duty of transportation and distribution managers is to ensure that stock arrives to expectant customers' on-time and in sound condition. Transportation and distribution managers play a crucial role in industries that deliver perishable goods, such as food and beverage distributors, medical supply companies, and chemical engineering firms.

Work Environment

Transportation and distribution managers work primarily in office settings, though their work may frequently take them to manufacturing facilities, distribution centers, or warehouses operated by their employing organizations. Transportation and distribution managers are in frequent communication with their fleet and related business operation centers, so much of their work is done out of a singular location where telephone, Internet, and radio communications systems are on hand.

Profile

Working Conditions: Work Indoors
Physical Strength: Light Work
Education Needs: Junior/ Technical/Community College, Bachelor's Degree
Licensure/Certification: Usually Not Required
Opportunities For Experience: Military Service, Part-Time Work
Holland Interest Score*: ESR

* See Appendix A

Occupation Interest

The field of transportation and distribution management traditionally attracts those who are interested in logistics and customer satisfaction. Like all managers, transportation and distribution management professionals must also possess leadership qualities that can motivate others.

A Day in the Life—Duties and Responsibilities

The main duties and responsibilities of transportation and distribution managers surround the supervision of shipments. In addition to planning, organizing, and managing shipping logistics, transportation and distribution managers must also direct warehouse and distribution staffs to ensure that orders of lading are properly fulfilled, safely packed, and sent to their intended destination.

Worker safety is an additional responsibility of transportation and distribution managers, who must ensure that goods are transported in accordance to state and federal laws protecting employee safety. Employees must also be briefed periodically on safety procedures in organizational meetings often directed by transportation and distribution managers. Documentation and legalities related to international shipping, including tariffs and security documentation also falls to transportation and distribution managers.

Transportation and distribution managers negotiate contracts with shipping and logistics firms based on their particular company's bulk shipping needs. They are also the point person for complaints related to merchandise received in poor condition or in incomplete or damaged supply. Lastly, transportation and distribution managers must coordinate with product designers and marketers to ensure that shipping containers and product packaging is shipped in the most economically viable manner possible, to maximize the efficiency of the shipping process and to keep costs reasonable.

Duties and Responsibilities

- Determining the most economical shipping methods, rates, and routes
- Selecting the route and carrier such as rail, air, road, water, pipeline, or combination
- Handling claims for lost or damaged goods
- Conducting studies of product planning, warehousing, packaging, and loading to reduce shipping costs
- Negotiating contracts with other companies to lease transportation equipment or property
- Evaluating and changing operating standards and procedures
- Keeping records of shipments, freight rates, product classifications, and applicable government regulations

WORK ENVIRONMENT

Physical Environment

Office settings predominate. However, given the supervisory nature of the role, managers may be required to visit manufacturing and shipping facilities on a regular basis.

Plant Environment

Transportation and distribution managers are employed across myriad industries, including industrial and chemical production, manufacturing, and agricultural processing.

Transferable Skills and Abilities

Communication Skills
- Speaking effectively
- Writing concisely

Interpersonal/Social Skills
- Cooperating with others
- Working as a member of a team

Organization & Management Skills
- Performing duties which change frequently
- Organization & Management Skills -Making decisions

Research & Planning Skills
- Developing evaluation strategies

Human Environment

Transportation and distribution managers routinely interact with fellow management staff and subordinate employees. Like all managers, they must be effective leaders who can communicate singular messages and motivate their staff.

Technological Environment

The technologies utilized by transportation and distribution managers include radio communication equipment, delivery tracking software, office systems technology, and global distribution programs.

EDUCATION, TRAINING, AND ADVANCEMENT

High School/Secondary

High school students can best prepare for a career as a transportation and distribution manager by completing coursework in algebra, calculus, geometry, trigonometry, biology, chemistry, physics, and computer science. Advanced mathematical and computer coursework can provide a good foundation for future work in logistics. Participation in extracurricular activities such as volunteerism and sports can also help students develop the leadership and motivational qualities that can be an important asset for careers in management.

Suggested High School Subjects
- Applied Math
- Business
- Business Math
- College Preparatory
- English
- Government

Famous First

The first transportation report was William Strickland's 1826 *Reports on Canals, Railways, Roads and Other Subjects made to the Pennsylvania Society for the Promotion of Internal Improvement*. It was a 51-page booklet, replete with 72 engraved plates, published by Carey & Lea, Philadelphia, Penn.

College/Postsecondary

Postsecondary education is traditionally a requirement for vacancies in transportation and distribution management, the occasional exception being in low volume corporations with small staffs. Postsecondary coursework that can contribute to the numerous skills and vast frame of reference required of transportation and distribution managers includes logistics, supply chain management, international business, finance, and economics. Exclusive master's level coursework is offered in some colleges and universities in the United States.

Related College Majors
- Business Administration & Management, General
- Logistics/Supply Chain Management
- Marketing Management & Research

Adult Job Seekers

Transportation and distribution managers work long hours, particularly during periods of the year such as the holiday season when demand for products is high and a high volume of shipping takes place. Even under normal circumstances, the breadth of responsibility required of the role requires a great deal of dedication and time, with frequent late work evenings and weekends required. Managers must also be on-call on a routine basis to assist in troubleshooting and dealing with discrepancies among staff members. The extensive experience and education required to be a successful transportation and distribution manager make it a difficult job for older professionals or those in a period of employment transition.

Professional Certification and Licensure

No specific certification or licensure is required, although this may vary from position to position given the nature of a transportation and distribution manager's employer.

Additional Requirements

Transportation and distribution managers must be skilled multi-taskers who can effectively manage multiple projects simultaneously. The leadership-oriented aspect of the position requires professionals who can motivate large staffs to complete complex tasks on schedule and within budget.

Fun Fact

Operations focuses on identifying and resolving the bottleneck in a process. One creation from this: the serpentine line (like the one at airport security) that funnels consumers through one large, demarcated line so that it's clear who has fairly reached the front of the line.

Source: http://www.slate.com/articles/business/operations/2012/06/queueing_theory_what_people_hate_ most_about_waiting_in_line_.html

EARNINGS AND ADVANCEMENT

Earnings depend on the size of the employer, the type of goods handled and the employee's qualifications and experience. Nationally, transportation and distribution managers had median annual earnings of $85,400 in 2014. The lowest 10 percent earned less than $50,640, and the highest 10 percent earned more than $146,110.

Transportation and distribution managers may receive paid vacations, holidays, and sick days; life and health insurance; and retirement benefits. These are usually paid by the employer.

Metropolitan Areas with the Highest Employment Level in this Occupation

Metropolitan area	Employment	Employment per thousand jobs	Annual mean wage
Los Angeles-Long Beach-Glendale, CA	4,280	1.06	$92,570
Chicago-Joliet-Naperville, IL	3,970	1.06	$90,620
New York-White Plains-Wayne, NY-NJ	2,850	0.53	$124,660
Houston-Sugar Land-Baytown, TX	2,750	0.97	$106,720
Atlanta-Sandy Springs-Marietta, GA	2,510	1.05	$92,470
Dallas-Plano-Irving, TX	1,910	0.85	$100,330
Minneapolis-St. Paul-Bloomington, MN-WI	1,740	0.95	$96,640
Seattle-Bellevue-Everett, WA	1,640	1.10	$102,730
Phoenix-Mesa-Glendale, AZ	1,630	0.89	$85,340
Washington-Arlington-Alexandria, DC-VA-MD-WV	1,540	0.65	$108,400

Source: Bureau of Labor Statistics

EMPLOYMENT AND OUTLOOK

Transportation and distribution managers held about 130,000 jobs nationally in 2014. Employment is expected to grow nearly as fast as the average for all occupations through the year 2024, which means employment is projected to increase 2 percent to 6 percent. As regulations governing transportation and distribution become more complex, companies will require transportation and distribution managers with expertise to direct shipping and receiving activities.

Employment Trend, Projected 2014–24

Business operations specialists: 7%

Total, all occupations: 7%

Transportation and Distribution Managers: 4%

Note: "All Occupations" includes all occupations in the U.S. Economy. Source: U.S. Bureau of Labor Statistics, Employment Projections Program

Related Occupations

- Production Coordinator

Related Military Occupations

- Transportation and Distribution manager
- Transportation Specialist

Conversation With . . .
LAURIE HEIN DENHAM

CTL, CAE, Sr. Director
Logistics & Supply Chain Academic Relations
APICS
Supply chain profession, 14 years

1. What was your individual career path in terms of education/training, entry-level job, or other significant opportunity?

I graduated from the University of Tennessee with a BS in education and a minor in psychology. I went on to earn a master's degree in social work at the same school. I couldn't find a job in my field so I worked for a staffing company. Three years later, I opened my own staffing company and we served a lot of non-profit associations. I sold the company to take the position of Executive Director of the American Society of Transportation and Logistics.

I was hired by an individual I met through a professional network who knew I'd had my own business; at that time, fourteen years ago, my field of expertise was business, not logistics. My logistics training has been on the job.

However, all of my schooling helped in my position. As executive director of a small association I wore a lot of hats: I oversaw governance with our Board of Directors and Board of Examiners as well as membership, certification, marketing, and business development. I worked with academics who wrote the exams for our certifications. I learned to ask a lot of questions, when to listen and how to get people to work collaboratively.

I was really impressed with the quality of people in the logistics industry. It's a relational business. You must have strong relationship skills to get goods moved; you must work together.

AST&L has now merged with APICS and my new role is to work with universities and K-12 schools globally to build awareness of the supply chain logistics industry. There are really good and plentiful jobs in logistics, and the industry does not have enough talent.

For instance, we worked with twelve high schools in the state of Florida to implement an entry-level credential program, the Global Logistics Associate (GLA). Through grant funding, we provided curriculum. At the end of their senior year, students took their GLA exam. Those who passed the exam received twelve hours of college credit to any state college in Florida. We'd like to see other states offer similar credit for industry credentials.

This is a fast-paced, always-changing business. There isn't anything that logistics doesn't touch. You could be a crane operator at a port, or do logistics analysis scanning data and trying to determine what mode of transportation will be most effective moving goods. You can negotiate for services, or sell services.

2. What are the most important skills and/or qualities for someone in your profession?

Agility and flexibility, because no day is the same. Soft skills are also very important because there's a lot of customer service involved and you're dealing with relationships. Analytical skills are also important.

3. What do you wish you had known going into this profession?

I wish something like the GLA program had been around because it offers a birds-eye overview of the industry that would have been helpful to me.

4. Are there many job opportunities in your profession? In what specific areas?

Recent statistics put logistics at the twenty-fourth fastest-growing career; U.S. News & World Report says this is the twelfth best business career with a $73,870 median salary. We're working to better define the jobs so the public better understands the field's career opportunities, because you could be a logistics manager in seven different companies and have seven different titles. Right now, logisticians are second to engineers as the most sought after graduates.

5. How do you see your profession changing in the next five years, what role will technology play in those changes, and what skills will be required?

I see huge growth in this profession. It's a global economy, and people are going to be moving goods. Manufacturing is returning to the U.S. and jobs are opening up because baby boomers are retiring. Technology is very important and changes rapidly. People worry that more robots will do their work, but advanced manufacturing will still need people to build and repair robots and people to make the parts. There are still going to be plenty of jobs.

6. What do you enjoy most about your job? What do you enjoy least about your job?

I enjoy that I get to work with academics, industry and students to have the necessary conversations to develop programs so students will have the skills and knowledge that employers need.

I least enjoy sitting at my desk but that's a necessary part of almost any job.

7. Can you suggest a valuable "try this" for students considering a career in your profession?

Check YouTube for videos that show the logistics process, starting with raw goods. Also, we have chapters all over the world so, working through them, you can find informational interviews, ask for a facilities tour, or attend an APICS event through our student scholar program. Many universities offer summer camps for a week that focus on the supply chain logistics industry, as well as advanced manufacturing.

SELECTED SCHOOLS

Most colleges and universities offer programs in business studies related to a career in transportation and distribution management. The student may also gain initial training in the field at a technical/community college. Graduate programs, too, are becoming increasingly available. Interested students are advised to check with their guidance counselor for information on relevant schools and programs.

MORE INFORMATION

APICS
8430 West Bryn Mawr Avenue
Suite 100
Chicago, IL 60631
773.867.1777
www.apics.org

International Society of Logistics
14625 Baltimore Avenue, Suite 303
Laurel, MD 20707
301.459.8446
www.sole.org

**National Industrial
Transportation League**
1700 N. Moore Street, Suite 1900
Arlington, VA 22209
703.524.5011
www.nitl.org

**The BWI Business Partnership,
Inc.**
1302 Concourse Drive Suite 105
Linthicum Heights, MD 21090
410.859.1000
www.bwipartner.org

**Transportation Management
Association of San Francisco**
180 Montgomery St. Suite 2360
San Francisco, CA 94104
415.392.0210
tmasfconnects.org

John Pritchard/Editor

Upholsterer

Snapshot

Career Cluster: Manufacturing; Production
Interests: Fabric, Design, Furniture Design, Interior Design, Visual Arts, Industrial Design
Earnings (Yearly Average): $31,890
Employment & Outlook: Slower than Average Growth Expected

OVERVIEW

Sphere of Work

Upholsterers cover couches, chairs, and other furniture with fabric and leather, and repair or replace their springs, padding, and stuffing. Some also cane chairs, re-web lawn furniture, make slipcovers, or build footstools, cornices, headboards, and other commonly upholstered wooden items. Some upholsterers specialize in restoring antiques or commercial furniture. Others specialize in custom automobile upholstery, re-covering worn-out seats and other interior components, fabricating new convertible covers, and replacing carpeting. Marine upholsterers cover indoor and outdoor seating on boats, and also fabricate boat covers, tops,

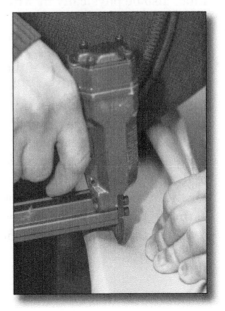

dodgers, and other items, while aviation upholsterers cover seats and the interiors of aircraft.

Work Environment

Upholsterers operate their own shops, are employed in government and various industries, such as tourism, and work in manufacturing settings. Most work a regular forty-hour week, although overtime might be necessary now and then. Self-employed upholsterers tend to work some evenings and weekends to accommodate their customers' schedules.

Profile

Working Conditions: Work Indoors
Physical Strength: Medium Work
Education Needs: On-The-Job Training, High School Diploma with Technical Education, Apprenticeship
Licensure/Certification: Usually Not Required
Opportunities For Experience: Apprenticeship, Part-Time Work
Holland Interest Score*: RCS

* See Appendix A

Occupation Interest

People who are attracted to upholstery careers are project oriented and enjoy solving problems with their hands. Their creativity allows them to visualize the final appearance of an upholstered item, such as a restored divan or bucket seats in a Corvette, while the ability to pay attention to details, measure accurately, and remain organized gets the job done. Upholsterers must also be physically fit with good eyesight at close range.

A Day in the Life—Duties and Responsibilities

Upholsterers spend most of their time reupholstering or restoring quality pieces of furniture. While customers usually bring small items to their shops, upholsterers typically make "house calls" for couches and other large pieces of furniture. They take along fabric samples and help each customer choose suitable fabric based on budget, fabric durability and safety, furniture style, interior decorating scheme, and other factors. They assess the condition of each piece, measure for the quantity of fabric and other materials that will be needed, estimate the price and time needed to make the repairs, and arrange to transport the furniture to the shop.

At the shop, the upholsterer removes the old cover from the piece of furniture and repairs the springs, frame, webbing, or support fabric, if needed. To reupholster the item, he or she prepares pattern pieces based on precise measurements, lays out the pattern pieces on fabric, and cuts around the pieces. The upholsterer also cuts out foam, cotton batting, or other cushioning material. He or she then attaches the cushioning material and the fabric to the frame with tacks or staples. Cushion covers, skirts, and other components are sewn with a sewing machine, with cording and zippers added as needed, and finished by hand. Some jobs involve special trims, buckles, or upholstery buttons, or special techniques such as tufting.

Specialty aviation, marine, and automobile upholsterers also cover metal frames and tend to work more with vinyl and leather, although they also sew cushions, valences, boat covers, and many other items from both natural and synthetic fabrics. Self-employed upholsterers must also perform many business tasks, including billing, bookkeeping, scheduling, marketing, and ordering supplies and fabric.

Upholsterers who work in manufacturing settings are more likely to perform assembly line work, where they handle just one or two operations, such as sewing, fitting, cutting, or installing.

Duties and Responsibilities

- Selecting and ordering materials
- Removing old covering, webbing, and padding from furniture
- Removing broken springs
- Replacing springs and webbing
- Covering springs with burlap, filling, and padding
- Measuring and cutting new upholstery fabric
- Covering and attaching fabric to frames
- Sewing or tacking ornamental trim or buttons to furniture
- Picking up and delivering furniture

OCCUPATION SPECIALTIES

Inside Upholsterers

Inside Upholsterers upholster inside sections of chairs and sofas, utilizing knowledge of upholstery materials and methods.

WORK ENVIRONMENT

Physical Environment

Upholsterers kneel, squat, and work in other awkward positions, and lift heavy furniture and bolts of fabric, and thus are prone to back and knee problems. They use sharp needles, powerful staple guns, and other hand and machine tools, which also put them at risk, especially for hand and eye injuries. The use of goggles, work shoes, and other protective gear is recommended.

Transferable Skills and Abilities

Organization & Management Skills
- Following instructions
- Making decisions
- Paying attention to and handling details

Research & Planning Skills
- Creating ideas
- Developing evaluation strategies

Technical Skills
- Working with your hands

Plant Environment

As the furniture industry has mostly moved overseas, and robotic systems have largely replaced humans in the automobile industry, few manufacturing positions exist for American upholsterers. Those who do work in factories are most at risk for repetitive injuries related to performing the same tasks over and over, as well as hand and eye injuries.

Human Environment

Apprentice upholsterers work closely with their supervisors. After becoming experienced, they might train assistants. Contact with customers is direct and usually involves some sales effort. Upholsterers may also consult with interior designers, textile artists, hotel management, and other professionals.

Technological Environment

Upholsterers use measuring tools, hammers, pliers, and other common hand tools; staple guns, button presses, grommet machines, webbing stretchers, hot knife cutters, and other tools of the trade; heavy-duty sewing machines and various hand-sewing tools and supplies; digital cameras to take photos of projects; and computers for ordering, billing, and other businesses uses, and sometimes for computer-aided design (CAD). Those who work in manufacturing settings use computerized sewing machines and additional industrial equipment.

EDUCATION, TRAINING, AND ADVANCEMENT

High School/Secondary

Students can pursue a vocational or academic program. Courses that are especially important include math, needed for measuring, determining square footage, billing, and other purposes, and sewing and textile courses, industrial arts, crafts, interior decorating, and courses that teach computer-aided design (CAD). Part-time or summer employment in used or antique furniture stores, volunteer work designing costumes or sewing theatrical sets, and other types of extracurricular experiences that build on sewing and industrial arts skills will be beneficial.

Suggested High School Subjects
- Applied Math
- Clothing & Textiles
- Crafts

- English
- Industrial Arts
- Shop Math
- Shop Mechanics
- Upholstery

Famous First

The first notable interior decorating firm was Herter Brothers, founded in New York City after the Civil War. The brothers, Gustave and Christian, began operating an upholstery business and branched out from there into furniture making and cabinetry. Later they incorporated paneling and ceiling design into their business, and eventually offered everything from flooring, carpeting, and draperies to general furnishings. Among their most prominent clients were the Vanderbilts and Jay Gould.

Postsecondary

Most upholsterers learn their skills in formal or informal apprenticeships, often in conjunction with some postsecondary training and independent learning experiences. Upholstery courses and programs are taught in vocational and technical schools, trade schools, and at some colleges, and are also offered through large fabric stores and craft schools. Students will have to learn sewing skills and techniques, including how to operate industrial-strength sewing machines, repair various frames, measure, cut, and attach different types of fabrics to different surfaces, and other skills. Students interested in self-employment should also consider taking business courses.

Related College Majors
- Upholstery

Adult Job Seekers

Adults with a background in woodworking or sewing are often drawn to upholstery work. Upholstery is also a common side business for interior decorators, antique dealers, car repair experts, and others. While a full-time job might offer a steady income, health insurance, and other benefits, many upholsterers with family obligations choose part-time self-employment, as they can set their own hours and work from home.

Apprentices typically become experienced enough to establish their own shops or move into supervisory positions after a few years. Some self-employed upholsterers have found that settling into a niche, such as antique furniture upholstery, is the best way to establish a reputation and thus increase their earnings, while others have found that broadening their services is the best route to success. Teaching and publishing books on upholstering techniques and designs are potential sources for additional income.

Professional Certification and Licensure

No license or certification is necessary, although some schools offer certification upon satisfactory completion of a program or course. The Industrial Fabrics Association International and the Marine Fabricators Association offer voluntary certification in the areas of Master Fabric Craftsman (MFC) and Industrial Fabric Manager (IFM).

Additional Requirements

A driver's license is usually needed; some upholsterers might need a commercial license for large vehicles used to transport furniture. Some amount of sales ability is needed for those who deal directly with customers.

Fun Fact

The earliest upholstered chairs and sofas were stuffed with all sorts of things: sawdust, grass, feathers, and the hair of horses, goats or deer. A far cry from the comforts of today, but so much better than the hard benches that came before.

Source: http://www.feathersdesign.com/the-history-of-upholstery/

EARNINGS AND ADVANCEMENT

Earnings depend on the geographic location of the employer and the employee's experience and skills. Median annual earnings of upholsterers were $31,890 in 2014. The lowest ten percent earned less than $19,940, and the highest ten percent earned more than $49,950.

Upholsterers may receive paid vacations, holidays, and sick days; life and health insurance; and retirement benefits. These are usually paid by the employer. Upholsterers may be required to purchase their own hand tools.

Metropolitan Areas with the Highest Employment Level in this Occupation

Metropolitan area	Employment	Employment per thousand jobs	Annual mean wage
Hickory-Lenoir-Morganton, NC	2,730	18.98	$38,680
Los Angeles-Long Beach-Glendale, CA	1,490	0.37	$29,540
Greensboro-High Point, NC	1,230	3.52	$33,560
Chicago-Joliet-Naperville, IL	680	0.18	$38,110
Elkhart-Goshen, IN	660	5.49	$28,340
Dallas-Plano-Irving, TX	650	0.29	$28,360
Houston-Sugar Land-Baytown, TX	600	0.21	$31,160
New York-White Plains-Wayne, NY-NJ	550	0.10	$40,340
Santa Ana-Anaheim-Irvine, CA	430	0.29	$30,310
Riverside-San Bernardino-Ontario, CA	400	0.32	$32,470

Source: Bureau of Labor Statistics

EMPLOYMENT AND OUTLOOK

There were approximately 40,000 upholsterers employed nationally in 2014. About one-third were self-employed. Employment of upholsterers is expected to grow slower than the average for all occupations through the year 2024, which means employment is projected to increase 0 percent to 3 percent. This is due to manufacturing firms using more durable coverings for furniture that do not need to be replaced as often, and as consumers now tend to replace worn furniture rather than reupholster it. Most job openings will be to replace workers who transfer to other occupations or retire, although some demand will be created by an increase in consumers who require the services of upholsterers to restore antique furniture or items with sentimental value.

Related Occupations

- Carpet Installer
- Textile Machine Operator

Conversation With . . .
RUSTY BERRYHILL

President, Kevin Charles Furniture
New Albany, Mississippi
Furniture and upholstery, 35 years

1. What was your individual career path in terms of education/training, entry-level job, or other significant opportunity?

When I was a kid, I never saw myself in the furniture business. I always wanted to be vet or a farmer, but the good Lord had other ideas. I got an associate's degree in industrial electronics, but it turned out I didn't like electricity. During that time, furniture manufacturing was the number one game in north Mississippi. A friend's father was vice president of a large company and offered me an entry-level position on an upholstery line. I steadily worked my way up until another company contacted me about becoming their quality control manager. Little did I know that the president and vice president of the company were leaving. At a young age, I got thrown into a VP of manufacturing position and learned all facets of furniture manufacturing.

In 2001, City Furniture in Florida contacted me about partnering up to start Kevin Charles Furniture. Fourteen years later, we're still manufacturing exclusively for City Furniture. I feel very fortunate that the position I'm in now wasn't just handed to me. The fact that I can have a conversation with an upholsterer about the best way to pleat an arm or how to make something happen is respected.

2. What are the most important skills and/or qualities for someone in your profession?

To be a good upholsterer, you have to be good with your hands, have excellent hand/eye coordination and pay attention to detail. Good communication skills are important—with customers, vendors and especially your coworkers, because it's a team effort.

There's a mindset that you have to get a college education or you won't amount to anything, but I don't have a bachelor's or master's degree. Whether or not you've got a degree, success depends on attitude and drive.

3. What do you wish you had known going into this profession?

There are so many management tools that teach better production techniques and process flow, but I wasn't aware of them. I wish they'd been made available to me earlier and I could have really studied them.

4. Are there many job opportunities in your profession? In what specific areas?

Upholstery is a dying art and there's an opportunity there. A good upholsterer is always in demand, not only here in Mississippi, but also in North Carolina furniture-making areas. Mississippi State University got a grant to create a training program for upholstery and furniture making. Older people are retiring, so we've got to entice the younger generation to learn these skills.

Seamstresses are also practice a lost art, due to overseas competition taking jobs away in previous years. We still need seamstresses to sew cushion covers together. Those positions are seeing a comeback here due to issues such as the rising middle class in Asia.

5. How do you see your profession changing in the next five years? What role will technology play in those changes, and what skills will be required?

The upholstery industry is increasingly utilizing the Lean Management System, an approach that improves efficiency and quality.

Today's workforce isn't like it used to be. In my early days, you had to work to make a living and you did whatever was needed to do so. Now we're trying to have a workplace with a good family atmosphere and trying to entice people to want to work here, while also remaining profitable.

Technology has evolved so much in the last twenty years, I can only imagine what the next twenty will entail. We rely on computers for scheduling, monitoring raw materials and instead of having to handwrite, you just scan a product onto a trailer. We use CNC cutting equipment to cut patterns, for cutting our wood frames and in the fabrication of foam products. We have high-tech sewing machines, but they still have to be fed and it takes a person to know which piece goes in there and to align it and run it through the machine with the proper stitches and flange. Furniture, for the most part, is still a hand-crafted product.

6. What do you enjoy most about your job? What do you enjoy least about your job?

What I enjoy most is the great sense of accomplishment I get upon seeing a finished product and knowing that I had a hand in creating something that someone will be placing in their home.

What I least enjoy, both as an upholsterer and a manager, is interacting and working with people who are not dependable and/or lack self-motivation.

7. Can you suggest a valuable "try this" for students considering a career in your profession?

Try to redo the bottom seat cushion on a rocker. Or, try to design and create a piece of furniture; you can get parts at Lowe's or Hobby Lobby and make anything you want. But more so, tour a plant or shadow someone in the business. I welcome that and I think most people do.

MORE INFORMATION

American Furniture Manufacturers Association
317 West High Avenue, 10th Floor
P.O. Box HP-7
High Point, NC 27261
336.884.5000
www.afmahp.org

American Home Furnishings Alliance
317 W. High Avenue, 10th Floor
High Point, NC 27260
336.884.5000
www.ahfa.us

American Society of Furniture Designers
144 Woodland Drive
New London, NC 28127
910.576.1273
www.asfd.com

Industrial Fabrics Association International
1801 County Road B West
Roseville, MN 55113
800.225.4324
www.ifai.com

Leather Industries of America
3050 K Street NW, Suite 400
Washington, DC 20007
202.342.8497
www.leatherusa.com

Marine Fabricators Association
1801 County Road B West
Roseville, MN 55113
800.209.1810
marinecanvas.com

Sally Driscoll/Editor

Welder

Snapshot

Career Cluster: Building Construction; Manufacturing
Interests: Welding, metalworking, electronics, construction, mathematics
Earnings (Yearly Average): $37,420
Employment & Outlook: Average Growth Expected

OVERVIEW

Sphere of Work

Welders cut, shape, and weld together a variety of metals to create and repair different parts for a diverse range of industries. Welders use various tools, such as a welding rod that utilizes heat to cut and fuse different materials. The most common form of welding is arc welding, in which heat is applied to two metals to join them. Welders work in several industries, including the construction, automotive, and engineering industries. The tasks performed by welders in the various industries are often similar.

Work Environment

Welders work in a wide range of environments, both indoors and outdoors. Some welders work in metalworking shops, where they are contracted to create or modify metal products for clients. Others may be hired to perform structural repairs in a residential or commercial building. Many welding jobs in commercial and residential buildings involve repairing and fitting piping systems. Welders can also work at construction sites, installing metal beams, pipes, siding, and other metal fixtures.

Profile

Working Conditions: Work both Indoors and Outdoors
Physical Strength: Medium Work, Heavy Work
Education Needs: On-The-Job Training, High School Diploma with Technical Education, Apprenticeship
Licensure/Certification: Usually Not Required, Not Hear and/or Talk
Opportunities For Experience: Apprenticeship, Military Service
Holland Interest Score*: RCS, REI, RES

* See Appendix A

Occupation Interest

The welding trade covers a wide range of industries and tends to attract people who enjoy working with their hands and would rather work on their feet than in an office. Welders must have great attention to detail and be able to adapt to different work environments. No two welding jobs are the same, so a welder needs to be a problem solver.

A Day in the Life—Duties and Responsibilities

There are dozens of different methods for welding, so once a welder is hired for a job, the first step is to determine the method and equipment needed based on the specifications or blueprints provided. One of the most common forms of welding is arc welding. This method uses an electrical current to heat metals and bond them together. The metals then cool and become fused. The electrical current is created at the tip of a tool commonly referred to as an electrical torch or a welding rod.

When the welder arrives at the job, he or she first examines where the planned welds will take place. Depending on the job, a welder may have to crawl, kneel, or assume other awkward positions in order to perform the weld. Then the welder sets up his or her equipment. The heat and sparks generated by welding equipment mean that a welder has to wear plenty of safety gear, including gloves, hoods, and masks. After the welder carefully performs the planned welds, he or she thoroughly examines them and makes sure they meet the quality standards and specification requirements.

Welders who work in shops also have to be able to accurately read specifications and schematics. They use the specifications to figure out which welding tools and materials will be needed to complete the job. Tools used in welding shops include industrial torches, grinders, and other heavy equipment. Strict safety regulations and practices must be followed.

Duties and Responsibilities

- Selecting proper welding equipment and accessories
- Adjusting equipment to properly weld materials
- Applying proper heat and/or pressure to bond the materials
- Aligning and feeding the work piece and removing it after the weld is completed
- Setting machine guides and work-holding devices

OCCUPATION SPECIALTIES

Arc Welders

Arc Welders join metal parts using electric welding equipment.

Gas Welders

Gas Welders use an intense gas flame to join metal parts.

Combination Welders

Combination Welders use arc, gas or resistance welding equipment on the same project depending on the materials and type of welding needed.

Production Line Welders

Production Line Welders join metal parts on a production line using previously set up gas or arc welding equipment.

WORK ENVIRONMENT

Physical Environment

Welders work in a variety of environments, sometimes in cramped spaces. Those who do not work in a shop may work at commercial and residential construction sites. Welders sometimes have to work high off the ground.

Transferable Skills and Abilities

Interpersonal/Social Skills
- Cooperating with others
- Working as a member of a team

Organization & Management Skills
- Following instructions
- Making decisions
- Paying attention to and handling details
- Performing routine work

Research & Planning Skills
- Developing evaluation strategies

Technical Skills
- Working with machines, tools or other objects

Plant Environment

Welding shops are well ventilated, although they tend to get hot due to the torches and the limitations on fans in the shop. Fans can interfere with the welding process, so welders can become overheated under their safety gear.

Human Environment

Welders frequently interact with others in the trade. They need to communicate with others working on the same job to ensure it is done correctly. A welder may also confer with clients who are requesting repairs and other modifications in commercial and residential jobs.

Technological Environment

Welders use a variety of materials, including various metals and alloys. Tools range from simple grinders and electrical torches to more complex tools involving lasers and computers.

EDUCATION, TRAINING, AND ADVANCEMENT

High School/Secondary

Most employers require a potential welder to have a high school degree or the equivalent before they will take him or her on as an apprentice. There are some basic high school courses that would benefit students interested in welding, including shop class, mathematics, and science.

Suggested High School Subjects
- Applied Math
- Applied Physics
- Blueprint Reading
- Electricity & Electronics
- English
- Industrial Arts
- Machining Technology
- Mechanical Drawing
- Metals Technology
- Shop Math
- Shop Mechanics
- Trade/Industrial Education
- Welding

Famous First

The first electric, or arc welding process was demonstrated by Professor Elihu Thomson of Lynn, Mass., who in 1896 obtained a patent for "an apparatus for electric welding." Thomson's arc welder came to be widely used in the auto, shipbuilding, construction, and home appliance industries.

Postsecondary

Most welders are not required to have a college degree, but there are several formal courses and programs offered at community and technical colleges that potential welders should consider taking. In addition, various welding associations offer seminars that would greatly benefit a potential welder.

At these courses and seminars, students are trained in the basics of welding. The different types of welding methods are covered, including arc welding, tungsten inert gas (TIG) welding, and metal inert gas (MIG) welding. Students are also instructed in different welding techniques, such as welding while on one's back, on a ladder, and kneeling. These courses may also cover the essential tools used in welding. Employers are more likely to hire a welder who has completed one of these formal courses.

Related College Majors
- Welding

Adult Job Seekers

There are a number of different industries in which welders are needed, and aspiring welders should look into these different work environments to see which best suits their interests. A person may want to specialize in fabrication shop work or may prefer working on construction sites. Additionally, welders should keep in mind the dangers and physical demands of the job and whether they will be physically able to do what is required. Welders often have to work in awkward positions, sometimes in tight spaces or high off of the ground.

Professional Certification and Licensure

Welding shops usually require someone with no welding background to go through a formal training or apprenticeship program. Many unions and welding associations offer such programs. These programs cover the technical skills required of a welder, including mathematics, measurements, and knowledge of electronics. Extensive hands-on training is provided during these programs, and trainees will also learn about safety standards and practices. Welding apprenticeships can last up to five years. At the end of an apprenticeship, a welder is considered a journey worker, which allows him or her to work without supervision.

Welder can receive certification in basic welding and specialized skills such as pipefitting and engineering. Those interested in receiving certification usually have to fill out an application, pay a fee, and then take part in several instructional seminars. Trainees will be tested on their knowledge and skills throughout the seminars. Different certifications require different employment and education documentation. Some programs may require a physical test, including an eye exam.

Once a welder becomes experienced and certified, he or she may apply to join a welding union. Joining a union will ensure that a welder receives benefits, a pension, and fair employment standards.

Additional Requirements

Since welders are usually responsible for checking their own work, welders should be perceptive and detail oriented. Incorrectly performing a weld can end up costing much more than the welder is paid. Welders should also be physically able to perform the duties and handle the necessary tools.

Fun Fact

Flashdance, the third highest grossing films of 1983, told the story of an 18-year-old Pittsburgh girl who worked as both a welder and an exotic dancer as she chased her dream of attending ballet school.

Source: http://www.rottentomatoes.com/m/flashdance/

EARNINGS AND ADVANCEMENT

Earnings depend on the type, size, geographic location, and union affiliation of the employer and the employee's skill. Welders had median annual earnings of $37,420 in 2014. The lowest ten percent earned less than $25,510, and the highest ten percent earned more than $58,590.

Welders may receive paid vacations, holidays, and sick days; life and health insurance; and retirement benefits. These are usually paid by the employer.

Metropolitan Areas with the Highest Employment Level in this Occupation

Metropolitan area	Employment	Employment per thousand jobs	Annual mean wage
Houston-Sugar Land-Baytown, TX	17,640	6.20	$43,230
Chicago-Joliet-Naperville, IL	6,300	1.68	$37,800
Los Angeles-Long Beach-Glendale, CA	6,230	1.54	$39,280
Dallas-Plano-Irving, TX	5,550	2.48	$35,980
Tulsa, OK	4,080	9.54	$41,990
Minneapolis-St. Paul-Bloomington, MN-WI	3,910	2.14	$42,700
Fort Worth-Arlington, TX	3,680	3.96	$37,330
Pittsburgh, PA	3,500	3.10	$40,930
Atlanta-Sandy Springs-Marietta, GA	3,400	1.43	$36,920
Portland-Vancouver-Hillsboro, OR-WA	3,370	3.19	$41,900

Source: Bureau of Labor Statistics

EMPLOYMENT AND OUTLOOK

There were approximately 400,000 welders employed nationally in 2014. Employment is expected to grow about as fast as the average for all occupations through the year 2024, which means employment is projected to increase 3 percent to 5 percent. Job demand is due to welders being able to use their skills in many industries and the growth of the defense industry, including the manufacture of aircrafts and missiles. In addition, job openings will occur from the need to replace workers who transfer to other occupations or retire.

Employment Trend, Projected 2014–24

Total, all occupations: 7%

Welders, cutters, solderers, and brazers: 4%

Metal workers and plastic workers: -5%

Note: "All Occupations" includes all occupations in the U.S. Economy. Source: U.S. Bureau of Labor Statistics, Employment Projections Program

Related Occupations
- Blacksmith
- Boilermaker
- Metal/Plastic Working Machine Operator
- Riveter
- Sheet Metal Worker
- Structural Metal Worker

Related Military Occupations
- Welder & Metal Worker

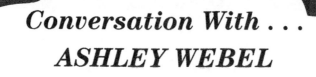

Conversation With . . .
ASHLEY WEBEL

Certified Welding Inspector/Certified Welding Educator
R&E Engineering Services, Macomb, Michigan
Welding, 11 years

1. What was your individual career path in terms of education/training, entry-level job, or other significant opportunity?

When I was in high school, I wanted nothing more than to go to art school or cooking school. Once I looked at job opportunities, what the pay would be and how much schooling cost, I changed my mind. Because I was so interested in art, I was more open to trying welding. Once I tried, I couldn't imagine doing anything else.

I started with an associate's degree in welding technology from Washtenaw Community College in Ann Arbor Township, Michigan. While in school, I competed in the SkillsUSA Welding and Fabrication Competition and learned how to read blueprints and use fabrication equipment. I was able to get an entry-level job cutting metal and doing some small metal fabrication jobs while I was still in school. After graduation, I was offered a job at a large welding equipment manufacturer in the training department. This wouldn't have been possible without my work experience and my involvement with the American Welding Society, which gave me the opportunity to network with and learn from the leaders in my industry.

2. What are the most important skills and/or qualities for someone in your profession?

Attention to detail has to be the most important skill when it comes to any job in the welding industry. We encounter welded products everywhere throughout our daily lives: cars, bridges, metal desks, even cooking equipment. Many different metals, and even some plastics, can be welded. It's immensely important to make sure it's done correctly and with quality in mind.

3. What do you wish you had known going into this profession?

I never realized all of the different opportunities within the welding industry! I have done inspection work in settings ranging from automotive plants to aircraft industries to metallurgy labs. I could work in a scientific lab or get my hands dirty building something different every day. The options are endless! Had I known this, I would have talked with a mentor to see which path was the best fit for me. I was lucky enough to have gained experience in many different areas, but I also jumped around a lot. Every position that I have had has been worthwhile, but not always a good fit. I work in a metallurgy lab now and love it.

4. Are there many job opportunities in your profession? In what specific areas?

Because welding is so necessary in the modern world, there will always be a need for people who can weld, design welded parts and products, and inspect them. Welding engineers are in high demand, as are welders to perform the work designed by engineers. Also, the robotic welding industry seems to be growing by the minute! I often hear of companies looking to hire welding engineers and welding robot technicians.

5. How do you see your profession changing in the next five years? What role will technology play in those changes, and what skills will be required?

A large number of manual welding jobs are becoming automated. Some see this as a bad thing, but I see it as an opportunity. These advanced automation jobs, such as laser welding and "advanced process" welding, are everywhere and the best people to fill them know how to weld. The added technology ensures that the welding industry will keep up with advances in the rest of the world. Opportunities are everywhere.

6. What do you enjoy most about your job? What do you enjoy least about your job?

The thing I enjoy most about my job is that it's interesting. It's hard to be bored when you're doing something new every day. It's gratifying to know that I get to make a positive impact on the world around me. On the flip side, the thing that I enjoy least is that the fast pace can lead to high stress. It's really important to get the job done right the first time. That can feel like a lot of pressure sometimes.

7. Can you suggest a valuable "try this" for students considering a career in your profession?

My best suggestion for anyone who thinks they might be interested in the welding industry is to seek out any opportunity to do manual welding. Whether it be in your uncle's garage, a metalworking class in high school, or a class at a community college, getting to actually try it will help you figure out if you'll truly like it. Even if manual welding is not really the route you want to take, you still may be interested in the metallurgy or design side. There are many internships available for those of you leaning toward the more scientific side. I also would urge you to reach out to a local chapter of the American Welding Society. It's comprised of the all of the "movers and shakers" in the welding industry. They'll be a great resource to reach out to for advice.

MORE INFORMATION

**American Welding Society
Foundation, Inc.**
550 NW LeJeune Road
Miami, FL 33126
800.443.9353
www.aws.org

**Fabricators and Manufacturers
Association, International**
833 Featherstone Road
Rockford, IL 61107
815.399.8700
www.fmanet.org

**Precision Machined Products
Association**
6700 W. Snowville Road
Brecksville, OH 44141
440.526.0300
www.pmpa.org

Patrick Cooper/Editor

What Are Your Career Interests?

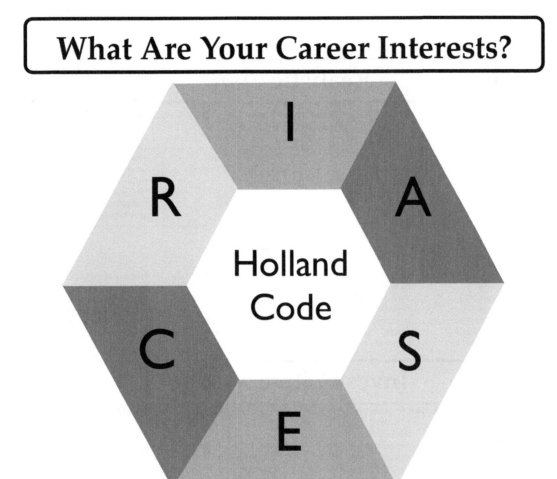

This is based on Dr. John Holland's theory that people and work environments can be loosely classified into six different groups. Each of the letters above corresponds to one of the six groups described in the following pages.

Different people's personalities may find different environments more to their liking. While you may have some interests in and similarities to several of the six groups, you may be attracted primarily to two or three of the areas. These two or three letters are your "Holland Code." For example, with a code of "RES" you would most resemble the Realistic type, somewhat less resemble the Enterprising type, and resemble the Social type even less. The types that are not in your code are the types you resemble least of all.

Most people, and most jobs, are best represented by some combination of two or three of the Holland interest areas. In addition, most people are most satisfied if there is some degree of fit between their personality and their work environment.

The rest of the pages in this booklet further explain each type and provide some examples of career possibilities, areas of study at MU, and co-curricular activities for each code. To take a more in-depth look at your Holland Code, take a self-assessment such as the SDS, Discover, or a card sort at the MU Career Center with a Career Specialist.

$\underline{\text{R}}$ealistic *(Doers)*

People who have athletic ability, prefer to work with objects, machines, tools, plants or animals, or to be outdoors.

Are you?		**Can you?**	**Like to?**
practical	independent	fix electrical things	tinker with machines/vehicles
straightforward/frank	ambitious	solve electrical problems	work outdoors
mechanically inclined	systematic	pitch a tent	be physically active
stable		play a sport	use your hands
concrete		read a blueprint	build things
reserved		plant a garden	tend/train animals
self-controlled		operate tools and machine	work on electronic equipment

Career Possibilities
(Holland Code):

Air Traffic Controller (SER)
Archaeologist (IRE)
Athletic Trainer (SRE)
Cartographer (IRE)
Commercial Airline Pilot (RIE)
Commercial Drafter (IRE)
Corrections Officer (SER)

Dental Technician (REI)
Farm Manager (ESR)
Fish and Game Warden (RES)
Floral Designer (RAE)
Forester (RIS)
Geodetic Surveyor (IRE)
Industrial Arts Teacher (IER)

Laboratory Technician (RIE)
Landscape Architect (AIR)
Mechanical Engineer (RIS)
Optician (REI)
Petroleum Geologist (RIE)
Police Officer (SER)
Practical Nurse (SER)

Property Manager (ESR)
Recreation Manager (SER)
Service Manager (ERS)
Software Technician (RCI)
Ultrasound Technologist (RSI)
Vocational Rehabilitation
   Consultant (ESR)

$\underline{\text{I}}$nvestigative *(Thinkers)*

People who like to observe, learn, investigate, analyze, evaluate, or solve problems.

Are you?		**Can you?**	**Like to?**
inquisitive	intellectually self-confident	think abstractly	explore a variety of ideas
analytical	Independent	solve math problems	work independently
scientific	logical	understand scientific theories	perform lab experiments
observant/precise	complex	do complex calculations	deal with abstractions
scholarly	Curious	use a microscope or computer	do research
cautious		interpret formulas	be challenged

Career Possibilities
(Holland Code):

Actuary (ISE)
Agronomist (IRS)
Anesthesiologist (IRS)
Anthropologist (IRE)
Archaeologist (IRE)
Biochemist (IRS)
Biologist (ISR)

Chemical Engineer (IRE)
Chemist (IRE)
Computer Systems Analyst (IER)
Dentist (ISR)
Ecologist (IRE)
Economist (IAS)
Electrical Engineer (IRE)

Geologist (IRE)
Horticulturist (IRS)
Mathematician (IER)
Medical Technologist (ISA)
Meteorologist (IRS)
Nurse Practitioner (ISA)
Pharmacist (IES)

Physician, General Practice (ISE)
Psychologist (IES)
Research Analyst (IRC)
Statistician (IRE)
Surgeon (IRA)
Technical Writer (IRS)
Veterinarian (IRS)

<u>Artistic</u> *(Creators)*

People who have artistic, innovating, or intuitional abilities and like to work in unstructured situations using their imagination and creativity.

Are you?		**Can you?**	**Like to?**
creative	original	sketch, draw, paint	attend concerts, theatre, art
imaginative	introspective	play a musical instrument	exhibits
innovative	impulsive	write stories, poetry, music	read fiction, plays, and poetry
unconventional	sensitive	sing, act, dance	work on crafts
emotional	courageous	design fashions or interiors	take photography
independent	complicated		express yourself creatively
Expressive	idealistic		deal with ambiguous ideas
	nonconforming		

**Career Possibilities
(Holland Code):**

Actor (AES)	Copy Writer (ASI)	Interior Designer (AES)	Medical Illustrator (AIE)
Advertising Art Director (AES)	Dance Instructor (AER)	Intelligence Research Specialist	Museum Curator (AES)
Advertising Manager (ASE)	Drama Coach (ASE)	(AEI)	Music Teacher (ASI)
Architect (AIR)	English Teacher (ASE)	Journalist/Reporter (ASE)	Photographer (AES)
Art Teacher (ASE)	Entertainer/Performer (AES)	Landscape Architect (AIR)	Writer (ASI)
Artist (ASI)	Fashion Illustrator (ASR)	Librarian (SAI)	Graphic Designer (AES)

<u>Social</u> *(Helpers)*

People who like to work with people to enlighten, inform, help, train, or cure them, or are skilled with words.

Are you?		**Can you?**	**Like to?**
friendly	cooperative	teach/train others	work in groups
helpful	generous	express yourself clearly	help people with problems
idealistic	responsible	lead a group discussion	do volunteer work
insightful	forgiving	mediate disputes	work with young people
outgoing	patient	plan and supervise an activity	serve others
understanding	kind	cooperate well with others	

**Career Possibilities
(Holland Code):**

City Manager (SEC)	Historian (SEI)	Park Naturalist (SEI)	Teacher (SAE)
Clinical Dietitian (SIE)	Hospital Administrator (SER)	Physical Therapist (SIE)	Social Worker (SEA)
College/University Faculty (SEI)	Psychologist (SEI)	Police Officer (SER)	Speech Pathologist (SAI)
Community Org. Director (SEA)	Insurance Claims Examiner (SIE)	Probation and Parole Officer (SEC)	Vocational-Rehab. Counselor (SEC)
Consumer Affairs Director (SER)Counselor/Therapist (SAE)	Librarian (SAI)	Real Estate Appraiser (SCE)	Volunteer Services Director (SEC)
	Medical Assistant (SCR)	Recreation Director (SER)	
	Minister/Priest/Rabbi (SAI)	Registered Nurse (SIA)	
	Paralegal (SCE)		

Enterprising *(Persuaders)*

People who like to work with people, influencing, persuading, leading or managing for organizational goals or economic gain.

Are you?		**Can you?**	**Like to?**
self-confident	ambitious	initiate projects	make decisions
assertive	agreeable	convince people to do things	be elected to office
persuasive	talkative	your way	start your own business
energetic	extroverted	sell things	campaign politically
adventurous	spontaneous	give talks or speeches	meet important people
popular	optimistic	organize activities	have power or status
		lead a group	
		persuade others	

Career Possibilities
(Holland Code):

Advertising Executive (ESA)	Credit Analyst (EAS)	Foreign Service Officer (ESA)	Politician (ESA)
Advertising Sales Rep (ESR)	Customer Service Manager	Funeral Director (ESR)	Public Relations Rep (EAS)
Banker/Financial Planner (ESR)	(ESA)	Insurance Manager (ESC)	Retail Store Manager (ESR)
Branch Manager (ESA)	Education & Training Manager	Interpreter (ESA)	Sales Manager (ESA)
Business Manager (ESC)	(EIS)	Lawyer/Attorney (ESA)	Sales Representative (ERS)
Buyer (ESA)	Emergency Medical Technician	Lobbyist (ESA)	Social Service Director (ESA)
Chamber of Commerce Exec	(ESI)	Office Manager (ESR)	Stockbroker (ESI)
(ESA)	Entrepreneur (ESA)	Personnel Recruiter (ESR)	Tax Accountant (ECS)

Conventional *(Organizers)*

People who like to work with data, have clerical or numerical ability, carry out tasks in detail, or follow through on others' instructions.

Are you?		**Can you?**	**Like to?**
well-organized	practical	work well within a system	follow clearly defined
accurate	thrifty	do a lot of paper work in a short	procedures
numerically inclined	systematic	time	use data processing equipment
methodical	structured	keep accurate records	work with numbers
conscientious	polite	use a computer terminal	type or take shorthand
efficient	ambitious	write effective business letters	be responsible for details
conforming	obedient		collect or organize things
	persistent		

Career Possibilities
(Holland Code):

Abstractor (CSI)	Claims Adjuster (SEC)	Elementary School Teacher	Medical Records Technician
Accountant (CSE)	Computer Operator (CSR)	(SEC)	(CSE)
Administrative Assistant (ESC)	Congressional-District Aide (CES)	Financial Analyst (CSI)	Museum Registrar (CSE)
Budget Analyst (CER)	Cost Accountant (CES)	Insurance Manager (ESC)	Paralegal (SCE)
Business Manager (ESC)	Court Reporter (CSE)	Insurance Underwriter (CSE)	Safety Inspector (RCS)
Business Programmer (CRI)	Credit Manager (ESC)	Internal Auditor (ICR)	Tax Accountant (ECS)
Business Teacher (CSE)	Customs Inspector (CEI)	Kindergarten Teacher (ESC)	Tax Consultant (CES)
Catalog Librarian (CSE)	Editorial Assistant (CSI)		Travel Agent (ECS)

BIBLIOGRAPHY

General

Brynjolfsson, Erik and Andrew McAfee. *The Second Machine Age: Work, Progress, and Prosperity in a Time of Brilliant Technologies*. New York: W.W. Norton, 2014.

DiMicco, Dan. *American Made: Why Making Things Will Return Us to Greatness*. New York: Palgrave Macmillan, 2015.

Ford, Martin. *Rise of the Robots: Technology and the Threat of a Jobless Future*. New York: Basic Books, 2015.

Lipscomb, Todd. *Re-Made in the USA: How We Can Restore Jobs, Retool Manufacturing, and Compete with the World*. Hoboken, NJ: Wiley, 2011.

Smil, Vaclav. *Made in the USA: The Rise and Retreat of American Manufacturing*. Cambridge, MA: MIT Press, 2013.

Industries and Applications

Anderson, Mary Ann, et al. *Operations Management for Dummies*. Hoboken, NJ: Wiley, 2013.

Ballinger, Jack T. *Chemical Operator's Portable Handbook*. New York: McGraw-Hill, 1999.

Chastain, Larry. *Industrial Mechanics and Maintenance*. Upper Saddle River, NJ: Prentice Hall, 2008.

Crowson, Richard. *Assembly Processes: Finishing, Packaging, and Automation*. Boca Raton, FL: CRC Press, 2006.

Cuffaro, Dan. *The Industrial Design Reference and Specification Book*. Gloucester, MA: Rockport Publishers, 2013.

Davis, Thomas B. and Carl A. Nelson. *Millwright and Mechanics Guide*. Indianapolis: Audel/Wiley, 2004.

Dinwiddie, Keith. *Basic Robotics*. Boston: Cengage Learning, 2015.

Harrison, Charles. *A Life's Design: The Life and Work of Industrial Designer Charles Harrison*. Chicago: Ibis Design, 2005.

Headley, James. *Forklifts*. Sanford, FL: Crane Institute, 2010.

Henry, Kevin. *Drawing for Product Designers*. London: Laurence King Publishing, 2012.

Hilyard, Joseph. *The Oil and Gas Industry: A Nontechnical Guide*. Tulsa, OK: PennWell Corp., 2012.

Lamb, Frank. *Industrial Automation: Hands On*. New York: McGraw-Hill, 2014.

Martin, Peter and Gregory Hale. *Automation Made Easy: Everything You Wanted to Know About Automation*. Research Triangle Park, NC: International Society for Automation, 2009.

National Center for Construction Education and Research. *Boilermaker Level 1 Trainee Guide*. Upper Saddle River, NJ: Prentice Hall, 2010.

Plog, Barbara, et al. *Fundamentals of Industrial Hygiene*. Itasca, IL: National Safety Council, 2012.

Speegle, Michael. *Quality Concepts for the Process Industry*. Clifton Park, NY: Delmar Cengage, 2009.

Thomas, Charles E. *Process Technology: Safety, Health, and Environment*. Clifton Park, NY: Delmar Cengage, 2011.

Underly, Kari. *The Art of Beef Cutting: A Meat Professional's Guide to Butchering and Merchandising*. Hoboken, NJ: Wiley, 2011.

Woodruff, Everett, et al. *Steam Plant Operation*. New York: McGraw-Hill, 2011.

INDEX

N